W9-CCZ-198

PSYCHOLOGY
AND
NATURAL THEOLOGY

BY

OWEN A. HILL

ETHICS, GENERAL AND SPECIAL

PSYCHOLOGY
AND
NATURAL THEOLOGY

BY

OWEN A. HILL, S.J., Ph.D.

Lecturer on Psychology
Natural Theology and Ethics at Fordham University

New York
THE MACMILLAN COMPANY
1921

Set up and electrotyped. Published, February, 1921

Imprimi potest.

JOSEPHUS H. ROCKWELL, S.J.,

Praepositus Prov. Marylandiae Neo-Eboracensis.

Nihil obstat.

ARTHURUS J. SCANLAN, D.D.,

Censor Librorum.

Imprimatur.

PATRITIUS J. HAYES, D.D.,

Archiepiscopus Neo-Eboracensis.

NEO-EBORACI, die 25 Novembris, 1920.

PREFACE

This volume on Psychology and Natural Theology is the result of years of experience in the class-room. It has at least the merit of being thoroughly tried out and tested, and that in itself means some commendation. With help from his teacher the average student can readily grasp its contents, and maturer minds can without any extraneous aid master its statements, and champion their validity against all opponents. It has been the author's aim to combine as far as possible the conciseness of the text-book with the fuller flow of the essay; and he indulges the hope that, while consulting the needs of the pupil in class, he has not entirely neglected the predilections of the general reader. Philosophy and rhetoric are no enemies; and the thought somewhat accounts for the extended notice Ingersoll and Verworm get, and for the separate article on Hypnotism. Theology contains no more important truth than the existence of God; and Ingersoll, with the help of empty arguments and glittering language, is responsible for not a few of the atheists in our own country. In all Psychology immortality and free-will are the dogmas of most practical worth; and their opponents appeal for support to the reputed learning of men like Verworm. Hypnotism and kindred practices of devil-worship will continue to work harm till stripped of their mystery; and right psychology is the single remedy.

While deriving no argument from Church or Scripture in matters purely philosophical, the author never hesitates, when opportunity offers, to mention a dogma of faith, or explain some truth contained in the catechism. When constrained to transfer a technical term of Scholastic Philosophy from Latin to English, he selects the best equivalent at his disposal. On occasions he multiplies proofs, not because they are individually weak, but because truth gathers strength and force when viewed from different sides.

When reading a book one wants to know primarily what the

writer himself has to say, not what others have to say; and this is the author's excuse for the meagre display of foot-notes, and references, and quotations in his work. As between men, the prestige of an opponent lends no intrinsic value whatever to his argument. In the field of philosophy every individual's authority is worth only as much as his arguments. Arguments from authority are, perhaps, the weakest in all philosophy, wholly subsidiary and corroborative, of no weight with the wise, without prior and independent arguments based on the very nature of things; and the common consent of mankind is only a seeming exception to this rule.

Psychology and Natural Theology, all the Metaphysics of Senior Year in Jesuit Colleges, are combined in the one volume; and this makes for economy as well as for convenience. Questions are thoroughly explained, without sending the pupil to other sources of information. The discussion of difficulties is unusually complete; and experience quite satisfies the author that nothing in all philosophy is more important than this solution of difficulties. It is virtually an application of the Case System to philosophy. The highest kind of knowledge, the only kind of knowledge really worth while, is certainty; and certainty is incompatible with concrete possibility of the opposite. Certainty is out of the question as long as any single opposing argument remains unanswered, no matter how many favorable arguments are urged in defense of a thesis or statement. Hence the supreme need of being able first to comprehend, and then to answer the arguments of opponents.

All the matter is done into set and concise theses, and the Scholastic method of presentment is strictly adhered to. In religion a good Catholic can be nothing but a devoted son of the Church, and in philosophy he can be nothing but a thorough Scholastic, an enthusiastic follower of St. Thomas. Pope Leo XIII forever settled that. Religion was not improved by the so-called Reformation, and Luther himself on no few occasions adverts to the fact. Luther and the Reformers worked no more harm to faith and morality than Kant, with his forerunners and followers, worked to reason and philosophy. Protestantism is a wilderness of religious confusion, and modern philosophy is a conglomeration of falsehoods, beneath the contempt of honest and healthy minds. We have small respect for modern systems in philosophy, with their pitiful mistakes and empty rant, culminating in mental obliquity and religious despair. Kant was a disciple of Luther, and all his philosophy is in substance an attempt on the part of the disciple to give an air of respectability to the master's principle about the right to private judgment. Kant's autonomy of reason is but a development of Luther's individual right to interpret Scripture. One is key to Protestant Ethics, the other is key to Protestant theology; and both are the crown and consummation of Subjectivism. Translated into plain English, Kant's categorical imperative runs this way, "Act as you think, and think as you like." With him speculative or pure reason is the faculty which thinks things in themselves, things as they are; and it has nothing to do with the categorical imperative, or with any other question bearing on conduct, God or the Soul. Kant writes it down the fruitful cause of all the aberration, confusion and superstition conspicuously abundant, he thinks, in Catholic philosophy and theology. With him practical reason is the faculty which thinks things not in themselves, not as they are, but as they are in us, as we want them to be; and it furnishes him with his categorical imperative, and with all his certainty about the existence of God, the reality and the immortality of the soul. His practical reason subjects thinking to wishing, and, because it partakes more of the nature of an appetitive than of a cognoscitive faculty, can with more propriety be called the will than the reason. And when a man makes his will the standard of his conduct, his descent into the abyss of wickedness is imminent and swift; when he makes his will the criterion of truth, whatever is desirable becomes true, whatever is undesirable becomes false, and the multiplication-table needs to be readjusted.

CONTENTS

PART I — PSYCHOLOGY

PART II — NATURAL THEOLOGY

PSYCHOLOGY AND NATURAL THEOLOGY

PART I—PSYCHOLOGY

INTRODUCTION

DEFINITION AND DIVISION OF PHILOSOPHY

A definition is a collection of words briefly setting forth a thing's nature. Division is the breaking up of a whole into its parts. Philosophy, in virtue of its Greek parentage, means love of wisdom, and this is called its nominal or name definition. Wisdom itself is a superior sort of knowledge, a knowledge that sticks not at the outward surface or external appearance of things, but burrows deeper, and in such sort sifts the very essence of the object known, that human effort can proceed no farther with the examination. *Philosophy, then, with us is knowledge of things in their last and most universal causes, so far as such knowledge is attainable by the light of natural reason; and this is called its real definition.* With the old Romans we distinguish three ways of knowing, set forth in the Latin terms cognitio, scientia, sapientia. The English equivalents are Knowledge, Science, and Wisdom. We cannot better illustrate their differences than by alleging an example. A man walks along a public thoroughfare. The common, unsophisticated citizen, viewing him from a distance, has knowledge to the effect that the being in motion is what we usually style a man; but he can give hardly any reasons for the knowledge within him. At most he can offer but very imperfect and superficial reasons, qualities, for instance, that might equally well exist in some certain animal as far removed from man as day from night. This common, unsophisticated citizen is possessed of knowledge in its rudest and simplest state, namely experiment and authority. Suppose a physiologist near, a man thoroughly acquainted with all the various muscles, bones, sinews, and the whole organism of the human frame. He is of opinion, too, that the object in front is what in every-day parlance we call a man. But he can substantiate his opinion with solid reasons. He walks upright, not on all fours. He has arms and legs, not fore-legs and hind-legs. He has fingers on his hands and toes on his feet, that preserve due proportions. These, indeed, are good reasons; but not final, not what our definition styles the last and most universal causes. They are not the last, because there is one farther removed, so far removed in fact, that, unless philosophy suggested it, the physiologist would be in continual danger of confounding men with beasts. They are not the most universal, because a large proportion of men are without one or other characteristic. Some men have no arms, others have no legs. Some men possess more than the requisite number of fingers and toes, others are wholly without them. The physiologist's knowledge is, of course, more perfect than that of the unsophisticated citizen. It is called scientific knowledge, or science. A philosopher now appears on the scene. He accosts the stranger, holds a short conversation and remarks, "Here in good sooth is a man, because he is a rational animal." His reasons are the last and most universal. It is quite impossible to hit on any reasons beyond. They are besides applicable to whatever man walks, has walked or will walk the earth. The intrinsic absolutely last cause of a thing is its essence; the extrinsic absolutely last cause of things is God. Things in our definition comprise whatever exists or can be conceived to exist. It is perhaps the most indefinite noun in our language. It includes God, the angels, man and the material world or universe, from the hugest brute in the jungles of Africa to the minutest grain of sand on the seashore. The word cause is taken to mean whatever by way of answer satisfies the question, "Why is this thing such or such?" Kant makes philosophy a fixed knowledge of the laws and causes of reason's spontaneity; and with him everything is merely subjective. Wisdom embraces all that God knows. It is an abyss that man can never hope to fathom. God knows everything capable of passage into an infinite mind. He knows things not only in their proximate or most palpable and apparent causes; but also in their last and most universal causes, and in all the intermediate causes ranking between the proximate and most universal causes. Our knowledge, of course, is less wide. Our imperfect philosophy must rest satisfied with knowing some few or many things in their universal and last causes, without attempting to trace these last and universal causes through such as are proximate and intermediate. Pythagoras on this account refuses to denominate men wise. He vindicates this attribute to God alone. He writes himself down not a wise man, but a philosopher, a man in eager pursuit of wisdom.

Division is the separation of a whole into its parts.

Plato divides philosophy into real, rational and moral; the philosophy of things, of mind, and of will; and they are called Metaphysics, Logic, Ethics. Hence our division:

- Philosophy
  - Logic
    - Minor, Dialectics
    - Major, First Principles
  - Metaphysics
    - General — Ontology
    - Special
      - Cosmology
      - Psychology
      - Theology
  - Ethics
    - General
    - Special

Sir Francis or Lord Bacon penned a wholesome truth, when he wrote, "Leves gustus in philosophia movere fortasse possunt ad atheismum, sed pleniores haustus ad Deum reducunt." "Sips of philosophy can perhaps lead a man to think there is no God, but fuller draughts tend ever to belief in His existence." We fancy with reason that the world of to-day is flooded with atheists, infidels, and empty theorists, only because the world of to-day, while spurring on its votaries to unparalleled diligence in things material, encourages them to skim lightly over facts that bear on the mind, the spiritual and nobler part of man. And the world will continue dark to life eternal, until it changes its method of studying philosophy. As long as men rest content with mere dabbling in this most sacred and most sublime of the natural sciences, so long will there be presumptuous scatter-brains, ready to scoff at truths too hidden and too abstruse to be taken in by a casual glance. This is all true even of the philosophy that Socrates, Plato, and Aristotle, long before Christ's coming, taught in the groves and the highways of Greece; but the remark gathers additional strength, when applied to what we style Catholic Philosophy. This latter is grounded in the natural resources of man's intellect, as was that of the pagans. Divine revelation, though it forms in Catholic Philosophy no real foundation or reason for the acceptance of truths, has nevertheless suggested to later times sublime ideas and sublime principles, that never entered into the mind of Socrates, Plato, or Aristotle. This fact led an English Jesuit, Father Clarke, to say: "Catholic Philosophy is not a system which can be explained in half an hour to the chance inquirer. Its principles are so intimately bound up with the Catholic Faith that it is to the non-Catholic a sealed book, an unintelligible mystery, which has for him no more meaning than an utterly unknown language."

DEFINITION AND DIVISION OF PSYCHOLOGY

Maher, pp. 1–26

Psychology is the second branch of Special Metaphysics; and, though less comprehensive than Cosmology, is far more important in its application. Like kindred expressions in philosophy, it is a Greek term, and means *discourse or reasoning about the soul, or the principle of life in living beings.* It is easy to falsely suppose that human beings alone possess souls. They alone possess rational souls, but the tree, as well, and the horse have within them a life-giving principle, that truly deserves the name soul. Psychology, however, pays small attention to beings other than human, and examines more in detail that most splendid of God's works, the soul of man, fathoming as far as possible its hidden secrets and veiled mysteries. It discusses the peculiarities of life in plants and brutes. It sets down and elucidates the properties and characteristics of life in man, describes the union prevailing between body and soul, strengthens beyond danger of loss our belief in immortality, offers a straightforward and satisfactory solution of what must forever remain a partial mystery, the joint operations of intellect and sense, and finally furnishes us with a clear insight into the workings of the will and its dread power of liberty.

The Greek word for soul means breath, the most attenuated substance within experience, and is another tribute to early philosophy's right appreciation of the soul's spirituality, and open condemnation of modern Materialism.

Psychology is twofold, empirical or phenomenal, and rational. The former proceeds by way of experiment, deals chiefly with results, and can well be called effect-psychology. The latter proceeds by way of reasoning and argument, deals chiefly with the faculties themselves, and can well be called cause-psychology. Two methods are in vogue for the solution of problems in empirical psychology, one subjective, the other objective. The first named is the more reliable of the two as well as the more immediate. It is wholly introspective, based on personal consciousness of individual mental phenomena, and borrows its information from inside sources. The other method, even if less reliable, and more mediate, is, when employed as an aid to introspection, quick and quite satisfactory. In this second method the student ranges beyond the field of his own personal consciousness, and, appealing to the consciousness of others, borrows information from outside sources. It finds material in other men's minds, in language, in history, in animal psychology, in physiology, psychiatry and psychometry. Psychology is likewise divided into Inferior and Superior. *Inferior deals with characteristics common to all three kinds of life, and with characteristics peculiar and proper to plant and brute life. Superior deals with characteristics exclusively proper to man.*

THESIS I

Life is that perfection in a being which makes self-motion or immanent action possible with it. We must recognize in plants a life-giving principle, essentially different from inert matter and its forces, physical and chemical. Brute animals are not mere automatic machines, but they possess the faculty of sense. They are, however, without intellect.

Maher, pp. 579–594; *Jouin*, pp. 151–161.

QUESTION

In this first thesis, which embraces all Inferior Psychology, we dispose of every living creature but man; and so make ready for the large work before us, by clearing from our field of view a multitude of beings that would otherwise darken our vision. Plants of whatever description, from the humblest mosses to the fern-like branches that seem to fold their leaves at the touch of a hand, fill the lowest department in the kingdom of life. Beneath them in creation are ranged anorganic or lifeless beings, such as stones and minerals, all far enough removed from them by manifest and specific differences to make the line of separation always possible to the master mind. Above them in creation are ranged beings endowed with a more perfect life, brute animals; while at the top and head of visible creation stands man, whom God, as Scriptural simplicity puts it, "made just a little inferior to the angels." The deep importance of this thesis may not at first sight be evident, but a moment's reflection about what Materialism proposes to itself to compass, can satisfy the most incredulous that it has a force of its own, which fully entitles it to the conspicuous place it fills in psychology. Materialism would persuade itself and us that spirit is a myth of fairyland, and that matter, physical and chemical agents, are quite equal to the task of producing thoughts or ideas, attributed by ordinary mortals to a spiritual agency, the soul, that cannot be weighed, or measured, or analyzed in the laboratory. If Materialism were true, regarding the highest kind of life falling under our immediate experience, we should scarcely hesitate to affirm that these same physical and chemical forces can produce whatever phenomena in the life of plants and animals elicit our wonder, and compel us to adopt the theory set down in our thesis. On the contrary, we base all psychology on the indisputable fact that even plants, the most imperfect sort of life known to us, contain within themselves a principle essentially different from inert matter and its forces. Of a surety, if plants call for such a principle, animals and men, endowed with a kind of life far superior to theirs, stand in still greater need of something such; and so Materialism in its attempt to level all distinction between mind and matter is absurd. Materialists take the highest order of life, man, and pretend to explain it by matter. We take the lowest order in life, plant, and show that mere matter is no adequate explanation.

TERMS

Life. The word life admits of as many and as various meanings as the word nature. At one time it means conduct, at another it is applied to creatures separated by an immense chasm from all notion of conduct. This much, however, may be said by way of reducing the expression to something like oneness of meaning. Life, as we use it here, is what lies at the base of all the conceivable notions suggested by the word. For it is quite plain that there is some peculiar feature common to all the beings known as living. Motion is this feature, and we are conscious within ourselves of acquaintance with this peculiar feature as often as the word life or living presents itself. An animal is alive when it moves; dead, when it is still, as St. Thomas says. Life is a substantial form, and, therefore, an incomplete substance, which, together with the matter, tree or body in brute and man, constitutes a single living substance. Life taken in a wider sense, and with a marked shade of difference in meaning, may be considered an accidental form; inasmuch as it gives essence and specific being to every concrete and individual act of a living creature. Accidental life is actual self-motion or immanent action; substantial life, the basis and support of accidental, is mere capability or possibility of self-motion. The former is a mere accident because it simply modifies or limits an accident, such as are all the actions of plants, brutes and men. Substantial life is for things alive being or essence; accidental life is superadded to the same, and is resident in every act put or placed by the living subject. *Substantial life is, therefore, capability of self-motion or immanent action; accidental life is the manifestation of this same capability in action.*

Life in actu primo is a substance; life in actu secundo is an accident.

Life in actu primo physically taken, is the soul; in actu primo mètaphysically taken, it is capacity. Parallels are, rational animal and rational animality.

Defective definitions of life:

Bichat describes life as a sum of the functions which resist death; Beclard, as a sum of the phenomena peculiar to organized beings; Owen, as the center of intussusceptive assimilative force, capable of reproduction by spontaneous fission; Comte, as a twofold internal movement, composition and decomposition, at once general and continuous; and Spencer, as the continuous adjustment of internal relations to external relations. All these descriptions are defective and wrong, because they halt at effects and touch only accidental life. Philosophy is the science of things in their last causes, not in their effects; and we want a description of substantial life.

Self-motion. Motion is of so many different kinds that the epithet self is absolutely necessary for the full conveyance of what we mean by life. There are a motion in place, a motion in time; self-motion and motion received from another; motion of mind, motion of body, and others too numerous to mention. But the idea common to, and invariably found at the bottom of, these several notions, is that of *change or passage from one state to another.* We must recognize here the difficulty, that God possesses life without experiencing change. Life is not univocal in God and creatures. Hence, two definitions are needed. We are now describing life as it exists in creatures. Created life is in God in an eminent way,— with all its perfections, without its imperfections. Immanent action is characteristic of life in God, too: and, though it produces no change in God Himself, since He is always in act, it fosters and promotes changes in others, outside of God; so including within itself the notion claimed above to be common to life in general. Creatures in even their vital or immanent acts are moved or influenced by object and end; God moves Himself altogether, and therefore, God's life is the most perfect conceivable. Agent in immanent act determines itself; sight is from eye; sight of this or that is from object. The Scholastics thus graphically put the thing. In Deo movens et motum sunt perfecte unum. Dei intellectus est Dei substantia. Deus est suâ vita in actu secundo. And they mean that God in all His acts is agent, action, object and end; that God's intellect is God Himself in substance; that in God there is no distinction between substantial life and accidental; He is actus purissimus, an utter stranger to mere potency or capability. Life can be viewed in a threefold way, as continuous improvement, as self-motion, and as immanent action. Its conspicuous feature in plants is continuous improvement; in brutes, self-motion; in man, immanent action. All three are manifestations of life, and therefore immanent action. Immanent action betrays itself in plants as continuous improvement, and so of the rest.

Immanent action. Immanent is only a Latin expression for indwelling or abiding within, and has for opposite the term transient, an exact equivalent for passing from one thing to another, or changing position. *An act therefore is immanent when it stays in or perfects the agent from which it proceeds, when the principle or originating cause of the act and its term are in the agent to which it is ascribed.* All really vital acts are immanent, and from this very fact contribute to their doer's perfection. The acts of inert or lifeless causes, like molecules in minerals, are transient, contribute nothing to their improvement, and either proceed from a principle outside the agent or have their finish or term in an outside object. Light proceeding from the sun is no vital act, and the sun is not a living body, because, though the light proceeds from the sun itself, the term of the act or illumination is in other bodies distinct from the sun. A flow of water is no vital or immanent act, because, though the term of the act is resident in the water, its principle is in gravity, or pressure, or some such external force.

Again, in this matter of life or immanence we recognize three different principles, the principium quod, the principium quo remotum, and the principium quo proximum; and immanence is secured, if the act proceeds from and terminates in any of these three principles. The first of the three is called the suppositum, or the whole being; the second, the principle of life or the soul; the third, the faculty employed. These three fix the varying degrees of immanence. An act terminating, like a thought or idea, in some faculty intrinsically independent of the being's material element, is more immanent than an act terminating in a faculty intrinsically dependent on such an element, or in the whole being. Vegetation terminates in the whole plant; sensation, in some organic faculty, like the eye; thought, in an inorganic or wholly spiritual faculty, the intellect. A blow is a transient act that begins in the agent and finishes in outside object; it is immanent, when viewed apart from outside object. A piece of stretched rubber, seeking its normal position, is not alive; because, though the term of the act is in the rubber, the force compelling it is in some external agency, namely in the pull that previously stretched it. Motion in the rubber is exerted to attain its connatural condition, no ulterior perfection. It is a case of flowing water and gravity. Immanence makes life, and three grades of immanence make three grades of life. With regard to the principle, mere execution makes plant life; execution according to a form sensibly known makes brute life; and execution according to a form intellectually known, with a view to some end not determined by the Creator, but fixed by the agent, makes human life. With regard to the term, its reception or residence in the whole subject or agent makes plant life; its reception or residence in a part or organ of the agent makes brute life; and its reception or residence in a faculty altogether independent of the agent's organism makes human life. Again, with term for viewpoint, living beings take to themselves something from without. Plants take elements of matter; brutes take material images or sensations, men take immaterial images or ideas.

Plants:

The order in life is, plants, brutes, men. St. Thomas says, the more self-motion, the more life. The three things in self-motion are, end, sensible knowledge, intellectual knowledge, with choice of means. Hence we have plants, brutes, men. There is no knowledge in plants, only execution; in their case end and form are from nature and from without. Knowledge is had in brutes, but at the highest mere instinct; they have no knowledge about the relation of means to end. Choice of means and knowledge of end as such, or universal knowledge, belong to men.

With the philosopher, plants are beings endowed with vegetable life; beings capable of that self-motion or immanent action, which manifests itself in growth by the peculiar process styled intussusception; beings able to nourish themselves, and produce other individuals of the same specific complexion. A snowball grows in size by successive additions from without, by juxtaposition, by aggregation. But it would be silly to expect the snowball to reach out for neighboring substances, like soil and moisture, put them through a series of transformations and change them into snow.

Plants are organic bodies without sensation; but distinguished from inorganic by evolution, propagation and structure.

Our adversaries are the Cartesians and modern physiologists.

It is a delicate matter to determine just where the world of vegetation leaves off, and where the world of inanimate or dead nature begins. Even the most learned quarrel among themselves and puzzle over the question whether certain beings, to all appearances dead, deserve the name of plant or not. The philosopher enters no such controversy. He is content to know that whatever tallies with the above description is a plant, and that whatever falls away from it belongs to some higher order of life, or is dead. There are three processes in plant life, nutrition, growth and reproduction or generation; and there are three corresponding faculties or powers. *Nutrition is that process by which an organic substance changes food into its own substance, to preserve itself in being.* It differs from growth and reproduction. This nutrition constitutes the vital stream, and mends the wear and tear entailed by life on the body and its organs. By virtue of waste and repair living bodies within certain definite periods undergo a complete change. Experiments show that the principle of life affects even the bones and such portions of the animal structure as seem least vital. Instances are poultry and pigeons from whose food calcareous salts were extracted. Nutrition includes absorption of food by root and leaf from soil and air, circulation of food-product, breathing and exhalation. By day the leaves absorb carbonic acid gas in the atmosphere, decompose it, and retain the carbon to exhale the oxygen. By night oxygen is absorbed and carbonic acid gas exhaled. Thus equilibrium is preserved in the vegetable and animal kingdoms. The waste product of plants or oxygen is food supply for animals, and the waste product of animals, or carbonic acid gas, becomes the food-supply of plants. Secretion and assimilation are other functions of nutrition. *Growth is that vital process by which organic substances attain to their due size by assimilation of food. Reproduction or generation is that vital process by which one living being derives its life from another living and conjoined being, with specific likeness in nature for result;* or, as St. Thomas puts it, "origo viventis a vivente principio, conjuncto in similitudinem naturae." 1. Q. 27. a 2. Explanation: Life alone can produce life, to exclude abiogenesis or spontaneous generation. The term must be alive, to separate generation from the production of sweat and tears. To be immanent action, the new birth must be conjoined with the parent during the process of generation. As soon as separation ensues, generation is over. The hen that hatches another's egg is not the chick's mother. Adam did not generate Eve, because the mere removal of a rib has no natural bearing on the production of a specifically similar being. Of the three functions, nutrition is first in point of time, last in point of dignity; generation is last in point of time, first in point of dignity. Generation is effected in three ways, by fission, by germination, and by ovulation; by multiplication, by bud, by egg. Some plants and lower animals are produced the first two ways. The third way, uncommon in lower orders of life and limited to their more perfect species, is proper to brutes and men. *In fission, original cell breaks into several; in gemmation, buds arise on outside of living body. Two principles conspire to the third process, the seed-cell or egg, and the fecundating principle. The result is the fecundated egg.* Here arises the old difficulty about the precise time of the soul's appearance in the embryo. Old writers were of opinion that a long or short delay had place. It is to-day a common opinion with theologians, philosophers and physiologists that the soul is present from the first moment of fecundation. *Spontaneous generation, or the derivation of life from dead matter, is a theory long since exploded.* Materialists and Evolutionists greedily swallowed the theory, to escape the admission of God and a soul. But scientists like Pasteur have proved conclusively that life always has its origin in antecedent life. Worms in putrified meat are due to eggs laid by flies, and the worms are the larvæ of future flies. Worms in apples and pears are larvæ of nocturnal butterflies. Pasteur showed by experiment that no life develops in a liquid, when germs are completely shut out. All appearances of spontaneous generation are due to germ-deposits from the air. Haeckel and Darwin admit that spontaneous generation is a postulate of Evolution. There is a wide difference between modern Materialism and the old Scholastics in this matter. Scholastics ascribed everything to God and the planets. Spontaneous generation is opposed to experience and reason. No instance of the thing can be adduced, and its advocates appeal to earlier times, ages back, when nature was younger and its forces fresher; as though the specific nature of these forces had undergone a change. Reason cries out against the theory, because no effect can be superior to its total cause.

About the first origin of life, it is then certain that living beings are not sprung from minerals or dead matter. God produced first life with the coöperation of matter. He made matter fit to receive life, and produced life in this prepared matter, not by creation, but by educing vital forms from it. These first organisms could have been seeds or perfect plants and animals of full growth. He could have made all the different species of plants and animals now extinct and as we have them, or He could have made a few inferior species in the plant and animal kingdoms from which the others were successively evolved. This much is certain, that man's soul is immediately created in every individual instance. Adam's body in the obvious sense of Scripture came immediately from the hands of God, without any process of evolution from lower life. Theologians commonly agree that at least the lower species of plant and animal life came immediately from God, and not from natural evolution. The souls of plants and brutes are substantial, but material and non-subsistent. They do not consist of matter, but are educed from matter, and are intrinsically dependent on matter for their being and activity. They cannot exist apart from matter. A thing's highest operation or activity settles the quality of its being, and the highest operations of plants and brutes are intrinsically dependent on matter. Nutrition, growth, generation, sensation, cannot be exerted without organs. *Man's soul is intrinsically dependent on organs for vegetative and sensitive life. In intellectual operations it is extrinsically dependent on the senses or matter, and this dependence is due to union with the body. Separated from the body, it can think without dependence on organs; and this constitutes intrinsic independence of matter.* Souls of plants and brutes are not created, but generated; because creation has for term either a complete substance, like an angel, or a subsistent if not complete substance, like the human soul. The souls of plants and animals are not immortal, because they perish with the body's organism.

Life-giving principle. Soul is another name for the same thing. The eyes cannot see this life-giving principle in plants, or brutes, or men. A plant cannot be boiled down to secure it by evaporation or any known process of chemistry. But our knowledge is not limited to the visible universe. It reaches beyond, to a world of beings too closely allied with the intellect to be grasped by the gross senses. Organism is not this principle of life, though it invariably accompanies the same; because organism perseveres after life's disappearance from the body. It is a substantial form, an incomplete substance, which escapes in its details our present imperfect vision.

This life-giving principle is a substance, because no accident can give species to living body.

It is a form, because it is not prime matter, which is potency and no act.

It is a soul, because the vital principle in living bodies.

It is a principle, or that from which another proceeds. Such a principle must be admitted; otherwise we have an effect without a cause, or we make God second cause of everything.

Adversaries: Materialists deny in all three kingdoms — Tongiorgi denies in plants — Cartesians deny in plants and animals — Materialists explain life mechanically, by local motion;

physically and chemically, by forces. We recognize this principle in a general way as the reality which restricts or limits living beings to their place or class in the universe of existences. St. Thomas with Aristotle describes this soul as "*Actus primus corporis physici, organici, potentia vitam habentis.*" Explanation: Actus is an imperfect translation of Aristotle's word which means finish or completion, entelechy. First act or finish, because it is a form which determines to species; matter without form is undetermined. The body in man is not a form, because it actuates no subject. First form, because it is a substantial form; because there is no form prior to it. Physical means natural, not artificial or mathematical. Scotus posits a forma corporeitatis. This is the question with Scotus, is the body prime matter or second matter? We maintain that one and the same soul constitutes prime matter a body and a living body, as substantial form and vital principle. The life mentioned in our definition of Soul is accidental life, not substantial.

This principle of life is not the body, because one perseveres in the other's absence, and in that event every body would be a living body. It is material in the sense of intrinsic dependence, not in the sense of three dimensions. A word about its faculties or powers. Vital acts are ascribed to three principles. The principium quod is the suppositum or whole agent, body and soul; the principium quo remotum is the soul; the principium quo proximum is some particular faculty of the soul. Faculties are organic and inorganic. Organic are in whole composite, and they are vegetative and sensitive. Inorganic are in soul alone, and they are intellectual. Faculties are active and passive. Active need no outside object as determinant, and they are vegetative. Passive need such an object, and they are sensitive. The intellect is both active and passive; passive, inasmuch as it needs a phantasm for the imprinted intelligible image; active, inasmuch as with this image it elicits the developed intelligible image or idea. From this point of view agens is passive, possibilis is active. All faculties are active inasmuch as they actively operate; for this reason the agens is active as well as passive, and the same is true of the senses. Act and formal object give name to faculty. Vital acts are six, vegetative, sensitive, intellectual, appetite, will, locomotion. Soul and faculties are really distinct with inadequate distinction, because soul is designed to inform body, faculties are designed to work; soul is faculties and something besides.

Essentially different. The physical and chemical forces of nature, blended with organism, differ indeed accidentally from the same forces, considered in themselves and apart from all organism; and Tongiorgi thinks these forces, thus accidentally modified, a sufficient explanation of life in plants. We contend for a still greater, an essential difference between the principle of life and these forces. The former, instead of being the latter, exercises the authority of a sovereign over them, and compels them to elicit, when under its potent influence, effects wholly different from ordinary results. Of course, the principle of life and material forces are in substantial union; not in accidental union, as Plato and others teach. Thus, oxygen in contact with anorganic bodies works havoc and destruction. It rusts iron, consumes wood, decomposes lifeless flesh. But oxygen is inhaled in thick volumes by ailing patients. Indeed, for diseases like pneumonia, repeated draughts of pure oxygen are most healthful medicine. We enumerate nine conspicuous differences between plants and minerals.

(1) *Make-up and constitution.* Plants are heterogeneous; minerals, homogeneous. Plants are made up of wood, bark, leaves, roots, cells, fibers. Minerals are the same throughout.

(2) *Origin.* Plants result from seed or generation; minerals, from chemical composition.

(3) *Reproduction.* By fission, gemmation, ovulation; minerals are multiplied by outside agency, by breaking asunder.

(4) *Growth.* Plants grow by intussusception, and are never born with their full size; minerals grow by successive additions from without and are of any size.

(5) *Size.* Each species of plant has its own fixed size; minerals attain to any size.

(6) *Duration.* Every plant has its own limited duration; minerals are of unlimited duration. Plants destroy themselves; minerals are destroyed by outside agencies.

(7) *Shape.* Every plant has its own fixed shape, and curves predominate; minerals assume any shape, and straight lines predominate. Most minerals are shapeless, some occur as crys-

tals or geometrical figures, and can always be broken into crystals of smaller dimensions.

(8) *Chemical composition.* In plants the chemical elements are complex; in minerals, simple. Protoplasm or life-stuff is made up of carbon, hydrogen, oxygen, nitrogen. Sulphur and phosphorus frequently occur. Iron enters the blood. Calcium and magnesium in the form of phosphates enter the bones. Potassium is required for muscular tissue; sodium and chlorine for the secretions. Minerals are made up of one or two elements, and their composition is stable.

(9) *The activity of plants is immanent; that of minerals, transient.*

N.B. If life were the product of physical and chemical forces, it would be possible to form a living body by suitable combinations. And yet no plant, not even the lowest moss, can be produced from the crucible. The chemical constituents of the animal body are well known, their proportions and affinities can be expressed in arithmetical formulæ; but no scientist has ever yet produced an organism. We know exactly the elements of an egg, how much oxygen, how much hydrogen, how much nitrogen; we can blend them in accurate proportions; but science cannot make an egg able to hatch a tadpole. No laboratory will ever create a cell, a muscle, a nerve. In life there is a something present that science cannot detect, and this something is the principle of life, the soul. The substantial changes manifest in life-action are Scholasticism's chiefest argument for the existence of matter and form. Without matter and form these changes would be a series of annihilations and creations, processes beyond the reach of mere creatures or natural agents. Hydrogen and oxygen are transformed by the electric spark into water; and water is transformed by the same agency back again to hydrogen and oxygen. The matter of a living being is changed by retrograde metamorphosis into inorganic substances to become the food of a plant, and the plant becomes the food of an animal. That animal may be the very one from which this traveling matter originally came. Carbonic acid in the air is decomposed by plants. These plants give back the oxygen, to retain the carbon. This carbon in the plant finds its way back to an animal in the form of vegetable food, and, brought into contact with the oxygen supplied by the lungs, is given forth in respiration in the form of carbonic acid. And the process begins all over again. All change postulates a subject common to each term of the change, unless we want to admit annihilation and creation; and this common subject is prime matter, materia prima.

Inert. Inert is here opposed to alive or living. Inert can mean inactive; but absolute inactivity is unknown among God's creatures. Every being, even the most insignificant in the universe of existences, a grain of sand, exerts a power proper and peculiar to itself. Inert therefore means lifeless, incapable of self-motion or immanent action.

Physical and chemical forces. Cohesion, attraction, repulsion, gravity, chemical union, affinity, proportions, and others of the same nature too numerous to mention, and discussed at great length in Physics and Chemistry.

Brute animals. As soon as a living being gives conclusive evidence of a sense, external or internal, with no pretensions to any superior faculty, we assign it to the category of brute animals.

Three operations in man and brute absent from plants: They apprehend bodies according to qualities, having external and internal senses with sensorial organs. They seek or shun bodies thus apprehended, having appetite. They move locally towards or away from bodies thus apprehended, having locomotion.

The recognition of objects manifest in brutes, is sufficient foundation for attributing to them the possession of senses; while absence of speech and of all mechanical progress induces us to deny them the possession of intellects. Transmigration makes brutes as intellectual as man. Pythagoras, Empedocles, Democritus, Anaxagoras, Epicureans deny man's superiority. Sensists, Physiologists and Materialists make all knowledge a physical and chemical process. Darwinists give inferior minds to brutes. Some animals are more perfect than others. They are commonly graded in our estimation by the fineness and number of their senses. Thus, while not a few are limited to the use of one single sense, others rejoice in the full exercise of all the external and internal senses we ascribe to man. But the most perfect never evince signs calculated to persuade the unprejudiced mind that they understand. They hear, they see, they remember, they dream; but they never elicit an idea, never utter a judgment, never give expression to a syllogism. Some brutes surpass men in the possession of a certain single sense, usually the sense employed for purposes of self-preservation. But no brute has all nine senses of the same uniform fineness as man's. Their soul, or principle of life, is material; not in the sense that it has quantity, can be weighed, or measured, or handled; but in the sense that for all its being and all its operations it is dependent on the body, or matter. It is derived from the parents in its entirety, because it possesses no specific property transcending the nature of material faculties, like the senses. It perishes with the body. Such dependence is reckoned intrinsic and extrinsic. Man's soul essentially connotes extrinsic dependence on body or matter. In its first operations it presupposes and demands as a necessary requisite some previous work of the senses. It is not the gift of parent to child, but is the result of a new act of creation in each individual instance. In itself it can exist, and after death it does exist, without any dependence whatever on the body, that crumbles to dust. Sensitive life presupposes vegetative. We note these several differences between the two.

1. Chemical elements in the animal combine in fours to form albumen; and these elements are carbon, hydrogen, oxygen and nitrogen; in plants, they combine in threes to form cellulose; and they are carbon, hydrogen and oxygen.

2. In brutes vegetative life is made more perfect by union with sensitive, and changes food into flesh, bones and nerves.

3. Animals feed on plants and other animals; plants feed on minerals. Organic food supports animals; inorganic, plants.

4. Sensation is specific difference between plants and brutes; and sensation is the perception of bodily substances in the concrete.

Automatic machines. No machine is strictly automatic, but only such in appearance. The word is of Greek origin, and signifies a thing gifted with self-will or self-motion. And yet there are machines, which from the nice perfection of their mechanism lead the superficial observer to conclude that they derive their motion from nothing external to themselves. Thus, the watch and locomotive to all appearances depend on no outside agency for their motion. But the watch will run down and stop, unless its owner at stated intervals applies the physical force needed to wind it up; the locomotive will come to a standstill, unless its cylinder is kept well supplied with steam. Brute animals differ from locomotives and watches in this, that, once in existence, they are capable of passing from one place to another and of eliciting various acts without any absolute dependence on beings or forces external to themselves. It was an opinion of Descartes that brutes are machines set in motion and kept in motion by the immediate influence of God.

Sense and Intellect. The intellect is a spiritual cognoscitive faculty, able to know immaterial objects and material objects in an immaterial, universal, abstract way; able to know the causes and essences of things; able to reflect on itself and its acts, to pronounce formal judgments, and to formally reason. A formal judgment unites or separates ideas; it affirms or denies; a virtual is matter for a formal, it comprehends without uniting or separating. Sensations are virtual judgments, and they deal with concrete qualities of individual things; e.g. color and shape of bread. Such a virtual judgment moves sensitive appetite.

Sense is a material cognoscitive faculty; knows material objects in a material way.

DIAGRAM

- Cognoscitive Faculties, Instruments of Knowledge
  - Senses
    - External
      - Sight
      - Hearing
      - Touch
      - Taste
      - Smell
    - Internal
      - Sensile Discrimination
      - Imagination
      - Sensile Consciousness
      - Sensile Memory
  - Intellect
    - Working
    - Receiving
      - Intelligence
      - Judgment
      - Reason
      - Consciousness
      - Memory

N.B. For explanation see Thesis II.

Division — Four Parts and a corollary —

I. Life is capacity for self-motion.
II. Soul of plant, essentially different from physical and chemical forces of plant.
III. Brute animals have senses.
IV. Brute animals have no intellect.
Corollary — Evolution is absurd.

PROOFS, I, II, III, IV

I. N.B. This first part is a definition, and definitions need not be proved, but explained. A definition is a principle, by supposition the subject contains the predicate. We need only show that our definition is correct, that it applies to living beings and none else.

It is the common opinion of mankind that things gifted with the capability of self-motion or immanent action are alive, and that things without the same capability are dead.

But what renders a thing alive is life, and in certain circumstances, here fulfilled, the common opinion of mankind is infallible.

Ergo life is capability of self-motion or immanent action; life is that perfection in a being which makes self-motion or immanent action possible.

With regard to the Major. To the average mind motion always suggests life; stillness, death. And the thing is clear in the case of a live or dead animal. With motion in evidence minds always satisfy themselves regarding the presence or absence of life by determining motion's origin. Flowing water is an instance.

With regard to the Minor. The judgment partakes of the nature of a moral judgment.

II. N.B. Recall notions regarding plants. Their principle of life is a substantial form called soul. They have three operations. They have no sensation. Their soul is non-subsistent. Their soul is indivisible in itself; divisible because of matter. Plants live because a one suppositum, in which activity begins and ends. One suppositum, because one activity, and everything concurs to produce seed and evolve organism. Activity begins and ends in plant, because organism takes up nutriment, assimilates it to own substance, and distributes it —

Plants possess a, energies, and b, qualities, essentially different from those of minerals or dead matter. But no effect exists in nature without its proper cause.

Ergo there is in plants some cause of these energies and qualities essentially different from those of minerals, namely, physical and chemical forces. In one word there must reside in plants a principle of life, designed to order aright and watch over these physical and chemical forces.

With regard to the Major. (a) The origin, growth and reproduction of plants are quite different from those of minerals. A plant begins as a minute cell, feeds on surrounding matter, grows, multiplies itself into other cells, which in turn combine to form the embryo. From the embryo a perfect organism arises. Besides, the plant mends whatever parts suffer loss, and keeps itself alive. Minerals betray no such energy. Their every act is transient, and they grow only from without.

(b) Plants are organic beings. Witness the cells in a tree, the roots, stalk, leaves, petals and intricate details of the flower in a rosebush. The chemical composition of plants is another feature distinguishing them from minerals. The shape of a plant is uniform and constant for the same species; minerals are indifferent to all shapes. Crystallization induces set and regular forms in minerals; but each crystal admits of division into others of the same character. Besides, the lines in a crystal are invariably straight, while in plants they are at one time straight, at another time curved.

III. 1. It is the common opinion of mankind, strengthened by most evident signs on the part of brute creation and by the wonderful structure of brute bodies, that animals possess the faculty of sense, a) external and (b) internal. They have organs, operations, effects, phenomena, like our own. But the common opinion of mankind thus strengthened is an infallible guide. Ergo animals possess the faculty of sense, and are not mere automatic machines.

With regard to the Major. (a) About external senses there can be no difficulty.

(b) Signs of internal senses follow. Sensile consciousness or central sense is evinced from the fact, that to hear, a dog uses his ears, not his eyes or tail; imagination from the fact, that a dog barks in his sleep and goes through all the motions of a street-fight. Sensile memory enables a dog to seek home, and to find his master in a crowd. With the help of sensile discrimination or instinct birds gather straw for their nest, and a young sheep dreads the wolf.

2. Brutes have sense-organs. Ergo they have sense.

3. Brutes have sensitive appetite, as their movements make evident. But appetite supposes knowledge. Ergo they have sense.

IV. Brutes give unmistakable evidence that they are possessed of (a) neither universal ideas, (b) nor psychological reflection. But beings without universal ideas and psychological reflection are without intellect. Ergo brute animals are without intellect.

With regard to the Major. (a, b.) (a) The fact that we have universal ideas is betokened by our use of arbitrary and conventional signs for language. But the use of such signs is unknown among brute animals. Ergo.

Brutes make themselves understood by natural signs, and are utter strangers to speech. Parrots can be taught by combinations of images in the fancy to emit a limited number of sounds, but these sounds do not constitute language.

(b) Psychological reflection, turning wholly on ourselves and our acts, leads us to change our methods, to indefinitely improve on our own works and those of others, and to make progress generally. But no such change of methods, no such improvement or progress appears in the lives of brute animals. Ergo.

Corollary — Universal Evolution or Darwinism is therefore absurd.

Evolution derives all the different species of plants and animals from one or a few primitive species. In his early work Darwin admits that the beginning of things is an insoluble problem, and declares himself an agnostic. When younger he acknowledged a Creator, to account for primitive species. Later in life he abandoned God altogether. This change was due to the logical development of his theory by men like Haeckel. Natural selection was the factor introduced by Darwin to explain the multiplication of species. The industry of man by breeding and crossing can effect changes in plants and animals. Nature, according to Darwin, can rival man in this process;

and nature's activity is displayed in natural selection. Variability, natural selection, heredity, struggle for existence and survival of the fittest are the magic terms occurring everywhere in Darwin's work. With him, natural selection is the prime cause of specific evolution; and natural selection is the preservation of favorable individual differences and variations, and the destruction of such as are injurious. All the young of plants and animals cannot reach maturity. A codfish lays 9,000,000 eggs in a season. In 750 years the elephants descended from a single pair would be 19,000,000. Our chief objections to natural selection are two. It is in itself insufficient, classes are not species; and it contradicts facts. Besides, it eliminates formal, final and efficient causality, to leave only material. It professes to get man from monkey. The form or essence of man is not latent in monkey as that of oxygen is in water, and such a man would be without a formal cause. No monkey can essay becoming a man, because that would mean self-destruction, and purpose would be wanting. No monkey can make himself a man, because effect would be superior to cause. Haeckel in Germany pushed Darwin's theory to its logical limit when, applying it to the world at large, he essayed to explain the origin of the universe, man included, from primordial matter; and Darwin was not long catching up with Haeckel. In this way, the theory of natural selection degenerated to the system of Realistic Monism. Monism, as the name implies, derives everything from one principle, matter. It is opposed to Dualism which recognizes spirit as well as matter. Monism is a gross mistake, because it denies God and immortality; because it advocates the fortuitous concourse of atoms, laughed to scorn by Cicero; and because it destroys all moral order. Haeckel himself was a mammoth fraud, and his open dishonesty robbed his old age of whatever prestige his early years enjoyed. Darwinists, with Haeckel, maintain that man is descended, body and soul, from the ape. One Friedenthal remarks that not only are we descended from monkeys, but we are monkeys ourselves. Advocates of the wild theory see an argument in the circumstance, that the differences between men of two races are greater and more striking than the differences between a man and an ape. They close their eyes to the fact that the difference between souls of men is one of degree, not of kind; while the difference between the souls of men and souls of apes is one of kind, not merely of degree. The soul of man is not descended from the soul of an ape. Reason and revelation bear loud witness that the soul of man is spiritual and created. Neither is man's body descended from the body of an ape. Arguments to the contrary are nothing worth. They are mainly two, resemblances and paleontology, or ancient remains. In their zeal to discover resemblances our opponents neglect differences. The differences between the body of a man and the body of an ape are too wide to countenance one's origin from the other. The skull-cap, the brain, and the bones are worth study. Muckermann, S.J., has tables to prove that the skull-cap of man is about three times as large as that of an ape. The circumference of a man's skull is twice that of an ape's. The human brain is three times heavier than that of the ape. In man it is the 37th part of his body's weight; in an ape, the 100th part. Speaking of bones, Virchow says, "The differences are so wide, that almost any fragment is sufficient to diagnose them."

Besides, no intermediate form occurs to bridge the chasm between man and ape. The missing link is still missing. The wisdom of the Creator is sufficient explanation for all the discovered resemblances. Man is the king of creation, and ought to embrace all kingdoms. *Infimi supremum debet attingere infimum supremi. Natura odit saltus.* The argument from paleontology is of as little weight. The Pithecanthropus erectus and the Neanderthal skull-cap prove nothing. The bones of the first were found in different places and put together, a farcical imposition. No ape ever yet regularly walked erect. Dancing bears are trained to walk on their hind-legs, but the attitude is unnatural and violent. The Neanderthal skull-cap might belong to anything, a Hollander, a German, an Icelander or a Celt. All paleontological finds prove man possessed of intellect. Hence the various implements of the Stone, Iron and Brass Ages.

N.B. Not all Evolution is Darwinism. Evolution itself is opposed to constancy or fixity of species; and Evolution is of two kinds, Universal or Sweeping and Particular or Restricted. Constancy holds that all species of plants and animals, as they now exist, were created. Sweeping Evolution holds that a few elementary organic bodies took their rise in matter from chance grouping of atoms. Restricted Evolution teaches that a few species of plants and animals were created, the others developed; God created first organisms and gave them special power to develop higher. Man and his soul are excepted. Man was created, body and soul. Mivart derives man's body from the ape. Of these theories, constancy or fixity of species is most in harmony with simple faith, and most in disfavor with modern science. Sweeping Evolution is Realistic Monism and downright ignorance. Restricted Evolution is semi-scientific, not opposed to so-called educated faith, and is held by Catholic scientists, like Wassmann, S.J. Hence our thesis: (*a*) *Universal Evolution or Darwinism is opposed to right reason; Particular or Restricted Evolution is* (*b*) *without foundation, and* (*c*) *contradicts facts.*

With regard to the terms. Species in Evolution means a collection of individuals more or less alike, capable of progeny without limit. The two requisite elements are, like shape and fertility. Members of the same species can have accidental differences. *A variety is such a collection of the same species as have the same accidental differences. The variety is called a race if these accidental differences are handed down by generation and become fixed.* By law of reversion, varieties return to primitive type, unless pairs of the same variety generate.

Fixity or constancy of species means that one species never becomes another. All the species of plants and animals, as they now exist, were in existence from the beginning.

Evolution means that all the species now extinct and now in existence are sprung from one or a few primitive species.

The language our opponents employ is about as follows: Variation in species is inherited by offspring. Nature by means of natural selection fosters some characteristics, and lets others disappear. The struggle for existence is nature's abettor in this task. As a result of the struggle, only the fittest survive. These survivors with the lapse of ages originate entirely new species of plants and animals, the series ending in man himself. Darwin has no explanation for the origin of life. Heredity, natural selection, struggle for existence are the factors he employs to explain the origin of species.

Proofs. (*a*) Universal Evolution or Darwinism denies God and immortality; postulates fortuitous concourse of atoms, and spontaneous generation; and destroys the moral order.

(*b*) Heredity is no explanation, because only specific characteristics are transmitted naturally. Accidental characteristics are transmitted only by the interference of an intellectual cause like man, and such varieties naturally revert to original type. Eventually the progeny of mulattoes is coal black. A donkey, as St. Thomas says, never essays becoming a horse, because that would mean self-destruction. Natural selection is no explanation, because in this case a blind agent would be able to accomplish what man has not yet been able to do, develop a new species. The struggle for existence would account for the disappearance of lower, not for the evolution of higher species.

(*c*) It contradicts present as well as past experience. Evolutionists admit that at present like generates like, and by no process can new species be gotten from old. They appeal to the past with as little success. Within history, Job and Aristotle describe animals and plants of the same complexion as our own. Plants, dogs, cats, birds and cows found in Egyptian tombs, and five thousand years old, are like our own. Fossils come down from prehistoric times are like present-day animals, unless they happen to be extinct; and there is no trace of intervening types, which ought to be numerous in the hypothesis of evolution.

Principles. Rudimentary organs can have ornament for purpose as well as utility. Sweeping Evolution is against faith. Some, like Lamy and Urraburu, think Restricted Evolution, even when not extended to men, against the faith; others see no opposition. Nearly all Catholic theologians vote it highly wrong to ascribe the origin of man's body to evolution from a monkey. It was immediately produced from slime of the earth.

PRINCIPLES

A. 1. The chemical elements in a molecule perfect themselves. Ergo immanent action.

2. The flame in a candle feeds on the wax. Ergo immanent action.

3. Sensation is determined by object, an extrinsic principle. Ergo no immanent action.

4. Motion is always from another. Ergo no self-motion.

Answers. (1) Each atom perfects another atom, or the atoms together make a new substance. Ergo no immanent act.

(2) The flame is not one substance, but an aggregate; and it does not feed on the wax by intussusception.

(3) The object determines sensation objectively, not subjectively. Sight is from the eye; the sight of this or that thing is from the object.

(4) Motion is from another, but that other can be united with the thing moved. The mind is not the man, but is united with him.

B. 1. Immanence is of only one kind. Ergo only one kind of life.

2. In brutes vegetative life produces sensitive substance; sensitive life, only accidents. Ergo vegetative is superior to sensitive.

3. Mere execution of motion is life for plants. Minerals execute motion. Ergo they have life.

4. Sensation is superior to vegetation because of forms assumed. But vegetation assumes forms, leaves and the like. Ergo no superiority.

5. Plants assume material substances; senses material accidents. Ergo senses not superior.

Answers. (1) Immanence itself is of only one kind; but acts vested with immanence are of three kinds, vegetation, sensation, thought.

(2) Vegetative life in brutes produces sensitive substance not by itself, but in conjunction with sensitive life. The accidents produced by sensation are in the order of knowledge, and therefore higher than mere vegetation.

(3) The motion of minerals passes to outside objects, it is not received in the minerals themselves. Principle outside. One molecule perfects another, it never perfects itself.

(4) The forms vegetation assumes are determined by nature, and in the material order; those of sensation are determined by the agent, and in the cognoscitive order.

(5) The material accidents assumed in sensation are of a

higher order than the material substances assumed in vegetation.

C. 1. Difference of origin proves no essential difference. An apple can be created or grown.

2. Difference in duration proves no essential difference. Men die at different ages.

3. Living beings tend towards quiet as well as minerals. Everything dies. Ergo tendency to motion is no sign of life.

4. Difference in activity proves no essential difference in being. Moderate heat cures, excessive heat kills.

Answers. (1) Difference in natural origin proves essential difference. Creation is supernatural in sense that it transcends the power of created natures. God alone can create.

(2) Duration constitutes essential difference between plants and minerals, not because long and short, but because determined and undetermined.

(3) Life when born never tends to quiet; when developed, it tends not to the quiet of death, but to cessation from vital changes.

(4) To cure or kill is not the formal effect of heat, but of a greater or less degree of heat. We argue from formal effects of plants and minerals.

D. 1. Difference in the combination of atoms can explain life, without any principle of life or soul. Letters and arrangement, meaning and no meaning.

2. Chemical analysis can detect no principle of life. Ergo none exists.

3. The soul is that at the disappearance of which life ceases. Life in the plant ceases when its parts are sundered and disturbed. Ergo.

4. The principle of life is neither a substance nor an accident, neither a body nor a spirit.

5. A plant is no more one substance than a machine.

Answers. (1) Difference in combination cannot explain generation, tendency to motion, necessity of union among parts, determined duration. Letters get meaning not from themselves, but from relation to men's ideas.

(2) Reason can detect what escapes the notice of chemical analysis. It is not the business of chemical analysis to detect souls.

(3) Cohesion and arrangement of parts are conditions of life, not its formal cause.

(4) The principle of life is an incomplete substance, it is neither a body nor a spirit; but it is something material or something spiritual.

(5) Unity in the machine comes from without; unity in the plant comes from within.

E. Some points of difference between the intellect and the senses. The senses acquire knowledge of only individual material objects without any generalization. They attain to the composite substance, inasmuch as it is a jumble of essence, properties and accidents; and are primarily affected by the properties and accidents in things. They are never capable of an explicit judgment; but only apprehend, without any union or separation of ideas. The intellect takes up sensible perception, and, separating the essence and substance from their properties and accidents, views them alone, and so acquires universal ideas. It compares one idea with another, and, when satisfied that a resemblance exists, units the two by affirmation, or elicits a judgment. The appetites follow the natures of their prime movers. Thus, the sensible appetite, wholly dependent on the senses for its every movement, never looks beyond material goods. The intellectual appetite, because intellect is the mainspring of its actions, soars beyond matter.

F. Mr. Broderip's story of a dog at crossroads seems to prove syllogism and reason. The dog tries in vain for scent of his master along two branches. Returning, he trots along third branch, with nose in the air. The dog would seem to argue thus: My master is somewhere along one of these three roads. He is not along two of them. Ergo he walks the third.

Answer. The phenomenon admits of a dozen different explanations. The dog may have detected ground or air traces of his master only after completing examination of first two roads. A dog can scent his master without keeping his nose to the ground.

G. The artistic effects of brute animals are due to the instinct they receive from God, and are wrought after so mechanical and unvarying a way that the animals themselves are rather passive than active with regard to the artistic element inherent in them.

H. Absolutely speaking, God could have created animals mere automatons; but at present such creation is an utter impossibility, unless we want to accuse God of wilfully and effectively deceiving us at every step.

(*I*) Identity of vegetative and sensitive souls. In a brute animal there is but one soul, the principle of vegetation and sensation. One and the same soul is the remote principle of growth and sensation; the faculties or proximate principles are several and distinct. The animal has but one being and one activity. It gets both from the principle of life or the soul. Ergo the soul is one. It has but one being, because it is one individual. It has but one activity, and therefore but one principle, because its activity is immanent, and this would be impossible in the event of several principles. Other reasons: When growth ceases, sensation is at an end; and vice-versa. Growth ministers to the organs of sense, and sensation is impaired when growth is disturbed by disease or drink. Growth and sensation are of uniform perfection in the different species.

(*J*) The souls of brutes are non-subsistent. They are not accidents, but incomplete substances and non-subsistent; that is, they have no being or activity independent of matter or the body's organs. Reasons: Growth and sensation are a brute's highest activity, and both are intrinsically dependent on organs. When an organ of sense is injured or diseased, the corresponding sensation is impossible. The senses are tired by frequent and intense application, they are disturbed by violent excitation, and these are signs of intrinsic dependence on organs.

Corollaries. 1. The brute soul is not created. Supernaturally, it can be created; but naturally, it calls for production from something of subject; and creation is production from nothing of self and subject. Naturally speaking, what cannot continue in existence without matter, cannot begin its existence without matter. In first production, the whole brute, body and soul, was created.

2. The souls of brutes are generated by their parents, because the whole suppositum is generated, and creation is out of the question.

3. Souls of brutes die with the body. They are corrupted by accident, not in themselves.

(*K*) *About the divisibility of souls.* *X. Y. Z.*

X. The soul of man is alone indivisible per se and per accidens.

Y. All other souls are divisible per accidens.

Z. The souls of more perfect brutes die in part when divided. *X.* The human soul is indivisible. Reasons: The part in an amputated limb would corrupt or remain; and neither supposition is tenable. The same soul thinks, wishes, sees, hears, and the like; and consciousness vouches for this. All the parts would think or only one part; and both suppositions are impossible. All the parts would be free or only one part; and the two suppositions are impossible. Simple acts call for simple principles; and thoughts are simple acts. Simplicity goes with spirituality, not vice-versa.

PRINCIPLES

(*1*) Man's soul has quantity, because it is received in body and is spread over body.

Answer. It is received and spread in such a way that the whole soul is in the whole body and in each part of the body.

(*2*) The soul is affected by bodies.

Answer. Not in itself, but because of union with the body.

(*3*) That would be multilocation.

Answer. Multilocation calls for several adequate places. The soul is in one adequate place, the whole body.

(*4*) The soul would move and be quiet at the same time.

Answer. Under different respects.

(*5*) The soul would have to withdraw from an amputated limb.

Answer. Soul simply loses one of its presences.

(*6*) The soul reappears in an affixed limb.

Answer. The affixed limb is all right for vegetative powers of soul in rest of body.

Y. In plants and imperfect brutes the soul is divisible. Reasons: Experience with worms and snakes; shoots and grafts. If parts of the soul animate cut portions of the plant or animal, the soul must have had parts in potency before the cutting. These parts because of union were actually one soul, potentially many souls. Actual simplicity is compatible with composition in potency, or indivisibility per se is compatible with divisibility per accidens. If the severed portion of the body is without the requisite organism for life, the soul in it ceases to exist, because intrinsically dependent on matter. Imperfect animals are such as have few senses and a ruder organism, like earth-worms. Even plants and worms, when cut into small pieces, die; because the organism is defective in minute portions. Plants and animals cannot be divided longitudinally but transversely, because of organism. *Z.* In perfect brutes the soul is divisible, but it dies in part. It has no parts per se, it has parts per accidens; and it dies in part because of intrinsic dependence on organism. Reasons: Souls in perfect brutes are as material as souls in imperfect brutes, and therefore divisible per accidens. After division parts die, because of more intricate organism. A part of the soul disappears from the severed portion. Not the whole soul. Ergo a part only. The whole soul would either corrupt, or subsist in itself, or retire to the live portion. Not corrupt, because whole soul exists in live portion. Not subsist in itself, because it is material. Not retire to live portion, because that portion already has a soul. Part of the soul corrupts, because corruptible by accident. *N. B.* Different in man, because his soul is spiritual and exists independent of matter. In an amputated limb man's soul neither corrupts, nor subsists in itself, nor retires to live portion of body. Man's soul admits of no composition in potency, or by reason of matter. It simply ceases to inform or actuate the amputated limb. In material souls, to exist and to actuate are the same; in a spiritual soul, to exist and to actuate are not the same. The human soul can cease to actuate without ceasing to exist.

P. S. When the organism in plant or animal is divided, the soul is by accident divided, because it intrinsically depends on matter and shares in matter's imperfection. The form or any quality of gold is divided in the same way. The soul, as form of plant or animal, is as dependent on matter for its being as the form or any quality of gold. The soul in a separated branch is no proof that there were actually several souls in the tree, but only potentially.

THESIS II

Sensation is an immanent and cognoscitive act. There can be no sensation without a faculty, an object, and union between the two in the faculty. Sensation perceives the object, not its species or image, not the organ impression.

Maher, pp. 63–208; 26–54. *Jouin*, pp. 161–171.

QUESTION

Division.—Three parts.

I. What is sensation? It is an immanent and cognoscitive act.

II. How is sensation accomplished? By union of faculty and object in faculty.

III. What does it perceive? The outside object.

Adversaries. I, II, III.

I. *Materialists deny soul, and make sensation a purely mechanical and transient act.* With them, sensation is motion transmitted to the brain and provoking modifications and reactions of a purely mechanical nature. In other words, sensation is molecular motion of the brain, whether phosphorescence, or electrical tension, or what not.

II. *With Descartes, the soul is always thinking. With Leibnitz, every thought has its sufficient reason in some prior thought.* Scholastics, whether in sensation or thought, demand union between faculty and object. Object cannot be united with faculty. Hence a substitute is needed, and this is the species impressa. Act must be immanent. Hence species expressa.

III. *Locke and Cartesians deny objectivity of sensations.* Species and organ-changes are that which is known, and in which objects are known.

TERMS

Faculties. Aristotle attributes five powers or faculties to the soul of man, vegetative, locomotive, appetite, sense, reason. The first four are common to man and brute. The fifth is proper and peculiar to man. The first two have no bearing on knowledge, and can for the present be neglected. St. Thomas emphasizes the difference between sensitive appetite and rational appetite. As sense and reason are two phases of knowledge, appetite and will are two phases of desire. Therefore, all question of growth and locomotion aside, the soul of man embraces these four faculties or powers, sense and reason in the cognitive order, appetite and will in the appetitive order. And with these four topics we are especially concerned in Psychology.

Senses and Sensation. The senses are the first of man's cognitive faculties to halt our attention. We met them in Major Logic, and we can best begin by recalling some of the notions there set down. *We then described the senses as material, organic, cognoscitive faculties, common to man and brute. They are instruments employed by man in his acquisition of sensations. Sensations in man are modifications of a living organ of sense, presenting to its owner some object affected with extension and resistance. An organ is any part of a living body possessed of a structure adapted to the performance of some function closely allied with life. The sense is called sight; the sensation, vision; the organ, the eye. Intellect is that spiritual, inorganic, cognoscitive faculty in man, separating him from brute creation; or the faculty attaining to all the knowledge peculiar to the senses, and furnishing man with a universal and abstract knowledge, to which the senses cannot aspire.* Returning to the senses, they are external and internal.

External, when organ is on surface of agent, and object is outside of agent; internal, when organ is in brain and object is inside the agent. The external senses are five, sight, hearing, touch, taste and smell, because there are five organs. There is no sixth sense, because there is no sixth organ. The internal senses are four, 1, sensus communis, sensile consciousness, or central sense; 2, vis æstimativa, sensile discrimination or instinct; 3, sensile memory; and 4, imagination. The one intellect exercises three different functions, called simple apprehension, judgment and reasoning. The resultants of these several functions, expressed in language, are the word, the proposition and the syllogism. In the production of an idea the intellect acts in a twofold capacity. Under one aspect it is called intellectus agens, or the working intellect; under the other, intellectus possibilis, or the receiving intellect. As working intellect, it conspires with the phantasm to effect what we call the imprinted intelligible image. As receiving intellect it coöperates with the imprinted intelligible image to produce the developed intelligible image, or idea proper.

Without wishing to lose ourselves in a labyrinth of questions, and with no desire to encroach on the domain of physiology, it will be enough for the present to merely note the organs and the objects of the several senses, external and internal. The organ of sight is the eye, its formal object is colored surface, or color. The organ of hearing is the ear, its formal object is sound. The organ of touch is the whole outer surface of the body, its formal object is manifold; roughness and smoothness, temperature, organic disturbance, pressure, resistance. The organ of smell is the inner surface of the nose, its formal object is odor. The organ of taste is the surface of tongue and palate, its formal object is sweetness, bitterness and the like.

Of the internal senses it may be said in general that their organs are the nervous system and special compartments of the brain. The formal object or purpose of sensile consciousness is to discriminate between and differentiate the operations of the external senses, while they are present. The formal object or purpose of instinct is to apprehend objects as fit or useful to satisfy the needs of animal nature, which qualities escape the knowledge of the external senses. Sensile memory retains and excites past sensations. It adds to imagination the recognition of old sensations as past. Imagination retains and combines past sensations without knowing them for past sensations.

In every sensation we recognize three distinct stages, the action of some outward body on the organ, disturbance in nerves forwarded to the brain, and the conscious sensation. The outward body falls within the domain of Physics. Physiology has to do with the nerve-disturbance, and Psychology is busy with the sensation proper, the finished product. Physiologists tell us that our nervous apparatus is twofold, the sympathetic system for purposes of vegetation or growth, and the cerebro-spinal system for purposes of knowledge. We remark in passing that, while these nerves with the body's organs are joint factors in the production of sensations, they are no adequate explanation of the same. Even sense knowledge, whether in brutes or men, postulates in addition to nerves, organs, physical and chemical forces, a principle of life, a soul, too subtle to be detected by eye or microscope, simple per se, divisible per accidens and material, not in the sense that it is measurable, but in the sense that it is intrinsically dependent on matter for its existence and activity.

Materialism is, therefore, wrong, when it professes to explain even sense-knowledge with the single help of nerves, organs, and physical or chemical forces. It is wronger still, when it ascribes the same origin to thought or intellectual knowledge. Nerve action and molecular movement are conditions, not the cause of thought, and non causa pro causa is a sophism. Sensation is the work of neither the body nor the soul alone, but of the composite being resulting from the union of both, the animal. There is no sensation in a soul separated from the body. In hell God supplies for sensation. Our ideas are dependent on our senses up to the formation of the phantasm. Beyond that stage they are entirely spiritual; organs and nerves play no part whatever in their final production, and a wholly immaterial faculty, the intellect, is their single explanation. Apart, therefore, from the body and its organs, the intellect can exist and operate; and its dependence on the body is merely extrinsic, due entirely to our present condition, and open to complete reversal after death, or separation from the body.

Omitting the sympathetic system of nerves, the cerebro-spinal system can be best described as a central mass, connected with all the different parts of the body by wires. This central mass is made up of brain and spinal cord, the wires are the nerves. The spinal cord is a column of white fibrous matter, enclosing a core of gray cellular substance called the marrow. The nerves are strings proceeding in pairs from the back and front of the spinal column. The front, anterior, efferent or motor nerves transmit impulses outward, and are the instruments of muscular movement. The back, posterior, afferent or sensory nerves transmit impulses inward, and give rise to sensations. These nerves branch to all parts of the body in such profusion that the finest needle, applied to any portion of the body's surface, will come in contact with a nerve. The brain contains four compartments, the medulla oblongata, a prolongation of the spinal cord, with nerves for the face, heart and lungs; the cerebellum, above and back of the medulla, with nerves for locomotion; the pons Varolii, above and in front of the medulla; and the cerebrum, or large brain, above all, with its two hemispheres and its two fissures, the Sylvian and that of Rolando. The nerves with ends in the head would seem to be located in the four different compartments of the brain; those with ends in the rest of the body, in the spinal column. The nerves are in pairs, efferent and afferent, like the wires in an electric circuit; and this would seem to be the process of sensation. An impression wrought on the end-organ of an afferent nerve is transmitted to a center in the brain. At its arrival in the brain a sensation is awakened. Conscious sensation produces an impulse, which flowing back along a motor nerve causes movement. Treading on the foot is an example.

Sensation is not in the brain, but in the organ proper to the sensation in question. Scholastics are against physiologists in this matter. The outward organ receives the impression, and sends it on to the brain; reaction follows in the brain, to inform central sense, and go back to the outward organ. This reaction is responsible for the two species, imprinted and developed. *Reasons:* 1. Experience and common sense; 2. A hurt in the brain is not felt elsewhere; 3. The brain can be removed and sensation continue; 4. Peculiar construction is in organ, not in brain; 5. The brain finishes its work with the internal senses.

The motion is too slow to be electrical. It is no faster than 80 or 200 feet a second.

Physiologists have mapped the different nerve-centers in the brain, and located with more or less accuracy the positions of the several sense-centers. Thus, while the upper portion of the brain is reserved for memory and imagination, the origin of the olfactory nerves is in the center of the base of the brain; that of the optic nerves, a little back of the first pair. The other nerves start in the medulla, and they control the skin of the face, and the muscles of the tongue and jaws. The auditory and gustatory nerves are rooted here. The tactual and motor nerves arise lower down in the spinal cord. St. Thomas, in his treatise on the internal senses, assigns each its own definite compartment of the brain, and in his own crude way foreshadows the work of modern physiologists. The ends of the gustatory nerves are on the surface of the tongue and palate, and the body to be tasted must be in a state of solution. The ends of the olfactory nerves are in the membrane lining the inner surface of the nose, and the stimulating particles must be drawn over the sensitive surface by inhalation. The ends of the tactual nerves are in the dermis, immediately under the cuticle or outer skin. These papillae are stimulated by pressure on the outer skin. The ends of the auditory nerves are in the liquid distributed throughout the labyrinth or inner ear. The ends of the optic nerves are in the inner strata of the retina, and are a layer of rods and cones, conveying the image on the retina as a neural tremor to the brain. The ear and the eye are the most complicated of our sense-organs. Obviously we cannot enter into a detailed explanation of each. That would be to trespass on physiology. We therefore dismiss the subject with these few remarks. The ear is made up of three parts, the pinna or sail and meatus; the tympanum, drum or middle ear; and the labyrinth, or inner ear. The eye contains the sclerotic, the cornea or pupil, the choroid coat, the retina, the yellow spot and the blind spot.

We recognize in sensation two values, the emotional, or pleasure and pain; and the cognitive, or knowledge. In the order of emotion the senses are thus rated, systemic, taste, smell, hearing, touch, and sight. In the order of cognition this rating is reversed to sight, touch, hearing, smell, taste, systemic. This order stands only when the senses are viewed directly, without taking into account appropriation by means of association and inference.

Idealism questions the validity of our sensations as instruments of knowledge, contending that they can furnish us with no solid certainty regarding the objective reality of things. But this wrong system, evolved by Berkeley and others from false principles advanced by Descartes and Locke, was abundantly refuted in Cosmology; and we refer readers to that treatise.

Many important discoveries with a bearing on the growth and development of sense perception are due to physiological research, and they are being daily multiplied. Thus, the weight of the brain at birth is about one-sixth that of the whole body. During the child's first year it almost doubles its size, and after-growth is much less rapid. It is full sized at the end of the seventh year. In normal European adults it weighs from 46 to 52 ounces. The child is born deaf, and in the matter of sight is able merely to distinguish light from darkness, without the ability to discriminate colors. Infancy covers the first two years, when the senses reach maturity, and locomotion and speech are imperfectly acquired. Childhood reaches to the seventh year. During this period memory and imagination grow, play-impulse appears, knowledge of personality, self-consciousness and use of reason. Boyhood runs from seven to fourteen. This is the plastic period. Habits and passions are hard to dislodge at fifteen. Youth ranges from fourteen to twenty-one. Character becomes set and fixed; the passions are prominent, and these years are the season of ideals. This period colors the man's whole future life.

The primary and secondary qualities of matter are only the formal and material, or proper and common objects of the senses. Thus, color, sound and the like are primary qualities; while extension, figure, motion, rest, number and the like are secondary.

In every operation of the senses we must distinguish two phases or elements, one in the subject, the other in the object. Odor in me and odor in the rose, are a familiar example. The object must somehow get into the subject, and the two must come into close contact. Sensation perhaps best expresses the act from a subjective; perception, from an objective point of view. The Scholastics explain everything with their species intentionales, knowledge-likenesses or images. They are called intentionales because with their help the faculty tends towards or goes out to the object. A species with them was no material efflux from the object. Objects, according to them, always act on the organ through intervening media. *A species was a modification of the faculty, helping to knowledge of outside objects. It was a transference of the object to the faculty.* With them, outside objects were the things known, not their species. Sense and intellect never know species, they know the corresponding outside objects, trees, horses, and the like. They never pass from a knowledge of species to a knowledge of outside objects. And all this was pithily and accurately expressed in the formula: "*Species est id quo res intelligitur, non id quod intelligitur, neque id ex quo vel in quo res intelligitur.*" Locke and idealists in general make the mistake of limiting our knowledge or certainty to these species, declaring the species, id quod intelligitur. The Scholastics were wiser, and based their position on the following argument, contained in St. Thomas, 1, q. 85, A. 2. "Every such purely subjective view of knowledge is wrong, because what we know is ultimately the subject matter of science, and science deals with outside objects, like the stars, the elements, trees and such, not with modifications of the agent, like the species. Besides, this false theory renews the error of whatever ancient philosophers maintained that everything is exactly what it is perceived to be; that honey is in reality sweet and bitter, with entire dependence on the normal or abnormal taste of the tasting agent."

These species are intentionales inasmuch as they are psychical expressions of material things. They are sensiles and intelligibiles, in accordance with the faculty employed. Impressae, or imprinted, are resultants from action of the object; expressae, or developed, are resultants from reaction of the faculty. Memory and its readiness argue the existence of impressae. Both kinds are affections of the faculty, not the object on the retina of the eye, not nervous disturbance. Hence the epithet, intentionales. If we want to escape the absurdity of innate ideas, we must maintain that material objects act on our faculties, and base our knowledge. The deaf cannot hear a sound or think it; the blind cannot see a color or think it. Ergo mind and sense do not altogether determine their own modifications. Furthermore, knowledge represents realities, unless we want to be skeptics; and sensation and thought are the psychical expression of things.

Imagination and sensile memory are important enough to deserve our special attention. *The imagination is that internal sense which stores away old sensations, preserves them, presents them when called for, and combines them to form new images.* It forms representations of material objects apart from their presence. Its energy results in what we call a phantasm. As compared with that of the other senses, the work of the imagination is faint in intensity, obscure in outline, transitory in character, normally subject to our control and without bearing on objective reality. Ordinarily the imagination is reproductive; when productive, constructive, creative, it assumes the name of fancy. Memory is not reproduction, but recognition. Illusions, dreams and reveries are due to the imagination. Illusion differs from fallacy and delusion. It is a spurious act of apprehension. Its causes are subjective or objective. Thus, strong anticipation of an event leads one to perceive the occurrence before it happens; as in the case of the butcher, who thought his arm torn by a meat-hook. Desire and fear can work kindred results in the case of a timid traveler and a child treated to ghost-stories. Ill health and disordered organs, along with irregularities in medium, are instances of objective influences. Hallucinations are illusions of an extreme and permanent kind. Dreams and reveries are due to the fact that the imagination usurps the functions of the external senses, which in sleep and drowsiness are inactive along with will, reflection, and the power to compare. Dreams seem real, because we are completely at the mercy of the imagination. They are incoherent and extravagant, with a tinge of consistency, and they regularly exaggerate actual impressions. The mind accepts as real the representations of the imagination, unless some faculty checks them; and in sleep no checking faculty is at hand.

Memory is the faculty that retains, recalls and recognizes past cognition or knowledge. If this past knowledge is sensation, the memory concerned is sensile; if it is thought, the memory is intellectual. We are at present dealing with memory taken as an internal sense; but what is true of sensile is easily applicable to intellectual memory. Aristotle distinguishes between memory, mneme, and reminiscence or recollection, anamnesis; between retention and recall or recognition. Modern writers call the first spontaneous, or automatic; the other, voluntary memory or recollection. St. Thomas restricts reminiscence to man, because it involves will and reason. If brutes have sense and appetite, we fail to see why they must be denied an inferior kind of reminiscence.

Logically, the first question demanding attention is the retention of past sensations. The Schoolmen were far clearer, simpler and wiser on this subject than moderns, who, because of their materialistic tendencies, render a plain and easy problem a tangled mass of confusion. The Scholastics meet the difficulty by supposing the memory a thesaurus specierum, a treasury of past experiences. When sensations disappear from consciousness, the soul with the help of the organism retains these modifications, images, species, as faint dispositions or habits. Reproduction and recognition are based on laws of association. They are three, the law of similarity, the law of contrast, and the law of contiguity in space and time. They mean that mental states suggest like, or different, or connected states in past experience; and our doctrine of species or psychical expressions of objects is ample explanation. Memory is likewise helped by the strength of the original impression, by frequent repetition, and by freshness of the experience. A good memory manifests itself in facility of acquisition, tenacity, and readiness of reproduction. Ben Jonson, Scaliger, Pascal, Macaulay, Mezzofanti, were remarkable in this particular. Children ought to be trained to judicious, not mere mechanical, memory.

Immanent act is opposed to transient. In a transient act, the effect is received in a suppositum really different and distinct from the agent. In an immanent act the effect is received in the agent itself. An act is immanent in broad sense when the effect is not a perfection of the faculty from which it proceeds, e. g. nutrition and locomotion; it is immanent in strict sense when the effect is a perfection of the faculty, e. g. to feel, to think, to wish.

Cognoscitive act means knowledge; it means to know; it means to become the thing known, e. g. I hold this in my memory. We become the thing known, not according to its material being, but according to its ideal or intentional being.

This intentional representation, its substitute in the faculty, is called a species, whether intelligibilis or sensibilis. *Hence knowledge is the vital expression of an object in the faculty.*

PROOFS I, II, III

I. Sensation is an immanent and cognoscitive act.

Immanent, from experience. Common or central sense is witness that sensation proceeds from me, and is received within me.

Cognoscitive, because it is a vital expression of the object, as in vision or imagination.

II. a. A faculty and object are needed; *b,* There must be union between the two. *c,* This union must be in the faculty.

[a] There can be no act without a principle and a term. Something must perceive, and something must be perceived. The faculty is the principle; the object is the terminating term; its substitute, the species, is the determining term.

[b] The faculty is indifferent, and must be determined by the object. This determination is impossible without union between the two, because action from a distance is repugnant; non datur actio in distans; the effect cannot be altogether separate from its cause; where a thing does not exist it cannot act; esse is prior to agere.

[c] Union must be in faculty, because otherwise sensation would not be an immanent act.

III. Sensation perceives the object, not its species or image, not the organ impression. We perceive objects not as they are in us, but as they are outside of us, e. g. trees. When we touch a sphere, the sensation is of a convex thing, not of a concave thing.

PRINCIPLES

I. A. Knowledge means a judgment. Sensation is no judgment. Ergo sensation is no knowledge. *Answer.* Perfect knowledge means a judgment, I grant; imperfect, I again distinguish. It means a formal judgment, I deny; a virtual, I grant;

B. Sense must know that the object exists. Impossible to

sense. Ergo. *Answer.* Must know in the concrete, I grant; in the abstract, I deny.

C. The ultimate principle of knowledge ought to be immaterial. *Answer.* Immaterial, in sense of not matter, I grant; immaterial, in sense of independent of matter, I again distinguish. In intellectual knowledge, I grant; in sensation, I deny. Sensation is organic, or material, in sense that it proceeds not from the soul alone, but from the composite or organ informed by the soul. Thought is inorganic, wholly immaterial.

II. D. The physical change induced in the organ explains sensation, without any union between faculty and object. *Answer.* It involves adaptation to sensitive cognition, I grant; otherwise, I deny.

E. Sense is no voucher for species impressa. Ergo species is not needed. *Answer.* The species impressa is demanded by reflection and reasoning combined.

F. Species impressa is enough. Ergo, there is no need of species expressa. *Answer.* It is not enough, because it is a virtual image, and transient, passing from object to faculty; the expressa is a formal image, and immanent.

III. G. It is not the work of the senses to judge about the nature of things. That belongs to the intellect. *Answer.* About inner essence, I grant; about outer accidents, I deny.

H. Light, heat, electricity are all explained by vibrations. Ergo, there are no sensible qualities, but vibrations. *Answer.* Sensible qualities are vibrations, I deny; are accompanied by them, I grant. Sensibles are proper, common and per accidens, e. g. color, shape, substance or man. Proper Sensibles are active forms and energies inhering in bodies. Vibrations and undulations are not these qualitates sensibiles, but accompany them .

I. Bodies are felt and perceived through vibrations. Ergo, there are no qualities. *Answer.* Sensibles are vibrations only, I deny; joined with vibrations, I grant.

J. Color blind see wrong. Ergo, there are no sensible qualities. *Answer.* In vitiated condition, I grant; in normal, I deny. They see only in part.

K. Senses reach bodies through species impressa. Ergo, they reach not bodies. *Answer.* As medium quod, or in quo, I deny; as medium quo, I grant.

THESIS III

There exists in man a cognoscitive faculty, essentially different from sense; and this faculty has truly universal ideas.
Maher, pp. 229–252; *Jouin*, pp. 210–215.

QUESTION

Division. Two parts: I. Intellect; II. Universals.

The soul is ultimate and radical principle of all man's life. It needs accidental principles or natural faculties to elicit vital acts. Faculty can be whole eye or soul-power in the eye. Whole eye, compounded of organ and power, is certainly distinct from soul by inadequate distinction. St. Thomas makes faculties real and distinct properties flowing from essence of soul. They are not the soul's substance.

Faculty is a proximate and connatural principle of vital operations; not remote like soul; not accidental like habit and species. Number of faculties is the same as number of aptitudes for vital operations. Faculties are denominated by acts and formal objects. According to Aristotle the soul's faculties are five, vegetative, sensitive, intellectual, appetitive, locomotive.

Question: Is the formal object of intellect different from formal object of sense?

TERMS

I. Intellect is a higher faculty than sense, because its knowledge is of a higher order; and causes are graded by their effects. Man is superior to brute, primarily because of what he can do, when he exerts his highest energy. All knowledge is not ultimately reducible to sensation, in spite of the popularity the opposite doctrine to-day enjoys. The materialistic tendencies of our age are altogether responsible for the sad mistake, and the penny-wise philosophers, who cater to the public taste, are variously known as Sensationalists, Associationists, Materialists, Phenomenists, Positivists, Empiricists and Evolutionists. Sensationists reduce all knowledge to sensation. Associationists make all knowledge a grouping of sensations by similarity, contrast, and by contiguity in time or space. Materialists hold that all knowledge turns on matter, and that the mind is a function of organism. Phenomenists restrict all knowledge to phenomena or appearances open to the eye, the ear, and the other senses. Positivists limit knowledge to positive science, to laws observable in phenomena or sense-occurrences, with no concern for metaphysics or ultimate realities. With Empiricists knowledge is bounded by what falls under the experience or notice of the senses. According to Evolutionists mind is evolved from matter, and therefore different from sense in degree only, not in kind. *Adversaries. Materialists* make intelligence motion in matter like sensation, with no essential difference. *Cartesians* make intellect and sense differ essentially from matter, accidentally among themselves. If brutes had sense, they would have intellect. They raise sense to intellect, sensation to intelligence. *Sensists* reduce intellect to sense, intelligence to sensation; making concept, judgment, reasoning, reflection sensations, associated or transformed; making intellect just as organic as sense, with no essential difference. So Locke and Condillac. With Locke, judgments are composite sensations; with Condillac, judgments are sensations transformed from imperfect to perfect.

We are capable of several acts that clearly prove intellect's essential superiority over sense. These acts are intellectual attention, comparison, and judgment, especially in the case of necessary judgments; universal and abstract concepts, reflection and self-consciousness. With regard to attention, we remark that active attention is a secondary act, an interior reaction of a higher kind, superadded to primitive sense-impressions, which induce a condition of mere passivity. An orange on a table can furnish forth a fair example. Comparison and judgment postulate intellect. These acts are impossible without a force holding the compared ideas together in the consciousness, and discerning the relation of similarity between them. Coexistence or successive occurrence of impressions is not enough. A third and distinct activity must be present, able to apprehend the common feature. And all this becomes clearer in the case of necessary judgments, as contrasted with empirical or a posteriori judgments, about the antipodes, a man's photograph, fire and heat, white snow, glass as a food. Sense tells us that a particular fact exists; intellect tells us that a universal truth holds. Universal and abstract concepts likewise prove intellect. Science without universal ideas is impossible. Imagination cannot form them. Berkeley logically admits this, and concludes that we have no universal ideas because we have no faculty for their formation. His catalogue of faculties is incomplete. The concept represents a thing's nature or essence without accidental conditions; the image sets forth concrete conditions. The concept is one applicable to many; the image is applicable to but one. The concept is immutable and necessary; the image, changeable, different in each individual of the same class. When we say that the whale is a mammal, we mean no particular whale, but every whale. Reflection and self-consciousness demand intellect. We can recognize ourselves as something more than our transient states. Something goes over from primitive condition to present condition of consciousness. That something is not sense. Ergo it is intellect.

The intellect is a spiritual, non-organic faculty; sense is an organic, corporeal, material faculty. Objects of sense are material phenomena, and sense employs bodily organs. The eye sees, the ear hears, or better still, the soul sees and hears by means of the eye and ear. The soul thinks by means of the intellect. It thinks by means of the phantasm only accidentally, or because of the present union in force between body and soul. Unity of consciousness is possible to only a spiritual agent, because matter cannot be turned back upon itself. Individual, concrete objects appeal to an organic faculty, like sense; universal ideas, necessary judgments appeal to only a spiritual faculty, an intellect. Extrinsic dependence of intellect on brain is far from making it material. Stimulation of sense is a conditio sine qua non in this life for intellectual activity, not a cause.

Balmes and Lotze refute the Sensism of Condillac. Condillac says, "a statue of gold with but one sensation has but one attention and no judgment. Two sensations would form two attentions, and would make comparison and judgment possible." In this theory all sensation would be attention, and all attention would be sensation. But attention is application of the mind to something. The perception of the difference between a pink rose and a red rose, is the effect of an activity of a different order from sensation, and that is intellect. Difference is an abstraction, and no proper object of sense. As Lotze says, attention has for purpose the discovery of relations, a work beyond the reach of sense.

II. Universals — Systems: Nominalism, Conceptualism, Exaggerated Realism, Moderate Realism. Universal is derived from the Latin phrase, unum versus alia, and means one with a relation to many, e. g. man, all essences are universals. Five different ways of being universal, in causando, God as cause of all things; in significando, words, James as standing for all of that name; in repraesentando, circle on blackboard as standing for all circles; in essendo, one existing of its nature in many, man taken as an essence; in praedicando, one of its nature predicated of many, man taken as an essence. Our present question is about last two; and they mean, one thing suitable to exist in many according to its whole being.

Essences are formal object of the intellect, without saying a word about their existence in many. We now discuss whether and how the mind conceives a universal, one existing in many. *Nominalism teaches that universals are mere words.* This system admits universals in significando, denies universals in repraesentando and in essendo, employing this argument: No universal idea is possible without a universal object. But there are no universal objects. Ergo there are no universal ideas, and universals are mere words. *Conceptualism teaches that universals are mere ideas, without any corresponding reality; they are mere figments or creations of the mind.* This system admits universals in repraesentando, denies universals in essendo, employing this argument: Universal words call for universal ideas, with no universal object. Ergo universals are mere ideas or concepts, with no corresponding reality a parte rei, circle on board. *Exaggerated Realism teaches that universal objects exist apart from and outside of us; that somewhere a universal man is just as much a concrete reality as an individual man among us;* employing this argument: Universal words call for universal ideas, universal ideas call for universal objects. Ergo universal objects exist apart from and outside of us. There are three schools of Exaggerated Realism. Plato taught that in another sphere man, horse, tree without individuating notes exist, like individuals here. Ontologists, Malebranche and the rest, held that universals are divine ideas immediately perceived by the mind. William of Champeaux maintained that individuals of the same species have numerically as well as specifically the one nature.

Moderate Realism teaches that universals are formally in the mind, fundamentally in things, employing this argument: We certainly have universal ideas, otherwise all science is out of the question. There can be no idea without its corresponding object, otherwise all our knowledge deteriorates to subjectivism and idealism. On the other hand there can be no physical universal a parte rei, as that would be a contradiction in terms, one and at the same time many under the same aspect. Hence universals are formally in the mind, fundamentally in things. Formally in the mind, because universality is not real but logical. Fundamentally in things, because the similarity of essences specifically the same, is foundation for conceiving many as one.

Universals are of two kinds, direct and reflex. The names explain themselves. A direct universal is the abstract essence, or the essence separated from its individuating notes, with never a word about its presence in one or many. A reflex universal is gotten from the direct by that operation of the mind called reflection. The mind reflects on the direct and discovers that it says a relation to many, that it is actually multiplied or capable of multiplication in many. Indeterminate would be the more proper name for direct. The reflex is the universal properly and strictly so called. The direct is in the individual, but with notes. The reflex is formally in the mind alone, it is an ens rationis, it is in the individual only in potency. The real universal is many actually, one in potency; the logical is many in potency, one actually. The real universal is the direct universal, as explained above; the logical universal is the reflex universal, it is the direct, considered apart from accompanying individuating notes. The essence of man is one, human, capable of lodgment in every individual of the race.

PROOFS

I. Intellect differs essentially from sense. Faculties are essentially different, when their formal objects are essentially different. But the formal objects of intellect and sense are essentially different. Ergo.

With regard to the Major. An orange, as reached by the different senses, is example.

With regard to the Minor. Intellect perceives unextended objects, and extended objects in an unextended way. Sense perceives extended objects in an extended way. Unextended objects are being, essence, existence, possibility, substance, right, duty, virtue. Extended objects in an unextended way are man as universal, all universals. Sense is an organic faculty, rooted in whole composite, and necessarily knows only extended objects in an extended way, e.g. Man as object of vision.

PRINCIPLES

A. Only material things are known. *Answer.* By act of phantasm, I grant; by intellect, I deny.

B. Intellect is intimately united with body. *Answer.* In unextended way, I grant; in extended way, I deny.

PROOFS

II. The mind has truly universal ideas.

Three things to prove. *A.* We have truly universal ideas, against Nominalism and Conceptualism.

B. There are no universals a parte rei, against Exaggerated Realism.

C. Universals are fundamentally in things; formally, in the mind. *A.* 1°, The common nouns in our language prove truly universal ideas. They stand for something. Otherwise most of our language is vain. They stand for nothing individual, like a man; they stand for no collection of individuals like an army. Every individual has its own particular name; and the name of a collection cannot be attributed to its component parts. An individual man is John Smith or something such, no single soldier is called the army. Ergo common nouns stand for something common to many, or for universals, and we have truly universal ideas.

2°. The collective nouns in our language, like army, prove truly universal ideas. No idea of a collection can be had without some enumeration of individuals, and this enumeration of individuals is impossible without universal ideas. A stone and a plant cannot be united in a collection, or enumerated as two in their capacity of stone and plant; but only in their capacity of corporeal substances or bodies, the note common to both. John Smith and James Brown cannot be united in the collection called army, or counted as two in their capacity of individual men; but only in their capacity of soldiers, the note common to both. Arithmetic can do nothing with a barrel of molasses and a ton of hay taken individually; but it can find their value in money or in weight, the notes common to both.

B. Exaggerated Realism is a contradiction, because it ascribes unity and plurality to the same thing under the same respect. Moderate Realism escapes blame, because it makes the object of a universal idea plural really and one logically; plural, inasmuch as it exists fundamentally in things; one, inasmuch as it exists formally in the mind.

C. 1°. Universals are fundamentally in things, formally in the mind. Things and mind coöperate to form universals. Things contribute the matter, mind contributes the form. Ergo universals are fundamentally in things, formally in the mind.

2°. The similarity of essences specifically the same and numerically different is in things, and this similarity is foundation for conceiving many as one. Ergo universals are fundamentally in things.

3°. Unity and communicability constitute the formality or essence of a universal. Both are due to work of the mind, and are not in things.

Ergo universals are formally in the mind.

With regard to Minor. Before work of the mind, essences specifically the same are numerically many, not one. They are as many as the individuals possessing them.

Before work of the mind, essences are not communicable, but individual; each essence is restricted or limited to the individual possessing it; the essence man in John Smith, belongs exclusively to John Smith, and to no other.

N.B. The whole universal, direct as well as reflex, is an ens rationis. John Smith is an ens reale. When we say, John Smith is a man, we mean that he is an ens rationis and something more, he is a direct universal along with individuating notes. The direct universal, on which reflection works to produce the reflex universal, though it is an individual essence, is not an ens reale. An individual essence is an ens reale, when taken as it exists in nature, with individuating notes. The direct universal is indeed an individual essence, but stripped of its individuating notes, and taken as it exists in the mind, not as it exists in nature. Ergo the whole universal is an ens rationis.

Corollaries. *A.* How we know our own body and singulars.
B. How we know our soul.
C. How we know God.

A. We know our own body and singulars by reflection. Reflection is twofold; strict and less strict. Strict turns on faculty's own acts; less strict turns on acts of another faculty. We know individuals as individuals by reflection on phantasms of them. Ergo we know singulars directly through the senses, indirectly through the intellect, reflecting on sensations. All this is plain from the circumstance that we define or cognitively grasp individuals with the help of notes falling under the senses, like time, place, shape, color.

Ergo intellect has knowledge of singulars from the senses. But the senses never lead into the intellect. Ergo the intellect reflects on the senses.

B. We know our soul through its acts, not through its essence. Otherwise we should always know our soul, and this knowledge at times escapes us.

C. We know God by negation, affirmation, and analogy. Our concepts of God are analogical and negativo-positive.

PRINCIPLES

A. No concept, unless object is real. Universal is not real. Ergo no universal idea.

Answer. Unless real with regard to what is conceived, I grant; with regard to manner in which it is conceived, I again distinguish; unless real fundamentally, I grant; unless real formally, I deny.

B. Manner of object's existence precedes act of faculty. Ergo universals a parte rei.

Answer. Fundamentally at least, I grant; formally, I deny.

C. One and many, of same thing, a contradiction. Ergo no universal.

Answer. Under same respect, I grant; under different respects, I deny. Entitatively and representatively.

D. Essence is one in many individuals before work of the mind. Ergo.

Answer. Specifically, I grant; numerically, I deny. Logical unity, and real unity.

The Soul — What It Is Not

THESIS IV

Monism in whatever shape is no adequate explanation of the soul.

Maher, pp. 474–524; *Jouin*, pp. 186, 187.

QUESTION

Our opponents are Kant, Hume, Mill, James, Monists

According to Kant our knowledge or certainty is limited to phenomena, or appearances, or experiences, whether they be sensible or intellectual. We have no certain knowledge about noumena, or things in themselves. In this question of the soul, or the Ego, as he prefers to call it, he distinguishes between phenomena and noumena by recognizing an empirical Ego and a transcendental Ego. In plain language, the first is the soul appealing to our notice in its several activities of thinking, willing, remembering, believing, loving, reflecting, hoping and the like. In this phase the Ego belongs to the class of phenomena, it can be studied with profit, and in its discussion we can compass knowledge or certainty. The second or transcendental Ego is the soul in itself, and apart from its activities. Thus considered, the soul belongs to noumena, it is beyond our mental reach, and time spent in its study is time wasted, and the whole thing ends in uncertainty, confusion and superstition. We contend that noumena are as much the object of knowledge as phenomena, that we have minds as well as senses, and that the mind's eye sees farther and better than the body's. We have immediate knowledge of the soul, and that is a distinct gain over our knowledge of outside phenomena. We have no intuition of a naked pure Ego, stripped of all particular forms of behavior, and we have need of no such intuition. It is quite impossible in our present condition of dependence on sense for knowledge. But, with the help of internal observation, combined with rational deduction from evident principles, we can prove to certainty that the soul is a real, abiding, simple, spiritual and immortal being; and that is what we purpose doing in the next thesis.

The Empiricists, with Hume for leader, make mind a succession of transitory feelings, because forsooth senses vouch for no permanent self or abiding basis of these changes, and knowledge vouched for by the senses is alone valid knowledge. At any rate, the senses vouch for these transitory feelings; and the mind, beginning work where the senses leave off, unequivocally informs us that judgment, reasoning, reflection, memory, with a bearing on these evanescent states, vouched for by the senses, would be absolutely impossible without the existence of a real, abiding subject, which puts together and holds together the terms of the judgment, which combines the premisses of the syllogism, which compares past with present states in reflection and memory. As well have a separate dynamo for each electric light in the city, for each car in the Subway, or Tube. *Mill makes the mind a series of feelings aware of itself as a series, and talks of a thread of consciousness, to secure the needed unity of mind in its different activities.* But a series always remains a series, and the Ego is with Mill just as much a mere succession of states as it is with Hume. In our theory the Ego is not, as Mill thinks, something different, in the sense of separate, from any series of feelings. The true Ego is the mind plus its states. It is an abiding existence, with a series of feelings. Its states are but modifications of the Ego. Hume flatly denies the need of a permanent subject for thought-activity. Mill sees permanency in a series aware of itself as a series.

James of Harvard, rejecting Hume and Mill, secures permanency of subject by conceiving the Ego as a stream of consciousness, in which each section knows the previous section and in it all that went before. And he illustrates ownership by appealing to the example of a long succession of herdsmen, coming rapidly into possession of the same cattle by bequest. Each thought is thus born an owner, and dies owned, transmitting whatever it realized as its self to its later proprietor. The chief features in James' theory are, stream, cognition of preceding states, and inheritance. The expression, series of states, is certainly more accurate than stream, because of interruptions by sleep and the like. Present thought's ownership of all former learning is a mystery, without the permanency of some subject that appropriated and retains all previous learning. My present thought was not in existence years ago to be vested with ownership in anything. In the case of the cattle the title was always in existence. It would be interesting to know what happens to the stream during six or seven hours of sleep and unconsciousness, unless some permanent, abiding subject bridges the gap. A man's ownership of cows is different from his ownership of past existence. It must forever remain hard to understand how each pulse of cognitive consciousness possesses the life history of the individual; and that is James' theory. It is a paroxysmal unintelligibility. The common sense theory is much less open to objection. The soul, the subject of past experiences, abides within me, and possesses the power to reproduce and recognize many of these past experiences, forever alive to its own identity in successive thoughts.

Arguments of James.

(*1*) No soul is needed. *Answer.* Persevering identity of conscious subject, judgments, reasoning, memory are impossible without it.

(*2*) The soul is worthless to explain thought. *Answer.* Conscious succession of thought is impossible without it. The notion of thoughts and feelings inhering in nothing is absurd and unthinkable. Were such thoughts and feelings possible, they would never constitute an enduring Ego.

(*3*) The argument from free will is nothing worth. *Answer.* It is worth much when deliberation, reflection, resistance, responsibility, remorse are taken into account.

(*4*) James stands for an anima mundi, a universal soul. *Answer.* (*a*) There is no evidence in favor of its existence. We argue from our own soul to that of others because of organism.

(*b*) It is an incoherent notion and in conflict with facts.

(*c*) It leads to pantheism.

Double consciousness doubles the difficulty for Mr. James. In the case of Felida I, and Felida II, the phenomenon is no doubt due to faintly conscious activities, or to reflex and automatic processes of the animated organism.

TERMS

Dualism and Monism.

Dualism { Ultra — Plato and Descartes.
Moderate — Aristotle, St. Thomas, and Scholastics.

Monism { Idealism — Berkeley.
Materialism — Cabanis, Vogt, Moleschott, Huxley, Buchner, Locke, Bain, Hodgson.
Realistic — Clifford, A. Bain, Spencer, Huxley, Hoffding.

Monism makes mind and body one. Dualism makes mind and body two. Ultra Dualism makes mind and body too separate, with Plato and Descartes for advocates. Moderate Dualism puts mind and body in substantial union, with Aristotle and Scholastics for advocates. Monism is of three kinds, Idealism, Materialism, Realistic Monism. Idealism teaches that there is no matter, that everything is mind. In Idealism the material world is an illusory creation of the mind; all minds are one, all are wavelets on the ocean of universal consciousness. Materialism teaches that there is no mind, that everything is matter. Arguments:

(*1*) Experience vouches for brain, not for mind.

Answer. Reason vouches for mind.

(*2*) Thought is dependent on neural functions.

Answer. Extrinsically; a condition is no cause.

(*3*) We cannot imagine how matter acts on mind and vice-versa.

Answer. We can understand.

(*4*) Conservation of energy and law of inertia are opposed to interaction.

Answer. These laws are meant for matter.

(*5*) According to *Cabanis* thought is a secretion of the brain; according to *Vogt,* the relation between thought and the brain is the same as between bile and liver; according to *Moleschott* thought is motion in matter, phosphorescence of the brain.

Answer. Thought is unextended; secretion is movement, a

material product, occupies space, result possesses weight and resistance, external senses can perceive process, results continue when unperceived. Conscious states are just the reverse, their esse is their percipi.

(6) *Huxley* makes thought a function of nervous matter.

Answer. The one function of matter is to experience movements or changes in matter. The brain functions or expends energy when we think, but this functioning or expenditure of energy is not thought.

(7) With *Buchner,* mind is a sort of steam engine, magnetism, electricity.

Answer. These things cause movement like the organism of the body; but consciousness is different; it is life centered in one single being, in a peculiarly indivisible unit.

(8) *Locke* teaches that matter has many unknown qualities, and that thought may be one of them.

Answer. Matter has no quality directly contrary to its own nature, God cannot effect a metaphysical impossibility.

(9) *Bain* argues that dependence on matter disproves spirituality. Mind varies with weight of brain, its convolutions, its phosphorescent activity; mentality increases and deteriorates with growth of brain.

Answer. Scholastics never conceived the soul an independent entity isolated from the body. The soul is the substantial form of the body, implying most intimate union and mutual interdependence. Therefore, bodily conditions influence mental operations. The intellect requires as an essential condition operations of sense and imagination, and whatever affects them affects the operations of the intellect. The intellect is, therefore, extrinsically dependent on organs for its material. Its activity, manifest in thoughts, judgments, reasoning, psychological reflection, consciousness, proclaims it spiritual and intrinsically independent of matter. We never find mind apart from the body, but we often find the body apart from mind.

N.B. About the size and weight of brain. Taken absolutely, the brain of an elephant or whale weighs more than a man's. Taken relatively, that of a titmouse or child weighs more than an adult's. Considering convolutions, the brain of an ox is superior to man's. In point of phosphorus, the brain of a sheep or goose is richer than a man's. The measurement of an average Parisian's skull is 1.5; that of a Cave-man 1.6. Gambetta's brain weighed only two and a half pounds. Four pounds are ordinary.

(*10*) With *Dr. Shadworth Hodgson,* conscious states never condition, modify or determine each other. All Materialists maintain that there is no reaction of consciousness on nerves. Neural or cerebral action conditions consciousness. He alleges as an example a man turning aside from a wheelbarrow. The image on the retina determines nerve-action, and nerve-action results in the appropriate movement. The mental state is a mere epiphenomenon. The only alternative is the admission of an immaterial agent, and we have no experience of that.

Answer. Take other examples besides wheelbarrow; novelist writing a novel, a detective gathering clews, a man seeking revenge in murder, premisses in syllogism and conclusion.

Real Monism teaches that mind and body are not two distinct realities, but merely two aspects, sides, phases of one being; and that there is no real interaction between mental and bodily states. In other words, mind and body are one; mind is body, and body is mind.

W. Clifford, A. Bain, H. Spencer, Huxley and Hoffding uphold Real Monism.

Clifford invented the word mind-stuff. Every particle of matter has a bit of rudimentary intelligence. The molecules of matter and appended morsels of mind have no mutual influence or interaction. Each goes it own way, and hence Parallelism. *Arguments:* (*1*) Parallelism is plain from Physiology. (*2*) Mutual interaction is impossible from Physics. (*3*) Origin of life in dead matter is plain from Evolution. In the jelly-fish mind-stuff rises to sentience. Elements of mind-stuff are enclosed in a film on under side of fish. In vertebrates mind-stuff rises to consciousness; in the human brain, to intelligence.

Bain restricts Parallelism to man. With him, mental life is a phase or aspect of neural changes. Mental and physical proceed together as undivided twins. There is no interaction between mind and body, nothing but unbroken material succession. Neural antecedents alone determine neural changes, mental sequence goes with material sequence, but never modifies it.

Spencer sees and acknowledges the impossibility of identifying mental states with neural processes, or mind with body. A unit of feeling, he says, has nothing in common with a unit of motion. And yet he concludes with Clifford and Bain that mind and nervous action are subjective and objective faces of the same thing, which is itself unknowable.

Answer. Clifford makes too large a call on our faith. Science never yet discovered a trace of feeling or intelligence in minerals or dead matter. Bain has to explain why bodies in conscious beings have this subjective aspect, while other bodies are without it. Consciousness cannot be a new form of material energy, unless he admits that material energy can issue forth from consciousness. Conservation of energy demands this mutual interchange according to physicists. The mind-stuff in molecules is either conscious or unconscious. If unconscious, no multitude of unconscious acts can constitute conscious intelligence. If conscious, all material things ought to own a mental existence. Plants and leaves ought to have minds, steam-tugs ought to rejoice, an abandoned coal-mine ought to entertain emotions of sadness. Besides, mental states are not composite; they are indivisible, as is evident in thought, judgment, reasoning, memory, self-consciousness; and their principle is not made up of separate minute intelligences.

Monism is absurd in its denial of mind's influence on body. In Evolution, its own pet theory, natural selection and struggle for existence suppose that pleasurable feelings, awakened by songs and colors in birds, determine and modify their bodily activity. If thought never influences action, we cannot argue to the existence of other minds besides our own. Mind and will, love and hate, would have nothing to do with the wonderful changes in history. Neural groupings would be their sole cause. All mental activity would be only an aspect or phase of body, with no efficient bearing on events beyond mere sequence and succession. The terms employed by Monists are ludicrous, crutches for halting theories, childish attempts to deceive with half-understood words, metaphorical phrasings expressive of the talker's ignorance. For instance, a two-sided cause is about as intelligible as a blue sound or a three-sided motion.

Hoffding appeals to two laws, Conservation of Energy and Inertia.

Conservation of Energy makes the sum total of energy in the universe remain always the same.

Inertia makes rest or uniform motion in a straight line continue, unless impressed forces change it.

Answer. Physical movement is modified not only by physical forces, but also by ideas. Witness the part ideas of justice, fair treatment and the like play in strikes and other economic upheavals. The first law is verified only in case of inanimate matter, and cannot be demonstrated for living organisms. Even in the case of inanimate matter it would not seem to be universal. Witness a cap setting off a ton of dynamite. The soul must not be considered a foreign agent acting on the body; it is the body's substantial form, most intimately united with it. It modifies not the quantity of the body's energy, but its quality; and the liberation and control of a man's physical activity by his mind, in the shape of thoughts and wishes, need not conflict with the law of conservation of energy. About the law of inertia, Hoffding changes Newton's formula to read thus, the state of a material point can be altered only through the influence of another material point; and thus worded the law is abundantly refuted by reference to natural selection in Evolution, to our knowledge of minds in other men, and to history's dependence on thoughts, ideas, principles and feelings. Newton was too wise a philosopher to make any such mistake. Luther, to suit his vile purposes, changed the wording of the Bible; small wonder if Hoffding changes the wording of Newton's formula. Finally, Monism rests not on reason, but on faith, with ignorant men like Hoffding for sole authority; and it finishes in Agnosticism.

The Soul — What It Is

THESIS V

The rational soul of man is an immaterial or spiritual substance, that is, in its existence and in its operations it is intrinsically independent of matter. The rational soul of man is a substance physically simple in point of essence and in point of extension. In man there is but one soul, the life-giving principle of his understanding, his sensible perception, and his growth. In man the rational soul and the human body are so united among themselves that from the union a single nature, or a single substance arises.

Maher, pp. 459–474; 544–579. *Jouin*, pp. 180–193.

QUESTION

This and the succeeding thesis are most important. They constitute the body of what we term Rational Psychology as opposed to Empirical; cause-Psychology as opposed to effect-Psychology. In them we determine what reason teaches regarding the nature, origin and destiny of the human soul. And the method we follow is at the same time inductive and deductive. From what the soul does we gather what the soul is.

In the preceding thesis we mentioned Materialism. Its defenders, if logical, are ultimately forced to the deplorable and unlovely expedient of denying first and foremost the existence of God, then the immateriality of the soul and its immortality. In Materialism man is only a more delicately elaborated brute, with organs favorable to nicer combinations of chemical elements, and an arrangement of parts conducive to a fuller application of the physical forces of dead nature. This is Materialism reduced to its barest simplicity. Some Materialists may repudiate this analysis of their system, and indignantly protest that no such tenets are theirs. They are at least unwilling witnesses to the repugnance ever evinced by reason to false and unsound theories; and, to the detriment of their reputation as logicians, they halt before a difficulty, that can be neither climbed over, nor gone around, nor removed. With us, matter is in the present imperfect condition of things an indispensable requisite for work of the mind. Man's soul is so wedded to his body, his intellect to his senses, that thought depends on sensible perception, and therefore mind on matter, in much the same way as the sculptor depends on his block of marble. But matter of itself is as incapable of thinking as the unshapen rock is of transforming itself into a Venus of Phidias or a Moses of Michael Angelo. Organs are not the cause of thought, they are a mere condition. Brain is to thought what light is to vision. Vision is impossible without light, but nobody ever thought light the cause of vision. Only a fool could be guilty of thinking or saying that light sees. Rain and sunshine are necessary for vegetation, without being its cause. If mind and will were organic, they ought to be for the organism. They are not for the organism, but for higher and spiritual good. Intellect and will cannot add an inch to a man's stature. They cannot improve his digestion or cure the body's ills.

Materialism, if true, would of course put outside of all question the other properties attributed by us to the soul. Its simplicity, its oneness, and the part it plays in the composition of man, would be foolish fancies, since it would be itself only the offspring of a dream. Plato, that master mind of antiquity, trusting to sensible emotions that arise within us when affected by one movement of the soul or another, recognized in man the presence of three more or less separate souls; the principle of knowledge situated in the brain, the principle of anger or impetuous desire situated in the heart, and the principle of milder desire and growth situated in the liver. The followers of Apollinaris and the Manicheans were content with two; the former, with principles of sensible perception and intellectual knowledge; the latter, with principles of good and evil. In this matter Pope Pius IX saw fit to condemn the teachings of a certain Gunther, who described man as a happy union of spirit and matter, resulting, however, from a process of evolution, by which matter in man, pushed to its utmost perfection, put on the nature of a spirit, and assumed the dignity of a human soul. Our doctrine, the only admissible doctrine on this point, is that man's parents make ready his body. On its completion, God by a separate and individual creative act breathes into the body a soul, the image of Himself, destined never to die.

The combined action of soul and body, and the influence they exert on one another, are full of difficulty. The one safe way of explaining these partial mysteries is that, which at the same time answers all reasonable questions, and avoids the rocks on which great minds split. Such an explanation we adopt. Plato, following his theory of the soul's imprisonment for some past offense, attributed to the rational soul of man about the same influence over his body as the sailor exerts on his ship, the rider on his horse. With him, therefore, soul and body were hardly more a unit than are the sailor and his ship. Malebranche applied Occasionalism to the intercommunication between soul and body. This theory makes God constantly work miracles, and is altogether opposed to our consciousness of the influence exerted by outside objects on our thoughts, and of the mutual interaction in force between body and soul. It makes phases of mind occasions provoking God to produce corresponding changes of body, and vice-versa. Leibnitz refers everything to the preëstablished harmony mentioned in Ontology. He solves the problem with one miracle, accomplished from the start, when soul and body are arranged to keep together like two clocks. All three, Plato, Malebranche, and Leibnitz, destroy the intimate physical union of soul and body, and the mutual interchange of influences between them, which we recognize, and for which in this thesis we contend.

TERMS

Rational Soul. The soul of man can be well and briefly described as the root and principle of his whole life. His life partakes of all three kingdoms, vegetable, brute and human; and its principle is therefore at one and the same time a vegetable soul, an animal soul, and a rational soul. Here we designate it by the last epithet, because it expresses his true dignity, and implicitly predicates of him the lower perfections, vegetation and animality or sensation.

Immaterial. Immateriality and simplicity are quite different notions. *Simplicity, formally and strictly taken, is the denial of composition, or of parts; immateriality is the denial of intimate, intrinsic dependence on matter, be it primal or second matter.* Extrinsic dependence on matter, such as is natural to man's soul during its sojourn on earth, or that necessity it lies under of deriving all its knowledge and exerting all its faculties through the agency of the body's organs, nohow lessens or interferes with its intrinsic independence of matter, or that natural right it possesses to existence or being with absolute freedom from matter. The brute's soul is both intrinsically and extrinsically dependent on matter; that is to say, it derives its original being from matter, and depends as well on matter for its every act. However, it is not matter, but something quite distinct from it. Neither is it necessary to know just what it is; since there are in the universe things innumerable, of whose essences we are wholly or partially ignorant; and this principle of life is one of them. To exact such knowledge of us would be as absurd as to demand of the scientist what is the precise nature of that mysterious force, which, generated by the rapid revolution of metallic plates, lights up a city and carries commuters home.

Substance. Man's soul is a substance. All beings are divided into substances and accidents. We are better acquainted with accidents than with substances, because they appeal to our senses. But we are more certain about the reality of substances, than we are about the reality of accidents, because our information regarding them is based on reason, a more reliable instrument of knowledge than the senses. Naturally speaking, there can be no accident without its corresponding substance. Accidents of their very nature inhere or subsist in another, and that other is substance. You can have no shape, no color, no pain, no thought without a something to base them. Motion is unthinkable without something that is moved. Thoughts cannot inhere in nothing, desires cannot proceed from nothing. Inner experience is testimony conclusive that there is within me an Ego or self, which is the center and source of my ever changing acts and states. Thoughts and wishes appear and disappear, the thinker or wisher goes on forever. What thought within me a year ago, thinks within me to-day. Substance is not a mere noumenon, which never reveals itself to knowledge. It is not a secret substratum, like the core of an onion; its primary element is not permanence without change, but existence in itself and not in another. It can be produced by another, but after its production it stands in itself without exigence of inhesion in another as in a subject. Permanence amid changes is a property flowing from its nature. In the case of an incomplete substance it can unite with another to form one complete substance; but this union is of a peculiar kind, not at all like the inhesion proper to accidents. The soul is an incomplete, not a complete substance. It is a substance, because it exists in itself; it is incomplete, because it is designed by nature to inform and enliven the human body, and so help to the finish of the complete substance, man. It is a spiritual incomplete substance or form, and differs from pure spirits or angelic forms only in this point, that nature intended it to be bound up with the human body, while angels are ordained to nothing such. In other words, angels are completely subsistent forms, the human soul is an incompletely subsistent one.

That the soul is a real unitary being, which abides the same during all the varying modes of consciousness, is plain in reflection on past experiences, and in that process of memory we call recollection. Judgments and the syllogism are impossible without the permanence of a being during the interval it takes to pass from subject to predicate, from premisses to conclusion. Our assurance about past events is as live and vivid as our assurance about the present. Material organism completely changes in a comparatively short time. It is therefore no enduring basis for reflection or recollection. Fleeting acts in the same way are no permanent foundation for linking the years. Apart from memory, self-consciousness discloses only the present existence of the Ego; but memory adds to consciousness persistent identity of the mind as a real being. The Ego always sails into view as the combining center of past and present experiences.

Physically simple. Simplicity is the denial of composition, and a good idea of physical simplicity as opposed to metaphysical simplicity, and of what constitutes the various kinds of simplicity and composition, can be gathered from an inspection of the diagram of wholes, set down under Division in Minor Logic. The soul is composed of metaphysical parts, essence and existence; it is composed, too, of various faculties which make it what was there described as a virtual whole. But these degrees of composition do not in the least interfere with its physical simplicity in point of essence and in point of extension. In other words, the soul is neither a physical essential whole, nor a physical integral whole. A physical essential whole is composed of matter and form; and the human soul is a pure form without any admixture of matter. A physical integral whole contains parts of a fixed quantity, size, magnitude; and no such division touches the human soul. Some are of opinion that the soul of a brute is thus composed of parts, and that in its entirety it exists spread over the whole body, without existing in any part of the body whole and entire. Scholastics in general, with St. Thomas, hold the contrary opinion; and we stand with them. According to them the brute soul is simple per se; and, because completely immersed in matter, divisible per accidens. All are agreed that the human soul enjoys definitive existence, existing at the same time whole and entire throughout the body, and whole and entire in each part of the same.

Location of the soul. The soul's simplicity settles its location. Because it is simple, the soul exists whole and entire in the whole body, whole and entire in each part of the body. This kind of existence, peculiar to spirits, is called definitive as opposed to circumscriptive, the kind peculiar to bodies. A body, because of its quantitative extension, fills its place in such a way that the whole body is in its whole space and only a part of it is in each part of its space. Reason is entirely responsible for our notion of definitive existence. The imagination helps only fundamentally, not formally; because imagination has to do with only extended bodies and their qualities. It would be vain, therefore, to strive to imagine definitive existence. The soul, therefore, exists whole and entire in the whole body, whole and entire in each part of the body.

The soul, we have already seen, is not a physical essential or a physical integral whole. It is, however, a metaphysical whole, composed of the three faculties, vegetative, sensitive and intellectual, which are functions of one and the same soul. Though the whole soul is present in each part of the body, it is not everywhere present in all its activity or force. Its vegetative and sensitive activities are intrinsically dependent on set and special organs; its intellectual activity is extrinsically dependent on the imagination and sensile consciousness, and they are situated in the brain. Though present whole and entire in all three organs, the soul sees only in the eye, hears only in the ear, and thinks only in the brain. This fact led some philosophers, who denied the substantial union of soul and body, to restrict the soul to definite locations in the body. Plato and Descartes made the brain its residence; others, the heart, the blood, the cerebellum, the spinal marrow and so on and so forth.

We prove in the fourth part of our thesis that body and soul in man coalesce as matter and form to make one complete substance, one complete nature. In other words, the soul animates the body, the whole body; and as this animation is a vital or immanent act, the soul must be present wherever it has place; in every part of the body, in even the hair, the nails and the teeth. The whole soul is in each part of the body, because, as a simple substance, wherever it exists it exists whole; and it animates every solid portion of the body at least by way of vegetative principle. Different faculties can be considered metaphysical parts of the soul, calling for organs of definite shape and efficacy; and the metaphysical parts have fixed locations in the body, determined by the seats of the several organs. Thus, the soul, as far as its power of seeing or hearing is concerned, is in the eye or ear respectively; and so of the rest. Were the reverse true, the body would be as capable of understanding as it is of growth. The intellect is in the brain, inasmuch as it is the seat of the imagination, on which the intellect extrinsically depends. It is in the foot, inasmuch as it is in the soul, which communicates life to the foot and actuates it. Man is what results from union of soul and whole body, not what results from union of soul and part of the body. The soul fills the body in much the same way as God fills Heaven and earth, not as air fills the room. When an arm or limb is removed, the substance of the soul is not diminished, because it is without quantity. It merely loses a presence, and its activity is limited in extent.

Phrenology attempted to locate in the brain the precise positions of various mental powers. Bumps may indicate sensation-development, they can never measure intellectual or emotional development, because intellectual faculties are not located in organs or intrinsically dependent on them. Cerebral functions can be located, and of late years motor-centers and sensation-centers have been settled with some definiteness. Stimulation by electricity in certain areas of the brain produces movement in certain limbs; and definite portions of the brain seem to be connected with the work of the eye, the ear and the other senses. Much of the brain, especially in the frontal region, is silent or not responsive, and this unoccupied territory may belong to memory, imagination, and the other internal senses already described and explained. St. Thomas centuries ago hinted as much, when he assigned each its own particular portion of the brain. The motor-center is usually found on the side of the head opposite to the correlated member.

One Soul. The unity proper to the soul is that of indivisibility. The human soul, besides being undivided or one, is indivisible per se and per accidens.

Substance and Nature. A substance is a being existing in itself. A nature is a substance, viewed as a being possessed of activity. Since, therefore, every substance, as soon as it begins to exist, contains within itself an activity peculiar and proper to its own species, every substance is a nature. The distinction between the two is only a distinction of reason.

Division — Four parts.

I. The soul of man is a spiritual substance.
II. The soul of man is a simple substance.
III. The soul of man is one.
IV. Body and soul unite to form one substance, one nature.

PROOFS I, II, III, IV

I. A thing's highest effort indicates the order and degree of its being. But the highest effort of the soul, the exercise of the intellect and will, is immaterial. Ergo the being of the soul, the soul itself, is immaterial.

With regard to the Minor. That work or operation is immaterial, which is consummated without any intrinsic concurrence of a bodily or material organ. But the work of the mind and will is without any such concurrence. Ergo it is immaterial.

With regard to this Minor. The mind attains to notions expressive of things, to which the senses can never attain, possibility, necessity, decency, duty and the like. It recognizes sensible objects that have not fallen, and may perhaps never fall, under the observation of the senses; when, for instance, it perceives in a cause the effect it is capable of producing, and in an effect the cause which gave it being. The mind, too, frequently corrects and checks the work of the senses. A faculty intrinsically dependent on a bodily organ can react only in response to a physical impression, and can form only images of a concrete character, of a purely here-and-now existence. In psychological reflection the Ego reflecting and the Ego reflected upon are the same. The Ego is at once subject and object. A sheet of paper cannot be turned back upon itself. A part can be folded back upon a part, but the whole sheet cannot be folded back upon the whole sheet. The will never confines itself to such material goods as influence the senses, but specially longs for goods that far transcend all mere bodily gratification. Hence truth, knowledge, virtue, honor, which make no impression whatever on a material organ, are prizes highest in favor with man's inclinations and desires. If our volitions were merely subjective phases or mental states inseparably bound up with organic processes, their moral freedom would be impossible, and man would be incapable of responsibility and morality.

II. (*a*) Physically simple in point of essence. (*b*) Physically simple in point of extension.

(*a*) The two parts would be either matter and form, or principle of thoughts and principle of wishes. But neither supposition can be admitted. Ergo.

With regard to the Minor. The first supposition is too absurd to need further attention. We just proved the soul a spiritual substance. If one of its constituents is prime matter, it must be at one and the same time spirit and matter, or spiritual matter, which is a contradiction in terms. Common sense and personal experience are loud in their denial of the existence within us of two separate principles or souls, one the instrument of our thoughts, the other that of our wishes; while the assertion of such duality is entirely without foundation, and rests on no solid proof whatever.

N.B. This whole argument is based on unity of consciousness. The mind cannot be an extended agent like the brain, and at the same time think, judge and reason. In the matter of thought three impossible alternatives present themselves. Different parts of the idea must belong to different parts of the brain or soul; each part of the brain or soul must contain the whole idea; the whole idea must belong to a single part of the brain or soul. First and second cases are evidently impossible. In the third case the part of the brain or soul in question would be either extended or simple. If extended, the whole question recurs again. Any judgment, any syllogism can as readily prove the brain an impossible subject or agent.

(*b*) The soul is capable of acts representative of things utterly simple in point of extension; as, for instance, that simplest of all notions, being, and the thought pondered in psychological reflection. These acts, to be truly representative of such objects, must be themselves simple in point of extension. If an agent quantitatively extended produced an effect simple and without all quantitative extension, the effect would be superior to the cause; and that axiom, at the root and basis of all philosophy, would be rudely torn away and demolished.

III. (*a*) Identity of the principle of sensible perception and understanding, meaning the remote principle or soul, not the proximate principle or faculty. (*b*) Identity of the principle of sensible perception and growth as above.

(*a*) Consciousness is witness that it psychologically reflects on sensible perceptions and on concepts or acts of the understanding. But this could not be the case, unless the principle of sensible perception and understanding were one and the same. Ergo.

With regard to the Minor. Sensation and understanding are immanent acts, and as such dwell in their entirety within their principle or subject. It would, therefore, be impossible for consciousness to psychologically reflect on sensations and concepts or mental acts, if one and the other sprang from different and distinct principles. In that case, either the sensation or the concept would cease to be immanent, and, passing from its own principle, would be received in another principle, and would so become a transient act. Furthermore, when the senses are very intensely employed, the intellect as a rule remains in profound quiet, and vice-versa. Dante in his Commedia adverts to this fact. All our intellectual knowledge takes its rise in sensible perception. Work of the outer senses and of the imagination is a necessary prerequisite and a tremendous aid to the acquisition of mind-lore. The inner struggle between sensible appetite and spiritual desire is another sign that the principles of sense and intellect are one. Like doubt, the state of suspense between two views, such a war supposes the battle-field to be one and the same principle or mind.

(*b*) Identity of the vegetative and sensitive principle in man is proved, if between growth and sensation there exists the closest kind of relationship in point of graded perfection, duration, subserviency and influence. But such a relationship exists. Ergo.

With regard to the Major. Unless the principles were identical, sensation and growth would now and then fail of one or other of the relationships just enumerated.

With regard to the Minor. These are recognized facts, that the more perfect the power of sensible perception in a man, the more perfect are his powers of nutrition; that man ceases to grow or to nourish himself when he ceases to use his senses; that in fact all three lives go out at once; that the faculties of growth are ordained by nature to repair and strengthen the organs of sense; that close application of the senses, as well as too absorbing study, ruins digestion and impairs all the organs of nutrition.

IV. Man, or what results from the union of body and soul, is capable of actions, which, possible to neither component taken separately, can belong only to the whole compound, as to a complete principle, one and undivided. But such a compound is a single nature and a single substance. Ergo.

With regard to the Major. Man is conscious of the fact that he is a being of a certain quantity or extension. The body alone cannot be the principle of this consciousness, since left to its own resources it is absolutely incapable of all consciousness. Neither can the soul alone compass this cognition, since left to itself it is just as incapable of conceiving itself made up of a certain quantity, and possessed of a certain extension. This act of perception, too, is one and undivided; not the resultant of two or more acts, derived from two or more principles. Man also has knowledge of large and small beings outside of himself. But knowledge of such beings requires an agent or principle, itself possessed of formal extension or quantitative parts. Such an agent the soul alone can never be considered, because of the simplicity, already proved its natural birthright. Neither can the body alone acquit itself of this operation, because its own unaided powers can never attain to knowledge of any kind whatever. Therefore, the only principle capable of acquiring this knowledge is the whole man taken as a unit, or that being compounded of body and soul.

PRINCIPLES — SPIRITUALITY

A. In spite of what Locke says to the contrary, matter is utterly incapable of understanding. Intelligent matter is as much an impossibility as a square circle; because it contains notes necessarily destructive of one another. Intelligent matter would be spirit and matter, and therefore an intrinsic impossibility. Voltaire thought Locke's theory solid, because matter can contain within itself such simple properties as gravity, and the various forces of nature. These properties are indeed simple, but they are not on that account spiritual. Spirituality and simplicity are quite different notions, and the forces adduced by Voltaire are intrinsically dependent on matter.

B. The soul's extrinsic dependence on matter, or bodily organism, makes it possible for a diseased brain, as in the insane, to disturb the course of its operations. But this is only an extrinsic and indirect effect, not directly or intrinsically affecting the soul, or that faculty of the soul known as the intellect. The action of the brain is not thought itself or its cause, but only a prerequisite condition for thought in present circumstances. The phantasm contributes only to thought's beginning, it plays no part in thought's finish. The species impressa and intellectus possibilis finish the thought. And this is what we mean by extrinsic dependence and intrinsic independence. Matter enters the constitution of a man's essence; and from this circumstance it follows that the natural exercise of his highest faculty must depend at least extrinsically, not intrinsically, on matter.

C. All our notions, coming as they must through the senses, are originally of things more or less material. Hence, when discussing and proving the spirituality of the soul, our arguments may appear weak from the fact, that we seem to substitute analogical for univocal notions. In other words, we prove the soul spiritual, though possessed of nothing but figurative notions of what spirituality is. Our concept of a spiritual substance, like the soul, is not intuitive and purely positive, as it is when a body or material substance is in question. It is what we call an abstractive and negativo-positive concept. In other words it strips bodies of triple dimension or quantity, to express spirit's substantial being; and at the same time keeps apart from spirit the imperfection attaching to quantity. And this arises from the need we lie under of beginning intellectual work with the senses.

D. Man understands, and man is a material and organic principle. Ergo the soul is not spiritual.

Answer. Man is the principium quod, not the principium quo. The soul is the principium quo remotum; the intellect, the principium quo proximum. Man is said to understand, because acts are attributed to the whole suppositum or person. Actiones sunt suppositorum. A man's thoughts belong to him, but his soul and its faculty of understanding are their principle or cause.

E. The soul is the form of the body in such a way that it is not totally buried or sunk in bodily matter, like the soul of brutes or plants; but in such a way, that, as root and principle of intellectual acts, it is intrinsically independent of matter.

F. The soul is the body's form in such a way that it has acts distinct from its informative activity. Its informare is not its esse, as happens in brutes and plants. It is the root of spiritual energies like understanding, in addition to being the body's form.

G. The soul sickens and grows old with the body. Ergo it is material.

Answer. Not with regard to its substance, but with regard to its faculties; intrinsically, with regard to vegetation and sensation; extrinsically, with regard to use in the case of intellect.

Vaughan illustrates with the example of a broken-down harmonium and a sonata. The player must use the defective instrument, because no other is at hand. It would be a mistake to think that the power of musical execution or the merit of the piece is in the instrument.

H. Children resemble parents in mind and will. Ergo soul is derived from parents, and material.

Answer. Children get organs from parents; mind and will extrinsically depend on organs. Hence resemblance.

I. Even rational appetite in man inclines more to material goods than to spiritual. Ergo soul is material.

Answer. Men without reason make this mistake. Men with reason sometimes go wrong in the matter, but always with full knowledge that they are insulting their true dignity.

J. There is no contradiction in intrinsic dependence for vegetation and sensation, and intrinsic independence for understanding, because not affirmed under the same respect.

K. The body receives the soul, not according to the soul's whole capacity, but according to its own capacity, vegetative and sensitive.

Simplicity

A. The soul moves the body, not by the kind of contact or touch most familiar to us, and styled that of quantity or mass; but by a kind peculiar to spirits, and styled that of power, influence, virtue. Only the first kind supposes quantity and extension in the agent or mover. The soul moves the body inasmuch as it is the body's form, not inasmuch as it is the principle of intellectual life and activity.

B. A spirit freed from all connection with matter, or a separate spiritual substance, should perhaps have force sufficient to move any mass or weight whatever. The doctors disagree in this matter; St. Thomas and Suarez deny angels the power, Scotus is against them. But our soul is not such a spirit. It is bound up with the body as its form. No wonder then that it encounters bodies offering resistance too great for any effort it can elicit. In the execution of movements the soul intrinsically depends on nerves and muscles. In ordering movement it is free from this intrinsic dependence.

C. St. Thomas remarks in one of his treatises that matter

and form can be said to have two meanings. Matter can sometimes be confounded with possibility or essence, and form with actuality or existence outside the mind. In this acceptation, matter and form can be attributed to the soul. But the composition thence resulting is only metaphysical, and that we agree to recognize in the human soul. The proper and strict meanings of the terms matter and form are not essence and existence; but essence itself is the result of their combination. Hence in this latter sense the soul cannot be said to consist of matter and form, since it is pure form, uniting not with anything in itself, but with the human body, to form the essence and existence called man.

D. The soul animates the body, the whole body; and, as this animation is a vital or immanent act, the soul must be present wherever it has place, in every part of the body, in even the hair, the nails and the teeth. There is some difficulty about the soul's presence in the blood. Cajetan is of opinion that the soul animates the blood. Others, like Bonaventure, Albertus Magnus, Suarez, DeLugo, Lessius, a Lapide, maintain the contrary. As usual, both sides appeal to Aristotle and St. Thomas. If the blood be actually part of the body, if it possesses organism and enjoys even vegetative life, it must be said to be animated by the soul. The Thomists, with the approval of some modern physiologists, ascribe all three qualities to the blood. Their opponents advance arguments to show that the blood is actually no part of the body, that it is without organs, and that it evinces no sign of growth. Quite the contrary, St. Thomas safeguards the integrity of the Blessed Virgin's body in the Incarnation, by urging that the body of Christ was made, not from the flesh or bones of His Mother, but from her blood, which is not an actual part of the body, but a part only in potency, and as such removable without detriment to the body. Physiologists are not agreed among themselves that the blood contains organs and betrays symptoms of growth. A few at most contend that the red globules, a small percentage of the whole supply, fulfill these conditions. Even the red globules are disjoined from the rest of the body, and on this score incapable of animation by the soul.

The chief arguments advanced by upholders of the negative are these three. The blood acquits itself of no vital act in even the vegetative order. The blood is nourishment for the body; and, therefore, has its own form before conversion into the body's substance. The blood is disjoined from the solid parts of the body. Transfusion of blood proves it possessed of its own form. (N.B. Grafting of skin would refute this last argument.) St. Thomas teaches that, like the different body-humors, the blood is not yet part of the body, but on its way to this dignity. Finally, there are weighty arguments for both sides; and, till the Church settles the matter, by an explicit definition, the two opinions must be voted probable.

To meet the theological argument, derived from the divinity's union with the blood in Christ, and its consequent assumption by Christ as part of the human body, defenders of the negative opinion distinguish between primary and secondary parts of the body. Primary parts have organic structure, and are animated by the soul; secondary parts, like the blood and humors, have no organic structure, are not animated by the soul, and still contribute to the wholeness or entirety of the human body. To be united with the divinity, the blood need only be part of the body in Christ, whether primary or secondary. In much the same way, the body of Christ in the Holy Eucharist postulates, in virtue of natural connection, the presence of His sacred blood in the Host, whether the blood be a primary or secondary part of the body. Though not animated or vivified by the soul, the blood gets its form, or is denominated human, from the soul. Hence, body and soul are not like a house and its form. The house is an artificial whole, and its form is an artificial form. Man is a natural whole, and his soul is a natural or substantial form. The parts of a house have their own form before union, the parts of the body are without form before the soul's approach. Or as St. Thomas puts it, a substantial form gives finish and perfection not only to the whole, but also to its parts.

E. The soul is in potency to accidental acts, not to substantial acts. It cannot change to another form. Hence it is physically simple in point of essence. It is its own formal cause, and has no other; though it has an efficient cause, God. As a simple form, it is simple act, but finite; unlike God, whose actuality is His essence. The soul's actuality is not its essence.

F. The soul is coextensive with the body. Ergo compound.

Answer. Definitively, not circumscriptively.

G. The soul has extended or quantitative faculties for vegetation and sensation. Ergo compound.

Answer. As root or principle, not as subject in which they inhere. The whole man is the subject in which they inhere.

H. Growth and amputation prove parts and quantity. Ergo compound.

Answer. New presences, not new substance. Amputation affects presence, not substance. Amputation is not to be understood as the soul's withdrawal from severed portion, but as sun's disappearance from room, when window is closed.

Unity

A. The word formally plays an important part in this branch of philosophy. Admitting many nice distinctions, and various interpretations, the word can easily lead a beginner astray. It has two senses, inasmuch as it sometimes prescinds from other perfections inherent in a being, and sometimes excludes from a being all perfections higher than that said to belong formally to it. Thus, the human soul is said to be in the first sense formally vegetative, sensitive and intellectual. In the second sense it is formally intellectual only. Souls formally vegetative and sensitive in the second sense, such for instance as those of plants and brutes, are perishable and subject to death. But man's soul, because not formally vegetative and sensitive in the second sense, but only such in the first sense, is not necessarily perishable and subject to death.

B. Some see in the war between man's passions and desires an argument for plurality of souls; because, forsooth, opposition demands at least two agents, and one soul cannot be at odds with itself. But they forget that the strife is not necessarily between souls, but between the different powers or faculties of the one soul. Man's soul, though in reality one, is virtually or in its forces and faculties many. There would be no quarrel, were there two souls. Each would go its own way.

C. The soul of man is wholly incorruptible. Its vegetative and sense-principles are not corrupted after separation from the body, but simply hindered from activity.

D. The notion of a vegetative or sensitive soul contains in itself no notion of corruptibility or incorruptibility, in much the same way as animality conveys no notion of rationality or its absence. Animality in man is rational, in brutes it is irrational. Even so vegetative and sensitive souls in plants and brutes are corruptible, in man they are incorruptible. Souls in plants and brutes acquit themselves of no higher life than vegetation and sensation, and they are on this account intrinsically dependent on organs, and corruptible by accident. The soul in man, which is at the same time vegetative, sensitive and intellectual, acquits itself of intellectual life, and is therefore intrinsically independent of matter and incorruptible.

E. Animal is said univocally of man and brute; because the soul of man, though generically different from the soul of brute, when viewed as merely intellectual, is similar and reducible to the soul of brute, when viewed as the root and principle of sensation. Man the compound is as corruptible as brutes, and therefore in the same genus. His soul is a spiritual substance, is in the genus of spirits, and therefore incorruptible. Genus is said of the whole compound, not of its form.

F. Man's soul is not a species of the genus spirit, a species of the genus animal, and a species of the genus plant. But it is a species of the genus spirit alone, and at the same time the root and principle of properties that belong to the lower genera, animals and plants.

G. Man is not an animal in virtue of one soul, rational in virtue of another. He is a rational animal in virtue of one soul, substantially spiritual, in root or principle vegetative and sensitive. Genus and specific difference are concept-beings, and a distinction of reason between souls is sufficient.

Composition of Man

A. We Catholics, relying on the promise made in person by Christ to St. Peter and his successors, that truth should be the Church's everlasting legacy, bow our heads and our hearts to her divinely secure guidance in matters as well philosophical as theological. In her representatives, the Popes and the Councils, she has at times seen fit to promulgate her tenets with regard to the composition of man, and we quote these few. Under Clement V, in 1311, an Oecumenical Council inscribed this definition among its decrees. "We condemn as false and directly opposed to the Catholic faith whatever system maintains that the rational soul of man is not truly and of itself the form (or actuating, determining principle) of man's body. If any man boldly presumes to contend that the rational soul is not of itself and essentially the form of the human body, let him be counted a heretic." In the 5th Lateran Council Leo X thus decreed, "We severely condemn all who assert that man's rational soul is subject to death, or that it is numerically one and the same in all men. Not only is it truly, of itself and essentially the form of the human body, but it is also immortal, and, in exact proportion with the number of bodies into which it is breathed, individually multiplied and necessarily so multiplied."

B. Soul and body, though a simple substance and a compound, though spirit and matter, though indivisible and divisible, can unite to form one complete and compound substance in the capacity of matter and form or incomplete substances. They could never unite to form a simple substance.

C. Substantial union is impossible, unless the soul somehow partakes of the body's material being, while the body somehow partakes of the soul's spiritual being. And, as a matter of fact, the body does partake of the soul's being; not inasmuch as the soul is precisely spiritual, but inasmuch as it is the root and principle of vegetative and sensitive life. In the same way the soul partakes of the body's material being not inasmuch as it is the root and principle of thought, but inasmuch as it is the root and principle of growth and sensation.

D. The body before union with the soul would seem to be matter with form, and therefore the soul is not the single form of the human body. Before union with the soul the body is not a complete, but an incomplete substance, under the aspect of a human body. It is an actual being only in a wide sense, not in a strict sense; and only an actual being in strict sense is constituted such by form. The dispositions, induced in the body by generation before union, are not accidents; but requisites for primal matter, adapted to the form called soul. The body's chemical elements before union are not complete substances, fixed in determined species; but a total subject, fit to be informed and given a fixed species, or made a human body by the soul.

E. It is impossible for a pure spirit to be a constituent part of a body. The same is not true of a spirit like the soul, which is a spirit naturally ordained to be at the same time root and principle of vegetative and sensitive life.

F. The body before union is not complete as a human body. It gets that completeness from the soul. It is complete, as a collection of elementary bodies, each with its own form, in such a way that the collection is an incomplete subject ready to be informed by the soul. These forms are latent during union, and are educed from the potency of matter after separation.

G. Body and soul are not two species under one genus, but they are two principles constituting one species of a genus. Therefore, body and soul are not of the same genus.

H. No corpse-form need be admitted, because after death the body ceases to be a body, and becomes rather a collection of bodies.

I. When faith teaches that the soul of Christ is in the Sacred Host not vi verborum, but per concomitantiam, it is talking of the soul of Christ, not inasmuch as it is the form of His body; but inasmuch as it is spiritual, or root and principle of intellectual operations. This is one of many probable explanations.

J. The dead body of Christ was truly one with the living body of Christ materially, not formally; because of union with the divine personality of Christ, not because of the form or soul.

K. When the soul actually informs the body, it informs it by virtue of its essence. It is, however, of the soul's essence to inform the body not actually but aptitudinally. Therefore, subsistence after separation is quite possible to the soul.

L. The body in union would seem to be an accident, because it accrues to the soul already created by God. But the soul, as the body's form, is not a complete substance; and accidents inhere in only complete substances.

M. Soul and body combine as matter and form, not as chemical elements. They do not perish like chemical elements to produce a third reality, the man; because the process of union is not mutual conversion or change, but mutual communication of their realities.

THESIS VI

The rational soul of man, even when separated from the body, is of its nature capable of existence and life, neither can it possibly be deprived of them. The soul of man will therefore live forever.

Maher, pp. 524–544; *Jouin*, pp. 193–200.

QUESTION

This thesis contains four parts, and is most important. It bears directly on man's moral life; and must, when carefully studied and thoroughly understood, produce a lasting impression for good. If our career is to begin and end with this shifting life, this round of joys and sorrows; if our thoughts, words and deeds are not to follow us beyond our deathbed; if no grim spectres in the shape of deeds ill done, of duties unfulfilled, are to confront us before the judgment seat, my present mode of life and yours are a hallucination and cruel self-deceit. Why deny ourselves, why restrain our passions, why say nay so many times a day to appealing self-indulgence, if we are candidates for the same blank fate as the dumb herd of dull sensualists, who pamper self, who give unbridled rein to their passions, whose self indulgence knows not what refusal or disappointment means?

It is an article of faith that these our bodies, after hiding away a space in the ground, will arise at the last day, be reunited with the soul, and with some few modifications, called for by their new sphere of existence, will last forever, the eternal companions of the spirits within us. But the immortality of the soul is a dogma of reason, and was recognized and contended for as such by ignorant and learned alike, long ages before the advent of Christ and the establishment of His Church. Pagans, who lived before the full light of divine revelation dawned on the world, to clear up mysteries and brighten up old truths, could without fault profess ignorance of the astounding favor gratuitously done human nature, the immortality of the body. The body, the soul's companion, is of itself heir to corruption; and had not our gracious Master, wishing to signalize His wondrous goodness, decreed to the contrary, it would forever tenant the cold grave. Small wonder that this consoling dogma, now so familiar to mankind, entirely escaped even the noblest geniuses of paganism. Guided by unaided reason, we can readily enough compass the notions of absolute and natural immortality. The first is peculiar to the infinite being known as God, the second is the birthright of such spiritual substances as angels and the souls of men. We, who hear God speak in the Scriptures, distinguish a third species of immortality, that of grace, accruing to an otherwise corruptible body only because God's free and limitless will was pleased to so dower it. Omitting for the present all discussion of the body's immortality and of God's immortality or eternity, we mean to weigh and prove the immortality of the soul.

Whether pagans or Christians, men with a claim to reason and its sober use have been a unit on the fact in question. A wide variety rules when the fact comes to be explained; and the crude notions of some ancient philosophers are scarcely more puerile than the theories advanced by not a few of the enlightened minds of our own time. These ancients at least recognized the utter impossibility of confounding thought with the products of matter, and thus soared worlds beyond the teachers, who to-day contend that dead matter can elicit concepts. The origin of this half mysterious principle they could not satisfactorily determine. Their attempts to surmount this first difficulty were many and curious.

One school, with the great Plato and Pythagoras, thought that human souls were beings from another sphere, that of the stars, who because of some unknown wickedness had been condemned by an offended Creator to drag out a miserable existence in this body, or prison-house of death. Another school, of a pantheistic turn of mind, reckoned human souls particles struck off from the divinity. Coming nearer our own age of Materialism, we meet with such theories as these. The soul is the result of generation in much the same way as the body; and this is Material Traducianism. The soul is the product of the parents' souls, which actually produce it from their own substance, and this is Spiritual Traducianism; or create it from nothing, and this is Exaggerated Creatianism. Rosmini undertook to split the difference between these two equally false systems, and maintained that the human soul, inasmuch as it is the principle of growth and sensation, derives its origin from the parents. God afterwards presents the idea of being to this vegetative and sensitive soul, and so renders it intellectual, rational, spiritual.

We need not remark that Plato, Pythagoras, and the moderns referred to, strangely deceived themselves in assigning so unworthy an origin to what is noblest in nature. Were Plato's hypothesis correct, the union at present in force between soul and body would be unnatural and galling. The imprisoned spirit would still retain some recollection of the happy hours it whiled away among the stars, before falling a victim to God's vengeance. But nobody is ready to grant that either of the above facts has place. The union of body and soul is wonderfully natural, and so pleasant withal that separation or death is the one evil against which man most strenuously contends.

Plato met our second difficulty by making it the foundation of his theory about the origin of our thoughts or ideas. Each soul, he says, comes into the world fully equipped with knowledge, stored away during its celestial sojourn, and elicited or recalled during the slavery of life on earth by constantly recurring suggestions. Discere est reminisci. To learn is to recollect. Fanciful fabric of this kind does credit to the poetic longings and aspirations of Plato, it ill becomes philosophy. Sober common sense in this particular matter, though it abandons him to the mob unfavored of the Muses, raises the ignorant farmer high above the sage Plato. He feels, and will stoutly maintain, that his ideas had no more claim to existence within him before their present production, than have the dollars and cents to existence in his ample pockets before he exchanges his crop for hard cash. Rosmini is wrong, because an accidental fact, like the presentation of the universal idea of being, cannot account for a specific change, like that of a sensitive into an intellectual soul. Besides, a sensitive soul is incapable of any such universal idea. Otherwise dogs and cats could change to men.

Evolution can have no part in the soul's production. If the

souls of parents cannot produce the child's soul, much less can the sensitive soul of brutes be producing cause of a human soul. Traducianism, whether it makes the bodies and the souls of the parents, or their souls alone, the efficient cause of the child's soul, is always a wide remove from the truth. For it is impossible to consider their bodies capable of such an effect, unless farewell is taken of the very first rule in all causation. Effects can never surpass in excellence the nature of their causes. Surely nobody will deny that a spiritual and intelligent soul is in a multitude of respects superior to a material and dumb body. The souls of the parents would accomplish this result in one of two ways. They would make the child's soul from particles of themselves, or would make it from absolute nothingness. But the human soul is a simple substance, and as such disclaims all connection with particles. Parents are not divine, and creation, or production from absolute nothingness, is essentially the work of God. Creation means production without preëxistent matter, power without limit, infinite might; and God alone is infinite. God, and God alone, is equal to the task of producing human souls. Because the man is said to be generated, it does not follow that the soul is generated. Because the man dies, it does not follow that the soul dies. Generation is said of the whole suppositum or resultant from union of body and soul, just as death is said of the whole suppositum; and as the man dies, while his soul goes on living, so the man is generated, while his soul is created.

We therefore maintain, with all sound Catholic writers, that, while each and every child born into the world derives its body from a father and mother, its soul is the workmanship of the supreme Artificer, and is immediately and individually created by God, and by Him breathed into the organism assuming shape. The soul of man is created by God, because it is finite and spiritual. As a finite being, it postulates an efficient cause. As a spiritual being, it can result from no substantial change in preexistent matter, because its constitution is altogether devoid of matter; from no substantial change in preëxistent spirit, because spirits are incapable of division and substantial change. Therefore it is created, and creative power belongs to God alone. Creative power is absolutely independent of everything outside the agent, and therefore infinite, impossible to creatures. No creature can in any single case create, because such power would be, in the nature of things, unlimited, and on a level with God's omnipotence. No creature can be employed as an instrumental cause in the work of creation, because in every such case the creature would be either a moral cause by prayer and petition, or in virtue of immanence a total cause by its own activity, an impossible supposition.

About the precise time of the soul's creation, St. Thomas, following Aristotle and his crude notions of embryos, teaches that the soul of the child is first vegetative, then sensitive, and last of all rational. In the case of a male child the rational soul appears only forty days after conception; in the case of a female, the interval is lengthened to eighty days. Physiology has weakened this opinion, and to-day philosophers and theologians commonly agree that the advent of the rational soul is simultaneous with conception. The theory of St. Thomas is at best only probable, and is no excuse for foeticide perpetrated at the earliest stage of conception. The opposite opinion is solidly probable; and to deliberately destroy even probable life is most certain murder. The rational soul is principle of all three kinds of life in man, and this is reason enough for its immediate creation.

Besides assigning the human soul a wrong origin, ancient philosophy likewise erred in its conception of the soul's destiny after man's dissolution. It never once questioned the fact of the soul's immortality, and all its mistakes turn on the kind of future awaiting the soul. Its notions are wonderfully close to the truth, and marvels of intellect, unaided by the floods of supernatural light ushered into the world by God's advent among men. Our untutored Indians and the ruder Chinese entertain notions of a hereafter analogous to those of ancient paganism and heathendom. Rome's greatest epic loves always to depict life beyond the grave as a boundless playground, where warriors, hunters, lovers, pursue in unbroken bliss the sports and pastimes, that filled out their little round of years on earth. His picture is invariably accompanied by that companion-piece of the lonesome lot ahead of rash mortals who presume to offend the deity.

"Lo, they reach saints' dwelling places, where a greener turf o'erspreads
Lawns, that level lie to spirits; where sweet virtue fragrance sheds.
Broader smile the glowing meadows, lit with light to men unseen,
And with stars, whose waning vigor dark would make moon's fullest gleam.
Some in grass-grown rings their prowess test in bouts with friendly foes,
Others on the glinting sea-sands wrestle, box, deal ponderous blows.
Merry here the nimble dancers pound and pat the echoing ground,
Sing to shells attuned by Orpheus, when he woke a world with sound."
Æneid VI, 640–648.

"Tortures dire assuage with anguish wounds self-will on earth cut deep;
Hanging high, some sate God's justice; others stifling vigils keep,
Deep adown in lakes of brimstone, hot with vengeful Heaven's ire;
Each and all are prod by Furies, births of unfulfilled desire."
Æneid VI, 739–743.

Or would you have the liquid numbers of rare old Horace, who in the midst of his wine and his loves found sweetness in soberer thoughts like these?

"I hammer out a chain of song,
To fasten me to fitful time;
With soulful words and ringing rhyme,
I link it tight, and weld it strong.

"It renders life an endless day;
No rain, no wind can rust or wear,
No ages can its strength impair;
It binds me to my kind for aye.

"I steal away from meaner men;
I die to live; my body sleeps,
My spirit, winged with fame, o'erleaps
Dull bounds, too thick for mortal ken.

"As long as priestess-virgins tread,
Beside gray years, the sun-flecked stair,
That winds up to Jove's house of prayer,
Green laurel grows, to wreathe my head."
Odes III, 30.

Cicero, the most eloquent man in all Rome, when every public-spirited citizen was an impassioned orator, thus completely unsatisfies his mind about the certainty of a future state of unending bliss: "Happiness which can slip away is half misery.

Who persuades himself that stability and continued existence pertain to a period of time admitting interruption or end? Heap wealth untold on a friend, bid him be happy. If a momentary doubt, touching the mere possibility of losing his fortune, find asylum in his mind, that friend must needs experience all the wretchedness of actual loss. Happiness cannot dwell with the anxiety attendant on uncertain possession."

The same Cicero in a profound treatise, descriptive of old age and its pleasures, introduces Cyrus consoling his children from a death-bed in language like this, "My boys, do not imagine that on my departure from your sight I shall exist nowhere, and be reduced to empty nothingness. Even while I moved among you, you failed to discern my soul; but none the less clearly did you understand from my conduct that it lived in this old frame. Believe, therefore, that it continues the same, though no longer seen of you. Heaven and earth could not persuade me to fancy that souls enjoy life only in these bodies of death, and die when they break off all commerce with them; that souls fall away from knowledge, when they take farewell of dull bodies that know not a thought. I hold fast to this fundamental truth, that souls only then are wise, when they begin that second stage of existence, freed from all admixture with material bodies."— De Senectute, c. 22.

All the old pagan writers of repute recognized the necessity of a future life, and inclined to even our faith in the resurrection and immortality of bodies. But, as before remarked, they adopted various strange notions and explanations of the manner of life in store for the soul, and of its gradual processes of development. Pythagoras suggests a very curious fancy, artistically described by Horace and Ovid. Horace is recording the address a dead sailor makes to some passing stranger.

"Pantho's son, Euphorbus brave,
  To hell again is flown;
Dead at Troy, to death he gave
  But muscles, pelt and bone.
Life restored, the sage he played,
  Pythagoras, nature's seer;
Knew the shield, with which he stayed
  Dread Trojans, mailed with fear."

Odes I, 28.

Ovid in one of his Metamorphoses, or Wonderful Changes wrought in human forms, leads in the celebrated philosopher Pythagoras, and makes him speak as follows:

> "Souls, unloosed from prison houses, flit away to fuller life;
> Leave the cold abode of bodies, with diseased discomfort rife.
> I myself, I well remember, used to fight in front of Troy;
> Pantho's son, Euphorbus; old in wisdom, though a boy.
> Atreus' younger son in battle launched the spear, that pierced me through;
> And the shield, that then betrayed me, late in Juno's shrine I knew."
>
> Metamorphoses XV, 161.

Briefly, the absurdities of metempsychosis and transmigration of souls are derived from the earliest promoters of philosophy. Men, they thought, whether conspicuously deserving during life, or conspicuously wicked, merely changed their first estate for another in the same or a different order of being. Like Euphorbus in the story, the good were wont to abide awhile in the nether world; whence, after a period of moral cleansing, they issued as heroes of later periods. They died blameless warriors or kings, and reappeared on earth, marvels of thought or founders of nations. The bad assumed the shapes of various brute animals, instinctively prone to the several vices cherished by them. It is highly useful to note that though reason, because of its natural weakness, failed to fully grasp the dogma's intricate meaning, there is apparent all through their writings a deep devotion to, a reverent regard for, that grand old truth taught by unerring nature, the immortality of the soul. With all their wanderings from the path of rectitude, with all their vicious inclinations and abominable turpitude, they were men enough to acknowledge that a destiny for better or worse awaited them, that they were to undergo a reckoning for their misdeeds, and that feigned ignorance was no secure refuge against the loud reproaches of a conscience, not to be stifled or hushed. In this particular they were heroes of a far more lovable type than the dullard agnostics of our time, weeds in the luxuriant growth of modern civilization and progress. Men's minds have undergone no essential change with the ages, and nature's lessons are the same for ancients and moderns.

TERMS

The rational soul of man. The soul of man is an incomplete, not a complete substance. It is a substance, because it exists in itself; incomplete, because it is designed by nature to inform and enliven the human body, and so help to the finish of the complete substance, man. It is a spiritual incomplete substance or form, and differs from pure spirits, or angelic forms, only in this, that nature intended it to be bound up in the human body, while angels are ordained to nothing such. In other words, angels are completely subsistent forms, the soul is an incompletely subsistent one. The souls of plants and brutes are incomplete non-subsistent substances. They are substances, and not accidents, because, though incapable of existence apart from the complete substance, rose or horse, they play a necessary and intrinsic part in the constitution of the one and the other. They cannot like accidents be present or absent without specifically influencing the being, rose, or the being, horse. These principles of plant and beast are simple per se, divisible per accidens; they have no parts in themselves, but exist whole and entire in each part of the being they actuate; but, unlike the soul of man, they are material; the plant and the animal are capable of neither thought nor volition, nor of any act in itself independent of and transcendent to matter.

Of its nature capable of existence. In the order of the universe angels stand next to God. They are capable of existence without a material body, and cannot like the human soul be so clothed with matter as to constitute a single complete substance.

They are complete substances in themselves; and can assume the appearance of man, only as man can assume this or that shape; they can assume the appearance or shape of man as an extrinsic accident. However, their existence was not actual from all eternity; but, till God first created, was a mere possibility. Herein consists the difference between God's being and theirs. He has been and is an actuality from all eternity, and never consisted of mere possibility. Man's soul remained a mere possibility longer than the angels; and Adam possessed the first human soul, that passed from capability to actuality of existence. Another difference between this human soul and angelic spirits lies in the fact that it never loses its capability of informing a material body, and constituting with it a single complete substance, man; though this capability can remain for a space unsatisfied, as happens in the interval between death and the resurrection of bodies at the last day. The souls or life-principles of plants and brutes are incapable of actual existence outside of material bodies. Their dependence, therefore, on matter is most complete, it is intrinsic as well as extrinsic. They are simple substances, but not spiritual. They exist whole and entire in each part of the plant or animal, as the case may be; but are debarred from eliciting a thought or other spiritual operation. Thus, their utter dependence on matter makes it impossible for them to actually exist, separated from the bodies they inform, and is our foundation for denying them immortality. Their simplicity or freedom from parts, would, if not interfered with by their materiality, ensure to them the possession of this rare quality. They are incorruptible per se, but corruptible per accidens. From this it may be gathered that the immortality of human souls depends not so much on their simplicity as on their intrinsic independence of matter. Souls nowise transcending the dignity of matter can be communicated to effects by material causes. Hence we hold that the parent-flower and the parent-animal give complete being to their offspring.

Life. Life is substantial and accidental. Here we are most concerned with accidental. The soul's existence is substantial life; its activity, manifest in thought and wish, is accidental. Substantial life is a substantial form, and therefore an incomplete substance, which together with the matter, tree or body in brute and man, constitutes a single living substance. Life, taken in a wider sense, and with a marked shade of difference in meaning, may be considered an accidental form, inasmuch as it gives its essence and specific being to every concrete and individual act of a living creature. Accidental life is actual self-motion or immanent action; substantial life, the basis and support of accidental, is mere capability or possibility of the same. The former is a mere accident, because it simply modifies or limits an accident, such as are all the actions of plants, brutes and men. Substantial life is for things alive being or essence; accidental is superadded to the same, and is resident in every act put or placed by the living subject. Substantial life, therefore, is capability of self-motion or immanent action, accidental life is the manifestaton of this same capability in action.

Cannot possibly be deprived. The creature, who would attempt to annihilate a human soul, would present as sorry an appearance as the madman, who contemplated annihilating the universe. The one and the other undertaking are the prodigious results of a divine act, and the Maker reserves to Himself the power of annihilation, or reduction to primitive nothingness. God's all embracing power reaches to every possible effect, and appears to be bounded by only such empty imaginings as result from combining notions mutually destructive. God's power considered merely in itself can accomplish everything conceivable, everything not an intrinsic contradiction. But God's power must not be considered merely in itself. It is essentially necessary always to take into account His other attributes, His wisdom, His justice, His kindness. These several qualities are never disparaged by any motion of God's omnipotence. Hence, though the annihilation of a human soul would result in no intrinsic contradiction, speaking absolutely, it would nevertheless be in palpable want of harmony with divine wisdom, divine justice, divine kindness. Since, therefore, God can admit no such want of harmony into His works, we may say with positive assurance that the soul cannot possibly be deprived of life or existence.

To save God's wisdom from flaw in the annihilation of a soul, opponents search for motives sufficient to induce Him to depart from a law, that He manifestly made for Himself from the beginning. But their search is vain. God in destroying human souls could consult neither His own interests nor those of souls. By their eternal preservation the divine glory will be forever celebrated in hell as well as in Heaven. Wicked souls would, of course, a million times prefer to their interminable woe utter disappearance from the world of being. Desire to comply with this preference of theirs would indeed be a motive, and a strong motive, inducing God to annihilate them. But God can yield to no motive, however weighty it appears to us, if that motive collides with a higher duty, He owes Himself and His divine attributes. God's justice could not admit the influence of such a motive. The wicked by a full and deliberate choice, in direct and downright opposition to God's will, have cleaved to sin, and only reap the reward allotted to Heaven to the abuse of its benefits and graces. Justice calls for a reparation or penalty as closely commensurate as possible with the damage done. But the damage done is infinite in intensity, viewing the person wronged, and eternal in duration, looking into the future. No creature can undergo pain of infinite intensity, but every creature can suffer finite pains throughout eternity. Hence it happens that any punishment short of eternal hell-fire would leave divine justice only partially sated, and therefore no justice at all. Thus would the annihilation of condemned souls defeat God's plans, and despoil Him of His most dread attribute.

Division — Four parts. I. Capable of existence.
II. Capable of life.
III. Cannot be deprived of them.
IV. Will live forever.

PROOFS, I, II, III, IV

I. Ontological Argument. The soul, separated from the body, is of its nature capable of existence, if it admits of corruption neither essentially nor accidentally. But the human soul admits of corruption neither essentially nor accidentally. Ergo.

With regard to the Minor. Only beings made up of physical parts admit of corruption essentially. The soul is a simple substance. Only beings intrinsically dependent on matter admit of corruption accidentally. The soul is spiritual, or a substance intrinsically independent of matter. N.B. Proofs for the soul's simplicity and spirituality are contained in preceding thesis.

II. Ontological Argument. The soul can of its nature live after separation from the body, if able to elicit thoughts and wishes. But after separation from the body it can elicit thoughts and wishes. Ergo.

With regard to the Minor. If death, or separation from the body, deprived a soul of its thinking and wishing faculties, or of all objects apt to serve as foundations for thoughts and wishes, or of every conceivable method of performing these operations; then, in sooth, would it be impossible for the soul to live after separation from the body. But the faculties, intellect and will, remain in the separated soul whole and sound as they were before the change of condition. Indeed, as Cicero well says, they put on a new activity, when released from the bonds of clay that before enveloped them. After death the human soul no longer exercises its vegetative and sensitive powers; it no longer helps the eye to see, simply because the body and the eye are disappeared from its influence, simply because growth and sensation are operations intrinsically dependent on matter. But thought and desire are operations peculiar to an agent in itself free from all dependence on body-organs or matter of whatever kind. If this agent during life on earth seems to depend on sense for the material of its thoughts, this dependence is only extrinsic, and does not at all enter into its nature or essence. Organs are not the cause of thought, they are a mere condition. Vision is impossible without light, but nobody ever thought light the cause of vision. Only a fool could be guilty of saying or thinking that light sees. Rain and sunshine are necessary for vegetation without being its causes. If mind and will were organic, they would be for the organism. They are not for the organism. Mind and will cannot add an inch to the man's stature, they cannot improve his digestion, or cure his body's ills. The law still holds Christian Scientists for criminal neglect.

Neither will objects be wanting, to give occupation to the mind and the will. God and the angels never had a body, and yet the mine of their intellectual treasures is inexhaustible. There are in material bodies qualities that cannot be perceived by the unaided senses, which can well be perceived by the unaided intellect, truth, virtue, the whole world of abstractions. God Himself can furnish forth food for thought, commensurate only with eternity. The soul can contemplate itself, recall and examine previous argumentations and notions, heaped away during life on this sphere, and jealously preserved by intellectual memory. In the present order of things, what the eye never sees the heart never craves for, nothing exists in the intellect but what previously in some shape or other existed in the senses. But, as is occasionally foreshadowed here below, the heart shall then long for objects unseen of the eyes, the intellect shall ponder knowledge far beyond the ken of the senses. Then the human soul shall adapt itself to a method of knowing and wishing peculiar to the angels.

III. Theistic Ontological Argument. To lose existence, the soul should have to either corrupt or be annihilated. But the human soul can neither corrupt nor be annihilated. Ergo.

With regard to the Minor. We have just seen that the soul, because of its simplicity and spirituality, admits of no species of corruption, whether essential or accidental. It can certainly be annihilated by no mere creature. Annihilation is the prerogative of the Creator. Man can annihilate nothing. He can induce modifications into existences, but the result of his utmost endeavor is always a change of condition, never total destruction. God alone is therefore equal to such a task. No atom is lost in a tree's decay. No drop of water is missing in evaporation, freezing, passage from sea back to sea. Weight of the universe is the same to-day as it was the first day of creation. Annihilation and creation are parallel acts. It is just as easy to get something from nothing as to get nothing from something. Only God can annihilate. But God's various attributes make it quite impossible for Him to expend His energies on such an effect. His justice, His wisdom, and His goodness render annihilation of human souls a manifest absurdity.

IV. From St. Thomas — a, b, c, d.

a. Theistic Ontological Argument. God, who is the artificer of nature, never withdraws from beings characteristics belonging to their essence. But immortality is an essential characteristic of the soul. Ergo the soul of man will live forever.

With regard to the Major. It is of the essence of everything created, angels and the human soul alone excepted, to undergo various changes, and finally be resolved into constituent elements, or suffer corruption. The composite being, man, is no exception to this rule. Unending duration would therefore be for every creature, but an angel and a human soul, the withdrawal of a characteristic essential to it. Hence we contend that the destructions and renewals everywhere apparent in nature are no arguments against our Major, but strong arguments in its favor. Could God act otherwise than as described in our proof, He would be a Maker inferior in point of skill to many a humble artisan we know. Such inferiority cannot without blasphemy be predicated of God.

b. Theistic Teleological Argument. Argument based on man's natural craving for perfect happiness, and consequently for immortality.

God cannot in justice render it absolutely impossible for man to satisfy that desire for perfect happiness, implanted in him by nature.

But if He annihilated the human soul, He would render it absolutely impossible for man to satisfy that desire.

Ergo God cannot annihilate the human soul.

With regard to the Major. A natural craving or desire has these several marks. It has its origin in human nature, not in education, prejudice, ignorance, and the like. It is unavoidable, so much so that no man can escape its influence. It is universal, not restricted to this or that class of men, this or that period of life, this or that condition; but common alike to the whole race, to rich and poor, to good and bad, to young and old, to slave and master. It is widely different from an acquired or accidental craving, such for instance as a craving for drink, for tobacco, for sensual pleasures, for intellectual wealth. All these lower cravings have for object goods not unmixed with evil; but the craving of which we speak in our proof has for object unmixed good, good that repudiates all commerce with evil, good therefore that cannot be coupled with the slightest chance of loss or disappearance, ever-enduring good. If God could render such a desire absolutely impossible of fulfilment, He could break His promises, and could make of man, His noblest creature in the visible world, a plaything of folly and the laughing-stock of the universe.

With regard to the Minor. Perfect happiness for man and the annihilation of the human soul are absolutely incompatible. As long as our happiness does not tally with the degree of which we know ourselves capable, so long does it fail of being perfect. We know ourselves capable of happiness without end, and are conscious of no absurdity when we wish to be forever happy. To use the words of St. Thomas, "Brute creation desires life and being inasmuch as they are a present possession, not as a lasting possession, because they are wholly ignorant of what ever-enduring life is. We, however, who know well what such existence is, long for it with a longing born of nature. Each and every creature has its own natural measure of desire. In intellectual beings, intellectual or abstract knowledge is the completest measure of desire. In man, this intellectual knowledge reaches to a notion of existence without end. Hence his aspirations to immortality. Our desires in this matter are not bounded by mere existence, but include also the notion of perfect happiness. This perfect happiness results from the fixed union of these three elements, absence of all evil, possession of every good compatible with our nature, unquestionable security against ever falling away from this state of blessedness."

Apart even from this desire of perfect happiness, man's perfectibility, his capacity for progress and improvement, indicates immortality. He seeks truth, and life is too short to compass all the truth. St. Augustine says, "Quid enim fortius desiderat anima quam veritatem?" Hence man's name, animal curiosum, the inquisitive being. Nobody can be said to have acquired all knowledge, to have nothing more to learn, to be beyond improvement. Hear Newton, "I know not what the world will say of my labors; but it seems to me I was like a child playing on the seashore, that finds now a smoother pebble, and then a more brilliant shell, while the great ocean of truth lay unexplored before me." Man is not capable of infinite development. He cannot grasp all truth simultaneously, and that is limitation enough. When Strauss insists on the saying, old people are done, old people outlive themselves, he may not know that he is adducing an argument in our favor. These sayings are declarations that the old people left their work incomplete, or went a little way into the other life. History knows no golden age realler than a dream. Man's imperfectibility in this life means impossibility, unless another life supplements this. Strauss sees in wasted seed, trampled apples, lost fish-eggs, an argument against the need of a soul's full development. But the cases are different. Things material perish before maturity, and this is true of man himself; because there is not enough water, air, earth, to support all. In spirit-land there is no crowding; feeding only whets appetite, and promotes health; one man's accumulation of intellectual wares beggars not another. It would be a wonderful world, indeed, where no seed would germinate, where no young apple would develop, where no fish-egg would grow to maturity. And this would be the case with the mind, were there no immortality.

c. Theistic Ethical Argument. Argument drawn from the moral order of the universe. Man in pursuit of his end ought to be bound by a perfect moral necessity to follow the dictates of right reason. But such bond supposes the unending duration of reward and punishment. Ergo.

With regard to the Major. God imposes on human nature this obligation. His consummate holiness makes it absurd to think that He can be for a moment indifferent to compliance and non-compliance with the duty. Worldly rulers can, perhaps, become so remiss as to view with equal pleasure observance and violation of their laws, but God can never descend to such imperfection.

With regard to the Minor. If the reward of the virtuous is to cease after a period, and the punishments of the damned are to have an end, men would not hesitate long between choosing the service of God and going over to the camp of His enemy. They would desert in a body to the devil. There is not, perhaps, on earth a man, woman or child, who has not already experienced, or will not in the near future experience, one of those ordeals which try the soul to its utmost. Saints and sinners have presented to them alluring temptations, resistance to which even bends the body to the ground. Nothing short of Heaven, and an eternal Heaven, can prevail on man in some circumstances to forego a present sinful gain, an enticing sinful pleasure. In the lives of the saints there are recorded temptations, overcome only with closed eyes or hasty flight. How many men would sacrifice the gratification of a passion, the enjoyment of an awfully vivid and awfully present pleasure, if a thousand years in hell were the only penalty, if the gnawing consciousness of moral guilt were the only consequence? Few, few indeed. Even as matters stand, with hell wide open before them, pleasure-seekers whose passions cannot brook delay, rush over the precipice with full deliberation and full assurance of results.

Eternal punishment is, then, the only sanction at all capable of deterring man from breaches of the moral law. It is, besides, the only penalty commensurate with the weighty importance and pressing necessity of that law. Whoever dies in sin, foolishly casts himself into circumstances that leave him an enemy to God, and preclude whatever chances he might have had before to help himself. He is, therefore, in a state of perpetual separation from God, and there is no help for it. God Himself is powerless to change these relations, when once the period of probation is over, and man has reached the term of his earthly existence. Justice, too, whose claims God cannot after death disregard, demands that between the offense and the punishment as perfect as possible a proportion have place. The malice of sin is so heinous that malice more heinous cannot be conceived. Its punishment, therefore, should be the most painful that can be pictured. Man's nature is finite, and cannot suffer pain of infinite intensity. The only particular in which he partakes of the infinite, is the unending duration of his soul. Nothing, then, remains for the lawmaker to do but inflict on His rebellious subject woes of finite intensity, of infinite or eternal duration.

d, Consent Argument. Argument drawn from the universal consent of mankind. A judgment, taking its rise in rational nature as such, cannot be affected with error. But our judgment concerning the immortality of the soul is such. Ergo.

With regard to the Major. This first premiss cannot be denied without making God, the artificer of nature, a most wayward tyrant and a most inartistic Maker.

With regard to the Minor. In the Minor we simply maintain that our judgment concerning immortality has all the elements of what was described in Major Logic as a judgment ratified by the common consent of mankind. The four elements there specified and their discussion follow. (1) A claim to universality, to long duration and unchangeableness, as well among the ruder as among the more civilized nations. During all ages, and among all peoples the immortality of the soul has been considered a truth beyond all question. Variations have occurred in the kind of life awaiting the soul, but these variations little affect the main point at issue, the fact. (2) A claim to exact agreement with all the rules of right reason. This claim we made good in preceding remarks. (3) A claim to absolute freedom from any such cause as prejudice, ignorance, and the like. Its universality is sufficient guarantee for this claim. Education, prejudice and ignorance are not so widespread in their influence. Education cannot overcome nature; and, in the hypothesis of our opponents, immortality would be against nature. "Naturam expellas furca, tamen usque redibit." (4) Inculcation of moral and social truths exclusively, not of scientific truths, such as the earth moves, the sun stands still.

Belief in immortality is too solidly established a historical fact to be overthrown by scoffers at religion and things holy. Monuments raised to the memory of departed friends, funeral-rites, sacrifices, pretended and real communication with the dead, all are standing proofs of nature's promptings in the matter. With certain tribes, wives were burned alive to accompany their husbands to the other world. Slaves were killed to serve their dead masters. Feasts were set to celebrate their happiness. Tombs in Egypt were meant for enduring mansions or palaces. Inscriptions congratulate the dead on their entry into peace and blessedness. Only a few select passages bearing immediately on the subject were set down at the beginning of our remarks. No one book could contain the unnumbered tributes paid this world-old belief by historians, philosophers, and poets. This historical fact has also peculiarities of its own, that commend it particularly to credit. In spite of the errors and mistakes, with which the belief is mixed up, especially among ruder peoples; in spite of the obscurity, that in earlier ages enveloped it; in spite of the seemingly contradictory views taken of the circumstances attendant on future existence; about future existence itself the persuasion has ever been deep-rooted and unshaken. Skeptics have labored hard to eradicate it from among men, the wicked have striven to prove it a bugbear; but the more their flimsy arguments were multiplied, and the deeper the search instituted, the purer and stronger grew the unanimity of mankind. The senses are dead set against immortality; passion is dead set against it; high-handed oppression is dead set against it. It is, therefore, vain to compare this belief with the long since exploded theory about the motion of the sun and the fixity of the earth. What booted it to the senses, or the passions, or sin, whether the earth moved or stood still? The whole social fabric depends for its permanency on this single dogma of immortality.

PRINCIPLES

A. A word has been already said about God's omnipotence with reference to annihilation of human souls. To repeat, it is plain that, absolutely speaking, God has power sufficient to end a soul's existence. In fact, mere refusal of coöperation on the part of God would work the soul's destruction. But the question here is not so much what God can do in the abstract, but what He will do in the concrete. He has clearly enough made known His intentions; and, in connection with His other attributes, He will not, and cannot annihilate human souls.

B. When the soul leaves the body, a form is removed from its matter, and begins an existence peculiar to itself. This peculiar existence is entirely natural, due to the human soul's very nature. The case, then, is altogether different from that urged by opponents, when they say that a form cannot exist apart from its matter without experiencing a condition of violence, wholly inconsistent with nature. Forms intrinsically dependent on matter cannot exist apart from matter; but forms like the human soul, intrinsically independent of matter, can readily enough exist and act without the help of matter. Separation becomes highly natural and expedient, when the diseased or maimed body ceases to be a fit dwelling place for the soul. Union with the body is natural to the soul in our present condition. Change of condition calls for change in natural mode of existence. One being can have several natural modes of existence, as is evident in caterpillar, pupa and butterfly. Separation is just as natural to the soul as union, though union is more perfect, because the soul can then exercise all three of its functions. A separate soul loses in extent of activity, to grow in intensity. The butterfly is more a thing of beauty than the caterpillar or pupa. The soul's activity is less, inasmuch as it fails of growth and sensation; but incomparably greater, inasmuch as it enjoys unhampered use of its intellectual strength.

C. Notwithstanding the certainty that a future eternity is ahead, man cannot but meet death with pain, discomfort and anxiety. It is a violent rending of soul from body, a penalty for original sin; and was therefore meant by God to be accompanied by disagreeable symptoms. But the bitterest pang attaching to death, is not the bodily torture, but the mental uncertainty about the sort of future in store for the departing soul; and, if it was during life addicted to sin, the utter abandonment of all the old haunts of pleasure. Saints, conscious of duty done and unstained innocence, the pledges of a glorious immortality, go out to meet death with little or no concern; they often hail it with joy. The fear attendant on dissolution has its origin, not in uncertainty about life beyond the grave, but in uncertainty about the kind of destiny the soul has worked out for herself. This dread uncertainty is on occasions vivid enough to make even men of God tremble. What must its terrors be for half-hearted Christians, for out-and-out reprobates!

D. Strauss argues: A finite being is in naught infinite. Ergo. *Answer:* Immortality like the soul's is not infinite, because it had a beginning and is communicated by another. The soul can never say, Now I have lived an infinitely long time. St. Thomas answered Strauss 700 years ago, De Anima, a. 14, n. 4.

E. Biedermann says: Whatever originates in time, must also pass away in time. Ergo. *Answer:* It can cease in time. Whether it will or not, depends on the good pleasure of its creator; and we know His pleasure from the soul's spirituality and its aspirations. St. Thomas again, 1, Q., 75, a. 6, n. 2.

F. Strauss denominates our argument an arbitrary reverie; a mere assertion; empty babble, called by the honest a prevarication. He that does not inflate himself knows the finiteness of his nature, and infinite duration terrifies him. *Answer:* Immortality is not infinite duration. Honest men, with Strauss and with Materialists in general, are civilized apes; and he forgets the long record of the past. It is good to be humble; but to have lower aims than those set for us by nature, is not modesty; it is hypocrisy mixed with cowardice. Immortality frightens only the reprobate, it has no terrors for the just. Sinners dread, not long duration, but hell.

G. The Jews knew nothing about immortality. Witness Eccles. 3.19. "The death of men and beasts is one." *Answer:* Preacher is showing vanity of the world. In things material, food, clothing, wealth, the death of men and beasts is one. The Jews were stout believers in immortality, and needed no reminder. Even the Egyptians believed it.

H. Philosophers have denied immortality. Ergo. *Answer:* Man's will is free and influences his statements. Denial seems better to the immoral; and, therefore, sways their judgment and will.

I. Whole nations have made mistakes in this matter. No two agree in their conception of a future life. Ergo. *Answer:* Their mistakes turn on the manner of immortality, not on the fact.

J. Souls alike in origin and subsequent duration are probably alike in finish. But man's soul, like the souls of plant and brute, begins in matter, and elicits vegetative and sensitive operations. Ergo, like souls of plant and brute, man's soul is mortal. *Answer:* Man's soul has its origin in creation, and along with vegetation and sensation it enjoys intellectual activity. Ergo it ought to be different in finish, or immortal.

K. Souls differ in degree of mentality; but these variations are no sign of possible dissolution, because they are rooted not in the soul's substance, but in organs the soul employs. Substantially all souls are of the same perfection.

L. In this life, the soul cannot think without phantasms; but in a higher life God can and will supply the place of phantasms. Actual vegetation and sensation disappear, potential remain; and they are not the soul's single activity.

M. Erroneous consent regarding the sun's motion was a scientific judgment, not moral or natural; and, being a mere hypothesis, was far from firm. Sanction in another life is per se sufficient to safeguard morality; by accident, and on account of free will, it sometimes fails of this effect. History proves the natural consequences of insufficient sanction. Men are content with the goods of this life because of their animal nature. They dread death, not because insecure about immortality, but about a happy immortality. The desire a young man has to reach old age is natural in another way, dependent on free will.

N. Kant argues: The soul weakens with the organism. Ergo. *Answer:* It weakens, not in substance, but in application of its powers; and this means extrinsic dependence.

O. The separated soul is the body's form in potency, not actually.

P. The soul's being is the body's being, and something more, namely being proper to it as a spirit.

Q. Immortality is no incentive to selfishness, because God, not self, is man's last end.

R. As a contingent being, the soul tends towards nothing negatively, not positively. It needs conservation on the part of God.

S. The wicked desire not annihilation, but surcease of pain.

T. Eternal punishment is just, and not opposed to the mercy of God.

U. Desire of happiness is not to be confounded with its accomplishment.

Dr. Verworm and Immortality

Columbia University lately harbored a distinguished physiologist from the University of Bonn in Prussia, Dr. Max Verworm by name. On October 26, 1910, with the approval, no doubt, and encouragement of the University authorities, he undertook to show a large audience, presumably made up of Columbia students, that individual souls are no more immortal than individual bodies. We venture to think that many of his listeners were sons and daughters of devout Christians, who hardly know that they are paying good money of the republic to have their children's minds infected with the deadliest brand of paganism's poison. We should hate to learn that any educated Catholic sat the frivolous and impious lecture through, without raising his voice in protest. Certainly, the publicity given the thing by the morning papers ought to open the eyes of Catholic and Protestant parents alike to the hellish enormity of entrusting the education of their growing boys and girls to advocates or abettors of a doctrine, that found favor with only the grosser minds in paganism. The following statements are taken verbatim from the *Times'* account of the lecture, and for purposes of convenient reference we number them.

1. "The soul is no more immortal than the body." 2. "Every act of consciousness is intimately dependent on the brain." 3. "A complex phenomenon ceases when a single con-

dition fails." 4. "Paralysis completely inhibits consciousness." 5. "A mournful faith in a future reward or punishment awakens fear. Hell and purgatory, inventions of a gloomy fancy, must give place to nobler incentives." 6. "Thought of death ought not to arouse fear. Pain and fear are physiological properties. The anguish of death would disappear. Cowards fear death." 7. "Causal view must yield to condition-view. Science neglects causes, to be content with conditions. Vitalism is last example of causal view. It proclaimed life from life, till science discovered that life can proceed from death." 8. "External factors of life are plain, internal factors are a hopeless complication. We do not know the exact chemical structure of a single cell. If an engineer lacks but one part of a complicated machine, he cannot put the machine together. Hence we cannot make living substances artificially in a laboratory. If we could succeed in assembling internal and external factors, the artificial system would live like the natural amoeba, and eventually a human being would result." 9. "Life is continual destruction and continual construction." 10. "Media vita in morte sumus, sang the monk of St. Gall." 11. "All life must die, and all life is death." 12. "Dust thou art, and unto dust thou shalt return."

And now we respectfully submit to Materialism's attention the following comments. 1. "The soul is no more immortal than the body." There can be no doubt regarding the body's mortality. Any graveyard can satisfy the most skeptical. But we presume to think it quite within reason to doubt regarding the soul's mortality. Any one of the arguments advanced in favor of its immortality, even the arguments based on universal belief, ought to be able to pause the most rabid Materialist, and urge him to at least waver in his position. Nobody ever saw a dead soul; and, till he sees the phenomenon, a physiologist ought in conscience to refrain from proclaiming the soul's mortality. Possibly man's soul dies, because it is identical with his body, or because it is totally submerged in matter, like the brute's soul. Identity of soul and body is gross Monism; and in all psychology nothing, perhaps, is easier to refute. Man's soul has simple and spiritual activities, that positively preclude as thorough a dependence on matter as that of the brute's soul. If man is body alone, if his soul is an empty nothing, there can of course be no question of the soul's mortality or immortality. In that case man's soul is the hole in a doughnut, and to talk learnedly about nothing ill becomes the wise. Materialists hold this opinion, and escape the whole difficulty by denying the difficulty's existence. And while on the subject, it does seem to me that the Materialist, though less refined and scholarly, is more logical than the Monist. He at least sticks to his colors, and goes down with a bad cause. And there is a certain amount of amiable, even if imprudent, courage in stupid perverseness. To deny the soul's existence, hurts logic less than to affirm its existence, and with the same breath dispute its immortality. 2. "Every act of consciousness is intimately dependent on the brain," because of the union at present in force between the soul and the body; but this is far from denying that the soul itself is intrinsically independent of matter, or spiritual. Consciousness is but an act of the soul, not the soul itself; and for this very reason a man can be unconscious without being dead. An act can cease to be, without involving its cause's destruction. Were the soul consciousness, dead and unconscious would be synonymous, a verdict that no reputable physician would countenance, whatever our learned Doctor may say to the contrary. When a person faints or sleeps, he is not by the very fact a candidate for the undertaker. Even so, when the brain is hurt, and consciousness is still, the soul's substance remains alive and intact.

3. "A complex phenomenon ceases, when a single condition fails"; and this is no reason why the cause of the complex phenomenon should cease, when the phenomenon itself ceases, or the single condition fails. Thought is the complex phenomenon, brain is its condition, the soul is its cause. Naturally enough, if the condition, or work of the brain, is wanting, there will be no thought; but this is far from proving that no soul remains. Brain is to thought what light is to vision, the soul is vision itself, or sight. Naturally enough, there is no seeing without light; but no man ever yet thought himself blind merely because he was seated in a dark room. Turn out the lights in a hall. There is no seeing, though every man in the hall has sight; and we can satisfy ourselves of this by turning on the lights again. Empty the hall of men, then flood it with light; and there is no seeing as well as no sight, because,

though the condition for seeing is verified, the cause of seeing or the seer is away. 4. "Paralysis completely inhibits consciousness"; but it leaves the soul whole and sound. To inhibit the act of an agent, is not to destroy the agent itself. For the information of surface-dabblers in philosophy, we again submit our proofs for the soul's spirituality, or intrinsic independence of matter or brain. We gather the soul's nature from what the soul can do, just as we get the measure of a man's psychology from the little he knows. The soul's activity is basis for our certainty about the soul's intrinsic independence of matter. The soul, therefore, is spiritual, because it has simple and spiritual ideas, ideas of things that cannot react on a material organ like the brain. As examples of such ideas we instance those of being, necessity, possibility, duty, honesty, all abstract and all universal ideas. Further, the mind has knowledge of material things that will never affect the agent's senses. It can see a cause in its effects, effects in their cause. It corrects the work of the senses. In psychological reflection the mind turns back on itself, and no material faculty can perform that trick. Whatever effects of the soul are patent to the senses, fail when the brain is hurt, because in this department of its activity the soul does allegiance to extrinsic dependence on matter. 5. "A mournful faith in a future reward or punishment awakens fear." Here the professor passes from psychology to ethics; and when a Materialist discourses ethics, he is laying down rules for brutes of the field, ill at ease when hungry, content when their bellies are full; with no higher aspiration than the ground, with no wider outlook than the present hour. For, when true to his character, he must maintain that man is only a more perfect brute, different from the monkey in degree, not in kind. If thought is a secretion of the brain, if man's highest faculty is sense, he is open to no subtler impression than physical pleasure and physical pain; and bodily fear would be as potent an incentive with man as it is with the dog and the horse, the lion and the tiger. It would be as arrant nonsense to talk to man of nobler motives, as to talk to dog or cat of decency. Nobility is a spiritual and abstract reality; and, appealing to no organic faculty, is eminently useless in the case of brutes. For this reason the trainer of a lion carries a sharp pointed instrument, the driver of a horse carries a whip; and both are abundantly supplied with lumps of sugar. The prod and the whip awaken physical pain, the sugar awakens physical pleasure.

But anon the Materialist forgets his part in the play, and slips the garb of a motley jester, to don the robes of a wise philosopher. Then he talks of fear as an unworthy motive, and eulogizes what he styles with unctuous severity nobler incentives to virtuous conduct. Fear is not by half the weak and ignoble incentive our friend paints it. One wiser than the professor from Bonn, is authority for the statement, that the fear of the Lord is the beginning of wisdom. Faith in a future reward is hardly mournful. The crape belongs with more right to Dr. Verworm's certainty about future nothingness. Faith in a future punishment is mournful only in the case of such as take no precautions to avoid it. Hell and purgatory are no inventions of a gloomy fancy. They are facts backed up with the undoubted word of God, and unprejudiced minds lean their way at the instigation of naked reason. Reason itself is prejudiced in favor of hell and purgatory, ancient literature is our warrant for the statement; and on this account revelation encounters small difficulty when it clamors for a hearing on these topics.

We further venture to suggest that two motives or incentives to moral conduct are better than one, particularly when the one selected is the weaker of the two. The Doctor in the heat of argument makes the usual mistake of thinking that believers in hell and purgatory altogether despise and neglect approval of conscience and remorse, the esteem and contempt of their fellows. We beg leave to assure him that we are just as much sticklers for respectability as himself, and we court everybody's and our own applause; but, in the impossible supposition of future annihilation, we hardly know whether we should welcome the pangs of self-denial, honest poverty, and life along the hard lines of the Ten Commandments, rather than risk a rebuff from conscience, sink in our own consideration, or expose ourselves to the remote danger of discovery by the neighbor. In the hypothesis of the Doctor, thought of death ought not to arouse fear; it ought to arouse despair, as it regularly does. In our hypothesis, thought of death ought to excite unease, because separation is not, in one sense, the soul's natural condition; it ought to excite anxiety and fear, because nobody is certain whether he is worthy of love or of hatred. It may not be known to the professor that, in the case of believers, death stirs less fear in the virtuous than in the wicked; and the circumstance is an indication that the dying dread not so much death as the future lot awaiting them. Suarez, a rascal Jesuit, from whom the Doctor could learn a vast deal of philosophy, died with these words on his lips: "I did not know it was so sweet to die." Whether pain and fear are physiological or psychological properties, makes small difference regarding the matter in hand; but the Doctor can rest satisfied that the anguish of death will never altogether disappear, and that Materialism is the most hopeless remedy in the world for the disease's cure.

6. If Dr. Verworm wants to meet death like a man, and not like a dumb animal, let him shake off his prejudices, study himself into the phase of mind regarding immortality, adopted by the wisest and noblest men in all history, and then soberly set to work along the surest path to a happy eternity, a life of faith, religion, and uniform virtue. Animals have no dread of death, because they know nothing beyond the present life. With the help of chloroform, or strong drink, or the stupefying principles of Materialism, men sometimes approach death with all the dull indifference of dumb animals. But their lot is not to be envied; and an ounce of the right kind of cowardice is worth more than a ton of the wrong kind of courage. It is the old story of the goat that stood on the track, to dispute right of way with the locomotive. The goat's owner, happening on his remains, dismissed the incident with the remark that his goat had a powerful lot of courage with a plentiful lack of prudence. In this case the goat were better a live coward than a brave carcass. We invite the professor to leave his shop a while, throw himself into a meditative mood, and calmly analyze, not nerves and muscles, but emotions. He will find that, after all, courage, like despair, is only a species of fear. Fear is reaction against impending evil. When the impending evil wears the aspect of avoidability or possible escape, fear becomes courage; when it seems inevitable and beyond peradventure certain, fear becomes despair. Neither the Materialist nor the Christian can escape death, or whatever evil the sad

fact contains. The Christian however feels that with God's grace he can still escape the evil consequences attendant on death in sin, or an eternal hell; and so he welcomes the end with courage. The Materialist can look forward to nothing more pleasant than blank nothingness, with a suspicion of something worse; and so despair is his lot. Be wise unto sobriety, not unto destruction.

7. The Doctor is back to philosophy, when he tells us that the causal view must yield to the condition-view; and, as usual, he is again wrong. Neither view must yield to the other. There is plenty of room for the two views, and they must be kept apart. The condition-view is peculiar to science; and we have no desire to do robbery. The causal view belongs to philosophy; and, as physiology is the science of life, psychology is the philosophy of the soul. Science has nothing to do with the last causes of things or their essences. Berthelot, Pasteur, Bernard, and others too numerous to mention, make wise acknowledgment of the thing; its business is entirely with positive facts and their mutual relations. And the sooner scientifists wake up to this sober truth, the better. When science tells us that brain is a condition of thought, it is venturing information it can well be supposed to have; and we accept its authority; but when it goes farther and proclaims brain the cause of thought, it is away from home, on forbidden ground, and deserves about as much credit as a ditcher discoursing on high art. Science ought to neglect causes, without denying them; and it ought to be content with conditions, without confounding them with causes. To deny a thing is a rather strange way to neglect it. Whether vitalism is a first, intermediate, or last example of the causal view, it is enough for us to know that vitalism, or the doctrine that life proceeds from life alone, is come to stay, and is surer now than it was when science was in its infancy. Science has actually strengthened instead of weakening the position of vitalists. The ancients and old Scholastics were somewhat staggered by the bogie of spontaneous generation, till modern science, in the person of Pasteur, clearly proved that seemingly spontaneous life actually proceeded from preëxistent germs. Science can examine till it grows blind, it will never discover that life actually proceeds from death; and when science gets away from facts, to talk

about possibilities, it deserves no attention. It is for philosophy, not for science, to talk about possibilities.

8. The professor's division of life-factors into external and internal has the merit of sounding erudite, though factors with him are a jumble of conditions and causes. His admission that the internal factors are a hopeless complication, is a tribute to the man's modesty, and almost tempts us to think that his case is not quite so hopeless as the complication. But in the next breath he makes bold to deny what leaders in his own chosen study seem ready to grant. He says that we do not know the exact chemical structure of a single cell, the quantitative relations of its substances, their positions in space and the like; whereas Liebig and others assert the contrary. In fact it would be but an imperfect kind of chemistry and physiology that failed of knowing these several items. All the chemical and physical forces of an egg can be determined with exactness, we can blend them in accurate proportions, positions and conditions, without ever producing an egg able to hatch even a tadpole. The one internal factor or cause, that escapes capture and defies science, is the principle of life or the soul, contended for by the Scholastics; and recalcitrants are rapidly coming over to their camp, acknowledging that the attempt to assemble elements with a view to obtaining life is a hopeless undertaking. Hence we cannot make living substances artificially in a laboratory, and the task promises to remain an impossibility for all time.

The Doctor's illustration of an engineer, unable to put a complicated machine together, because he lacks one of its parts, is but a lame subterfuge. If the engineer knew his business, he would not be long discovering the missing piece, or inventing a substitute, or acknowledging the machine an impossibility. If he afterwards found that another workman, by assembling the same parts, under the same conditions, produced a machine in full operation, he would at once suspect a hidden agency, a motor perhaps in the cellar; and he would take no rest till he solved the problem. Scientists are puzzling their heads over the egg and its contents, chemical and physical, without being able to hatch even a tadpole. A healthy hen can without much ado produce a chick from an egg of her own making. Scientists therefore ought to suspect in the hen and the egg a hidden agency, distinct from chemical and physical forces, a principle of life, the soul contended for by Scholastics. Otherwise, they have on their hands a fact that admits of no explanation.

9. When the professor says that life is continual destruction and continual construction, he is only repeating the mistake made by Comte and other positivists, who cannot see beyond their noses; and like a woful blunderer he hopelessly mixes causes and effects. Life is the principle or cause of continual destruction and continued construction, not the destruction and construction themselves. To hold his manner of talk is about as sensible as to say that the candle, or gas, or electricity is light, and that the man is the house he builds.

10. The monk of St. Gall, responsible for the touchingly beautiful expression, "Media vita in morte sumus," knew well what he was saying, though his materialistic interpreter altogether misses his meaning. The monastery were no place for him, unless he believed in the immortality of the soul; and he held meditative discourse on the death of his body, not on the death of his soul.

11. All life intrinsically dependent on matter or bodily organs must die; the soul of man, because intrinsically independent of matter, can live forever, and because of teleological as well as ethical reasons must live forever.

12. Let the poet answer his last fling, "Dust thou art, to dust returnest, Was not spoken of the soul." If he sets small or no store by poetry, let him turn to the second chapter of Genesis, the only authentic record we have of man's creation, and he will find, perhaps, to his surprise, that the body of Adam, not his soul, was made of dust. "And the Lord God formed man of the slime of the earth; and breathed into his face the breath of life, and man became a living soul."

We have been too busy with immortality's critic to urge in detail philosophy's solid arguments for unwavering certainty in this dogma of the ages. We have been answering objections, and it is hard to tear down and build up with the same hand. In our thesis we made good all our claims, and set immortality on a basis that cannot be shaken by feather-weights in the arena of controversy. We cannot close without recalling an incident that had place in Brooklyn, New York, soon after the publication of Dr. Verworm's views in the *New York Times.*

The same paper is responsible for the story. A reverend gentleman, Mercer, by name, undertook to enlighten some members of a Philosophical Society in that borough, and for his pains was told that he buncoed his audience, and that clergymen in general deceived their congregations to keep their soft jobs. We sincerely pity the Rev. Mr. Mercer. It is disappointing indeed to deserve bouquets, and get the decayed growth of gardens. Whatever it means elsewhere, wanton abuse is not considered in politer circles a manifestation of gratitude or a mark of chivalry. No doubt he left the gathering a wiser, even if a sadder man. The president of the meeting, a Mr. Rinn, vouchsafed Dr. Mercer the comforting and rather commonplace bit of information, that a blow on the head with a sledge-hammer, could make him a degenerate and a ruffian. The Doctor might have replied that, if the hammer applied to Mr. Rinn's own head were heavy enough, it might produce the same sad result. He preferred, however, to be more parliamentary, and suavely dismissed the difficulty with a reference to Paderewski and a battered piano. The illustration is well taken. We merely remark that it could be strengthened by working out the figure thuswise. As the artist, without detriment to his ability, necessarily coaxes poor music from a cracked instrument, on which his skill extrinsically depends; so the soul, without harm to its substance, is hindered of intellectual activity, when the brain, the organ on which it extrinsically depends, is reduced to misshapen pulp with a hammer.

THESIS VII

The intellect, to understand, has need generally of the imprinted intelligible image, as a determining principle. This imprinted intelligible image is the joint product of a phantasm and the working intellect, acting as partial, efficient, subordinate causes. The receiving intellect and this imprinted intelligible image so combine as efficient causes to put the act or idea, that the idea in its entirety proceeds from both as from subordinate causes.

Maher, pp. 252–378; *Jouin,* pp. 200–210.

QUESTION

The Origin of our Ideas. And now we approach a mystery, the profoundest in all psychology. It bears on the origin and genesis of our ideas. That we have ideas nobody can in reason doubt; but to explain just how they rise, is a delicate matter, and calls for the sharpest kind of study. After all, the heart of the problem is to know how the mind, an altogether spiritual faculty, equips itself with knowledge of material and particular objects, to afterwards pass to universal ideas; how to get a material object, man, into a spiritual faculty, there strip him of matter, spiritualize him, and hold up to view not this or that individual man, as he exists in nature, but a peculiar kind of man, a type representative of every individual in the human species.

Among the ancients no guide is safer than Aristotle, and since his time St. Thomas Aquinas is without an equal. Our theory is the joint product of both, and cannot be far wrong. It would be useless to look for the truth among modern writers. The race of metaphysicians is dead, and to it has succeeded a motley crew of biologists, physiologists, phrenologists, electricians; all mere mechanics, without a single pretense to the refinement of subtler thought. They can be called empiricists or experimenters. They limit our knowledge to sensation, and refuse to see in man any higher faculty than sense. In this connection they are called Sensists or Materialists. They have involved and intricate ways of establishing the identity in force between thought and sensation, between operations of the mind and operations of the senses; but the principles underlying their whole method are too openly and grossly wrong to deserve attention. They virtually reduce man to the level of a brute. No essential difference has place between one and the other. They differ only in quality of sensation. A man's senses are a little better than a horse's, and that is all. Like the brutes, men are born to enjoy themselves; and they ought to be content if they succeed in satisfying their animal instincts. They are subject to no law, amenable to no penalty, begin and end with this present life. Locke (1634–1704) is the reputed father of this system. Condillac (1715–1780), Comte (1798–1857) followed closely in his footsteps; and it is safe to say that, outside of Scholasticism, all of to-day's philosophy is more or less infected with the same poison. Sensism, far from undertaking to explain mind and the origin of its ideas, attempts to destroy the reality of both, and avoids the difficulty by refusing to acknowledge its existence.

There are, however, other wrong systems that have the merit of at least meeting the question squarely; and these have a claim on our attention. Chief among them is Plato's theory of innate or inborn ideas, a theory that does large credit to the man's poetic genius, without adding to his reputation as a philosopher. Leibnitz (1646–1716), Wolff (1679–1754), and Kant (1724–1804), have borrowed to a large or small extent from Plato. Rosmini (1797–1855), too, is indebted to the same master-mind for his method. Ontologism, with Malebranche (1638–1715), for founder, is another theory not without its supporters even at the present time. Traditionalism is another explanation ventured by a school with a respectable number of followers. We reserve for last place the true and correct theory, formulated by Aristotle, adopted by St. Thomas, and by the whole Scholastic world with him.

According to Plato, souls before their advent into the world enjoyed a higher life among the stars. In that superior air they owned a knowledge due to impressions made by their Creator. They had ideas of every conceivable thing. For some unknown crime these souls were after a term condemned to unlovely companionship with bodies as to a prison, and hurled headlong from sky to earth. These ideas they carried with them to their new home, and one by one they rise to view at the instigation of recurrent sensations. Hence all our present knowledge is but a grouping of old ideas, and to learn is to recollect. Des Cartes (1596–1650), is accused of adopting innate ideas, but without reason. The innate ideas he contends for are notions derived from neither outside objects nor the will's activity, but from the mind itself. However, many of his followers are amenable to the blame imputed to their master. It costs small trouble to refute Plato's system. Innate ideas are empty creations of the fancy and have no foundation in nature. They rest on the hypothesis that our souls lived before our bodies, that the union in force between soul and body is unnatural and a penalty, that there is a sphere or a planet where universals exist much as individuals here on earth. We certainly have no recollection of any previous life lived by the soul; union with the body is in such measure the soul's natural condition that it rebels against separation, and death is on all sides reckoned a penalty or punishment; and our universal ideas are easily gathered from individual objects without the intervention of any so extraordinary a world. Rosmini thinks that our universal ideas postulate the need of at least one innate idea, that of being in general; but, apart from the fact that his doctrine is dangerously close to pantheism, our universal ideas are easily derived from individual objects without the help of a single innate idea.

Ontologism, though it gets its name from Gioberti (1801–1852), was first mooted by Malebranche (1638–1715). The height of its offending lies in the circumstance that it ascribes the origin of our ideas to immediate vision of God. We have intuition of God, He is absolute Being, and in Him we have knowledge of all else. We must maintain, with all good Catholics, that immediate knowledge of God is reserved to the next life, and altogether impossible to mortals. The only knowledge of God within present reach is the kind deduced from the open book of creation, and therefore posterior rather than antecedent to our knowledge of created objects. Besides, were Ontologism true, it would seem to follow that, as we know everything in

God, we likewise wish everything in God, and all the movements of a man's will would be honorable and in strict accord with morality. The end of the story would be inability to sin, and the removal of everything like an essential difference between good and bad, right and wrong. Further, Ontologism furnishes a stout defense to Deism, Indifferentism and Rationalism. If the mind sees everything in God, and if it fails of the truths presented for belief by revelation, these so-called truths have no reality, and revelation amounts to just nothing. No truth would be absolutely beyond the reach of reason, and all need of supernatural revelation would be at an end. Pantheism likewise has an ally in Ontologism. It derives the mind's activity from the soul's close union with God. If things are knowable only in God, they have their being, not in themselves, but in God alone. In what measure a thing is, in that measure is it understood, and vice-versa. The expression, man is being, would seem to mean, man is the absolute being within certain bounds and limits, a particle of God.

Traditionalism has DeBonald (1754–1840), for author, with Bonnetty (1798–1879), and Ventura (1792–1861), for champions and exponents. Its purpose is highly commendable. It aims at tearing up Rationalism by the roots, but its wrong methods only strengthen the error it attempts to destroy. According to its tenets, the mind left to itself never rises higher than knowledge of sensible things; and to frame universal and abstract notions, particularly in the field of religion, morality and politics, needs the help of a higher mind. This higher mind is the reason holding sway in society; and because society, representing the garnered lore of ages, hands down or passes on these universal and abstract notions through the medium of language, the system is called Traditionalism, and language is a large factor in its economy.

Here are some of its most manifest absurdities. It is as impossible to think without the help of words as it is to see without light. Man is as much able to create, as he is to discover the truth. With the gift of speech, Adam got his first ideas immediately from God. Against Traditionalism we distinguish between quaestio juris and quaestio facti. As a matter of possibility Adam could have formed language. As a matter of fact, there are two opinions, 1, language was infused into Adam with knowledge, 2, language was formed by Adam with help from God. Traditionalists maintain that the mind cannot begin to think or continue thinking without instruction administered through the agency of language, that man is without the skill needed to formulate a language, or determine fixed signs for his ideas; that primitive revelation was altogether natural, because an absolute necessity to man's mental activity; that the mind is entirely passive in its acquisition of knowledge; that faith, or the acceptance of truth with society for single authority, is the basis and foundation of all philosophy and science. We answer: That instruction through the medium of language fails as an explanation of the origin of our ideas, must be plain from the fact that a child learns nothing when told that two sticks are of equal length, unless he knows beforehand what equality and length are. The same word in different languages gives rise to different ideas, and different words in different languages give rise to the same idea. A word is of no value without previous knowledge of the idea it represents. Ideas are not understood by means of words, but words are understood by means of ideas. If our ideas have their origin in divine revelation, every trace of difference between natural and supernatural truths is removed. No man can learn from another, unless he is able with his own unaided strength to grasp the truth proposed, unless he has ideas before he sits at the feet of his teacher. St. Thomas says, "Sicut medicus causare dicitur sanitatem in infirmo, natura operante; ita etiam homo dicitur causare scientiam in altero, operante ratione illius; et hoc est docere." "Every teacher is a doctor. Medicine is of no avail, without a constitution to coöperate with it; and teaching is of as little avail, without a mind to coöperate with it."

To know the reality of God, only three things are needed, notions of being, cause and effect, and the principle of causality; a look or a glance at the world; and the impulse needed to reflect on the spectacle, and search out its causes. According to the saner Traditionalists these three requisites are not beyond the mind's native and unaided strength. Order is the root and origin of every moral truth, and the mind is resourceful enough to compass the notion of order and its consequences. Religion therefore and morality are far from demanding any so extraordinary a help as revelation or instruction. While words are highly conducive to growth in knowledge and the accumulation of ideas, they are by no means absolutely necessary. To understand, the mind is dependent on phantasms, and words are the clearest, readiest and most flexible phantasms at our command. Because they are easily retained, words are of incalculable assistance to the memory. Words are the most convenient of symbols, representing as they do ideas of the widest conceivable variety. They are the key able to unlock the treasury of all knowledge, human and divine, gathered from every side by the learned at the expense of great labor, committed by God to mankind, and sent down through the ages in spoken and printed type. And yet, with all their advantages, words are not an absolute necessity to thought. We often think of things without being able to recall their names. On no few occasions we are driven to the use of circumlocutions and roundabout methods, simply because some single word has slipped the memory. At other times our thoughts are so swift that we cannot fit words to them as they rise.

Dismissing now the futile attempts made by Sensism, Platonism, Ontologism and Traditionalism to explain the origin of our ideas, we proceed to set forth and make good the one true and correct theory, current among Scholastics, borrowed by them from Aristotle, its first propounder, and St. Thomas Aquinas, its eminent elaborator. The intellect is indifferent to whatever ideas, all ideas look alike to it, it is capable in itself of thinking house, horse or man; and, to elicit a thought, it must pass from this phase or condition of indifference to determined and well defined relations with some set object. In other words, the intellect has all the power needed to apprehend whatever object; but this power will never bear fruit, it will never result in a thought, unless some certain object gets in the way of the intellect, and, as it were, restricts or limits its attention. Thus, a magnet is vested with the capacity or power needed to attract or draw all iron; but it will never, as a matter of fact, draw or attract iron, unless some particular piece of that metal is placed within the sphere of its activity. Therefore, the object on which this or that thought turns is the thing that holds the mind, determines it, restricts it, and so gives its apprehensive or thought-power a definite and concrete market value. In this respect the intellect is a passive faculty, inasmuch as it receives motion and influence from another.

In our present condition the mind's proper object is the essence of a material substance or body. Other objects can of course engage its attention, but essences of bodies are reserved to it in a special way, much as color is reserved to the eye, sound to the ear. Bodies are made up of essence and accidents. Sense has their accidents for object; mind, their essence. All the accidents in a body grouped together constitute what we call the material or less proper object of each of the five senses. In addition to this material object, we portion off to each particular sense its own formal or proper object. Thus, the eye deals formally and properly with the body's color; the ear, with its sound; the taste, with its sweetness; the touch, with its smoothness. The imagination remains always a sense, and its phantasms are mere reproductions of work done by the external senses. Whereas, the eye merely sees color, the ear merely hears sounds; the imagination sees, hears, touches, smells and tastes. Its formal or proper object can well be said to be the material object of the other senses.

To return now to the intellect. It passes from idleness to activity, from capability of thinking to actual thought, with help derived from its object, the essences of bodies. These essences are themselves material, the mind is spiritual, and there can be between the material and the spiritual no so intimate commerce as the kind called for by an immanent act like understanding, unless the material is first modified. Before these essences can enter the mind, they must be somehow or other spiritualized. The intellect must be, therefore, equipped with a faculty or virtue able to fit these material essences for entrance into a spiritual mind. Aristotle, therefore, ascribes to the intellect a twofold power, one active, the other passive; and names them respectively the intellectus agens and the intellectus possibilis, the working and the receiving intellect. The function of each is different and well defined. It is the business of the intellectus agens to make the material essence ready for the intellectus possibilis by modifying or spiritualizing the same. This it accomplishes by producing a species intelligibilis impressa of the essence, and this in turn is representative of the essence, now stripped of its material environment or concomitants. This power of the intellectus agens to abstract from the material elements surrounding body-essences ought to cause no wonder. The eye is able to contemplate a body's color without adverting to its other qualities. The mind ought to be able to view a body's essence empty of all its accidents; and, therefore, of all matter, in which its accidents are rooted. The process no more results in change of matter to spirit than the act of seeing results in the change of a body's sound, taste, smell and smoothness to color. As a matter of fact, the mind removes nothing from the body's essence. It leaves everything just as everything was before the process of change began. As the eye singles out the color in its material object, so the intellectus agens singles out the spiritual in a body's essence, shuts its sight to every material attribute it contains, and carries away a species intelligibilis impressa of pure essence without any admixture of matter. For purposes of thinking, this species intelligibilis impressa serves the mind as substitute for the body's essence, in much the same way as the species sensilis serves the eye as substitute for the body's color. The color of the seen body is not transferred to the eye. It remains where it belongs. But a substitute for the color, its species sensilis, finds its way to the eye, and vision follows. The body-essence is not itself transferred to the mind. It remains always where it belongs, in material surroundings. But a substitute for this essence, its species intelligibilis impressa, finds its way into the mind, and the thought or idea follows. This species intelligibilis impressa is the joint work of the imagination and the intellectus agens. This species is not what is understood or thought. The essence itself is that. The species is that with whose help the essence is thought or understood. To understand or think is not the same as to produce these species or receive them; but it is work the intellectus possibilis does, when equipped with the species intelligibilis impressa. In last analysis, the intellectus agens and the phantasm coöperate as partial and subordinate effective causes, by way of a single complete cause, to produce the species intelligibilis impressa. The intellectus possibilis receives this first species, and thus equipped it elicits a second, called, to distinguish it from the first, species intelligibilis expressa; and this last is in reality the idea or thought, the mind-waif, the mind-word, the close of the process called thinking, or the simple apprehension.

In our present condition, because the intellectus agens must always have play, we cannot think even spiritual things, though they give rise to no phantasm, without in some way referring them to sensible objects, capable of arousing phantasms. On this account our ideas of spiritual things are analogical or figurative; comparative, not proper. Intellectual memory is the intellectus possibilis, inasmuch as it retains old species impresses to elicit with their help new thoughts or ideas. And yet in all its operations, so intimate is the mind's dependence on work of the imagination, we cannot think or recall objects, though actually possessed of their species, unless the imagination first evokes corresponding phantasms. This remark serves to explain after what manner all our knowledge has its rise in the senses, and in what measure mind depends for its information on sense. St. Thomas thus elucidates the point, "Non potest dici quod sensibilis cognitio sit totalis et perfecta causa intellectualis cognitionis, sed magis quodammodo est materia causae." 1, Q., 84; A. 6. Sense supplies us with phantasms, from them as from material the intellectus agens derives species intelligibiles impressas, and these last with the intellectus possibilis are the real and efficient cause of thought or intellectual knowledge.

Tongiorgi, § 361, maintains that, while the axiom, "Nil in intellectu quod non fuerit prius in sensu," occurs nowhere in Aristotle or any conspicuous follower of Aristotle, it is of frequent use with Sensists. After the mind of Aristotle, it means that we know with the mind only what material things we know first with the senses; but what we discover with the mind in material things is different from what we discover with the senses. Moreover, the mind rises from its knowledge of material things to the knowledge of things altogether immaterial or spiritual, with dependence always on phantasms. In other words, our knowledge begins with the senses, but never finishes with them. According to Sensists the axiom means that our intellectual knowledge is no wider or more extensive than our sense-knowledge; it merely changes sense-knowledge in a variety of ways, leaving its nature always the same. In other words, our knowledge begins and ends with the senses, it is restricted to sensible, material objects; and things spiritual are an empty dream. This is in brief Aristotle's doctrine regarding the origin of ideas, and its main features are summarily set forth in our present thesis.

TERMS

The intellect is the spiritual, inorganic cognoscitive faculty in man, separating him from brutes, and capable of knowledge transcending the senses. The three powers in the soul, are set forth in the subjoined diagram:

1. Cognoscitive	Material, organic, is sense. Spiritual, inorganic, is intellect.
2. Appetitive	Sensitive, organic, is appetite. Spiritual, inorganic, is will.
3. Executive	When it moves own body, is locomotion. When it moves outside objects, is energy.

Imprinted intelligible image, or the species intelligibilis impressa, is a determining reality, superadded in the nature of a quality to the intellect, with the production of some fixed idea in view; it is the joint work of phantasm and working intellect; it paves way, it determines, it is the undeveloped photograph.

Finished intelligible image, or the species intelligibilis expressa, is the idea in its completeness; it is the joint work of first image and receiving intellect; it is the developed photograph.

Generally, because when object is spiritual, there is no need of a new imprinted intelligible image, an old image stored away suffices.

Determining principle, to enable the intellect to pass from idleness to activity, because without image it is indifferent to this or that particular idea.

Phantasm is the product of the imagination, the treasure-house of sensible images, the highest of the senses, an organic faculty seated in the brain.

Joint Work means that the phantasm and working intellect combine as partial, subordinate, efficient causes. The image and receiving intellect combine in same way to produce the idea. An efficient cause by real and physical exertion of its power produces another existence. Partial causes are opposed to adequate; subordinate, to coördinate. When two principles together are the whole or adequate cause of an effect, each of the two is its partial cause. Causes are coördinate, when they are of the same rank and nature with respect to the effect, and each produces its part of the effect independently of the other. Two horses drawing a chariot are partial, coördinate, efficient causes. One of two such causes can by successive additions to its strength become equal to the task of producing singly the whole effect. Causes are subordinate, when they are of different rank and nature, and each of them contributes in its own particular sphere to the whole effect, in such a way that one without the other can do nothing, neither ever becoming able under any supposition to produce the whole effect. The writer and his pen are partial, subordinate, efficient causes. Subordinates are partial, indeed, with respect to their efficacy; but they are whole or adequate causes, with regard to their result. Each bears on the whole effect, not on part of it.

To understand means the first operation of the mind, resulting in a concept or idea. We are studying our intellectual knowledge in its root or origin; and, therefore, restrict ourselves to concepts or ideas. These make up judgments, which in turn combine to form reasoning or syllogisms. We deal with direct, not reflex knowledge. Direct puts us in intellectual possession of some outside object, like a man, a horse, or a house. Reflex is a further improvement on, an elaboration of direct.

Knowledge, like every act, has what we call its term or limit, that in which the act ends, finishes, closes; and philosophy recognizes two kinds of terms in intellectual knowledge, or an idea. They are called the intrinsic or subjective term, and the extrinsic or objective term of the idea. The intrinsic term is the idea itself, the actual likeness of the outside object existent in the mind, and technically called the species intelligibilis expressa. The extrinsic term is the outside object, whose likeness exists in the mind; it is the man, the horse, or the house of which we have an idea.

The word species needs explanation. It means likeness, that

which makes some outside object present and visible to the mind, much as the photograph stands for the man, or chips for money. It is of two kinds. There is a species intelligibilis impressa along with a species intelligibilis expressa. The first is the joint product of a phantasm and the intellectus agens, or working intellect; the other is the joint product of the species intelligibilis impressa and the intellectus possibilis, or receiving intellect; and the difference between the two, to hold to the same illustration, is about the same as that in force between an undeveloped and a developed photograph. The species intelligibilis expressa is the idea itself, and it is called the mind-word, because the mind uses it as a symbol of the outside object, much as we use words for symbols of our thoughts. That thought results in this likeness, this species intelligibilis expressa or mind-word, is evident from the fact that thought is a true vital and cognoscitive act. Because it is a true act, it must have a term, or result; because the act is vital, its term must be immanent or within the mind; because it is cognoscitive, the term within the mind must be a likeness of the object outside the mind.

It is a dogma in philosophy, conceded on all sides and made good by experience, that knowledge arises when the mind pictures its object, or assumes towards it the relationship of resemblance. Hence resemblance enters the definitions of all three species of truth, logical, ontological and moral. In logical, the mind resembles the object; in ontological, the object resembles the mind; in moral, the word resembles the speaker's phase of mind. And the species intelligibilis expressa is only this actual likeness of the object struck off or delineated in the mind. In thought, the thing understood or known is not the species, or likeness; but the outside object, the man, the horse, or the house. When we use our eyes, we see not the sensile images of objects, but the objects themselves. And all this is borne out by the fact that we talk about these outside objects, not about our ideas, or mental acts; and what we talk about, that is topic of our thoughts. Philosophy sums up the whole thing when it says that the mind-word or idea is that, by means of which we understand or think; while the outside object is what we understand or think. Subjective concept and objective concept are the same as the idea's intrinsic term and extrinsic term respectively. The objective concept of a man is the man's essence, the man himself. The subjective concept of a man is the idea of a man, the act of understanding a man.

Our first ideas are derived from sensile experience, and immediately from phantasms, the products of the imagination, the chiefest among our internal senses. From these first ideas others can be evolved by process of analysis, comparison and argumentation; and with these last we are not concerned. Therefore, our external senses and our imagination contribute as primary sources to our intellectual knowledge. We have already disproved the existence of anything like innate or inborn ideas; and their rejection paves the way to coöperation of sense with intellect in thought-formation. The denial of mutual dependence between sense and intellect would virtually establish a twofold nature in man. Right order demands that the senses, or inferior faculties, minister or do service to their superior, the intellect. It is a matter of experience that children born deaf or blind never elicit ideas of sounds or colors, whereas such as fall deaf or blind a long or short interval after birth readily elicit ideas of both kinds. This is clear evidence that innate or inborn ideas are the idle suggestion of a poetic temper, and that our first ideas are derived from sensile experience, especially from phantasms. First ideas invariably deal with bodies, substances vested with extension and resistance, material for work of the senses. They are opposed to secondary ideas, which have spiritual things for object. These last are called anological, in opposition to proper, because we derive them from comparison with bodies, material substances gifted with extension and resistance, cognoscible to the senses. A phantasm is the product, the species expressa, of the imagination, the highest function of internal sense. We take phantasm here in its objective sense, inasmuch as it is the outside object actually perceived by the imagination. External sense can be called the remote medium of our intellectual knowledge; imagination, its proximate medium.

Again, we appeal to experience for proof that imagination is the proximate medium of our intellectual knowledge. Very young children and grown up idiots cannot acquire ideas, are outside the reach of instruction, in spite of the fact that their intellects are right, and their external senses are sufficiently well developed. The mind undergoes no intrinsic change with the child's growth, and it slaves to no natural dullness. The eyes and the ears of a young child are as clear and sharp as those of any adult. The difference, therefore, between very young children and adults must be due to want of development in the only remaining factor, the imagination; and phantasms are proximate means to man's intellectual knowledge. With the external senses sound and in good order, any hurt in the brain or disturbance in the imagination prevents the mind from reasoning out new knowledge or putting to good use knowledge already possessed. No hurt in the brain can hurt the mind taken by itself, because the mind is of its very nature inorganic, and therefore incapable of physical injury. Therefore, every such hurt interferes with the process of thinking, simply because the mind is in natural need of phantasms for its object or the material of its ideas. When engaged in intellectual work, we are conscious of immediate dependence, not on the external senses, but on the imagination; and the readier and richer the imagination, the better and easier our work. Finally, order vindicates to the imagination the prerogative of proximate means to our intellectual knowledge. It is the highest of the senses, while mere intelligence is the lowest of the mind's faculties; and there is a law in philosophy to the effect that the highest in a lower class touches or borders on the lowest in a higher class. Supremum infimi attingit infimum supremi. Therefore, the working intellect and the phantasm produce the imprinted intelligible image; this image and the receiving intellect in turn produce the idea, the developed intelligible image, the intelligible image in its completeness.

Our theory postulates two distinct functions of intellect in its first operation, simple apprehension or thought, namely the working and the receiving intellect. The Thomists contend for a real distinction between the two; Suarez denies every wider distinction than virtual, and his reasons commend themselves to our approval. One and the same faculty can be active and passive, as happens in the case of the receiving intellect and the will. The receiving intellect is passive with regard to the imprinted intelligible image, and active with regard to the idea or thought. The will is passive with regard to the influence exerted by the intellect, and active with regard to the wish it elicits. No contradiction has place, because they are active and passive under different aspects, sub diverso respectu. The images produced by the two are not in themselves complete and independent, but mutually incomplete and supplementary; another sign that they result not from two really distinct faculties, but from one and the same faculty capable of two different functions. Were the working intellect really distinct from the receiving, it would be forever idle after death, a thing hard to admit. Supposing mere virtual distinction between the two, the difficulty disappears. Because they are really identical, one would be as active as the other after death.

The working intellect is not formally or strictly cognoscitive; it is cognoscitive in a merely preparative way. All its efficiency centers in the active production of one of the two joint principles coalescing to form the intellectual act, the idea, the thought. Its work begins and ends with the imprinted intelligible image or likeness; and the idea or formal cognition is not this first image, but the joint product of it and the receiving intellect. For this reason it is called the working intellect, the intellectus agens; not because it understands, but because it makes outside objects ready to be understood, spiritualizes them after a fashion in the imprinted intelligible image, and thus paves the way for their entrance into a spiritual and immaterial soul.

And here another mystery confronts us, this spiritualization of the outside object. We must maintain that the mind understands not the imprinted intelligible image, but the corresponding outside object; and this latter never ceases to be material, a body, a substance vested with extension and resistance. Plato thought to solve the mystery by introducing innate or inborn ideas, conveyed to the mind from the first by the mind's maker. The difficulty seemed to be otherwise insuperable because of his formula, "Like knows like," or a spiritual soul can know only spiritual things. Aristotle, improving on Plato, changed his teacher's formula to the following: "The thing known assumes in the mind the mind's own quality." In other words, material things exist in the spiritual mind after a spiritual manner. In more general terms, the formula runs this way, "Whatever is received adopts the quality of its receiver." "Aequale cognoscitur ab aequali," says Plato. "Cognitum est in cognoscente ad modum cognoscentis," or "Receptum est in recipiente ad modum recipientis," says Aristotle. The upshot of the whole thing is that the imprinted intelligible image takes the place, usurps the function, of the outside object. One is the other, the image is after some fashion the outside object. We clear the mystery by recognizing in things a twofold value, entitative and representative. The agreement of image and object is not of course in point of entitative value, but in point of representative value; non in essendo, sed in repraesentando. And in the field of knowledge this agreement is sufficient basis for identifying one with the other. Agreement in essendo has place, when two things agree generically or specifically, as a man and a horse, a man and a man. Agreement in repraesentando has place, when one of the two contains a something able to lead us to knowledge of the other, as a man and his photograph, the imprinted intelligible image and its outside object. In the image its entitative value must be sedulously kept apart from its representative value. The marble in the statue is a different thing from the Cæsar it represents. In the same way the physical being of the image is a different thing from the being of the image inasmuch as it represents this or that outside object. Small need to recount the differences in force between the image and its object. The image is always an accident, the object is often a substance; the image is simple and without parts, the object is often a compound; the image is a particular and concrete thing, the object is often a universal and abstract entity; the image is a thing that can exist or cease, it comes and goes, the object is often a thing that goes on forever. Agreement in entitative value, in essendo, is not needed between the imprinted intelligible image and its object, because its whole purpose is to effect such a union between the mind and its object that the mind be prepared or made ready to elicit a vital or immanent likeness of the object; and such a likeness is compatible with generic and specific differences, or independent of agreement in essendo. The idea itself, the thought, lacks agreement in essendo with its object; and yet, when we think, we think the object. The imprinted intelligible image is in far less need of any so close agreement as entitative.

To return now to the intellectus possibilis, the receiving intellect. Unlike the working intellect, it is formally and strictly cognoscitive. It receives the imprinted intelligible image, and with its help elicits the idea or thought in a finished state. Because of this twofold process it is called in Latin, patibilis or possibilis. It is patibilis, or receptive, or capable of suffering at the hands of another, inasmuch as it receives the imprinted intelligible image from the working intellect; and possibilis or possible, or capable of becoming things, inasmuch as it has the power of transforming itself into everything conceivable in the universe by the vital and immanent expression of whatsoever reality. It can become everything in much the same sense as the photograph becomes the man it represents.

The reality of imprinted intelligible images once admitted, we must admit in the mind a certain inborn faculty able with the help of phantasms to evolve these images. We cannot assign the phantasm for adequate and complete cause of such images, because these images, as intellectual forms and therefore spiritual accidents, are of an essentially higher order than phantasms which are acts of the whole man, body and soul acting as a single principle, and therefore organic and material accidents. The reception of phantasms into the intellect cannot be assigned as adequate and complete cause of these images. First of all, it is quite impossible for the intellect to receive unmodified phantasms, phantasms as such. The intellect is an inorganic faculty and phantasms are organic accidents. As a matter of fact, phantasms undergo no change in the process of thought. They remain what they were, and the imprinted intelligible image is far from being a modified phantasm. It is a third entity, derived from the joint energy of the working intellect and the phantasm. Aristotle's formula, the thing known assumes in the mind the mind's own quality, is no proof that a phantasm received into the intellect is adequate and complete cause of the imprinted intelligible image. The phantasm is of its nature and essence organic, and to transform it into an inorganic being like the imprinted intelligible image would be not to change but to destroy it. Therefore the phantasm and the receiving intellect are not of themselves enough to account for the idea or thought, and we must admit the additional function denominated the working intellect. Aristotle dismisses the matter with this simple proof. The soul of man is intrinsically intellectual, and because nature is never lacking in necessary helps, and because she never imposes a task without at the same time supplying everything needed for its accomplishment, the soul of man must be intrinsically and abundantly equipped with all the requisites for intellectual acts like ideas and thoughts. But thought is impossible without the imprinted intelligible image, and this in turn is impossible without the intrinsic equipment we call the working intellect. Ergo the soul of man is equipped with the working intellect, or faculty able with the help of phantasms to produce the imprinted intelligible image.

The working intellect works only in conjunction with phantasms, and phantasms are possible only when there is question of objects perceptible to the senses. When the object of the idea or thought is spiritual, not sensible, the receiving intellect performs the whole operation, without any distinct employment of the working intellect. Old imprinted intelligible images stored away in the memory are called into play, and for this reason our ideas of spiritual objects are anological and not strictly proper; they are based on our knowledge of sensible objects and are evolved from it by comparison and kindred processes. The words in our language expressive of spiritual objects are figurative; for instance, idea, concept, notion. The energy of the working intellect is restricted to the imprinted intelligible image. Every other intellectual operation belongs immediately to the receiving intellect, mediately to the working intellect. Therefore ideas, judgments, syllogisms, the derivation of new ideas from old ones, memory, all are the work of the receiving intellect. The Scholastics ascribe a triple efficacy to the working intellect; it lights up the phantasm, it makes the object of the phantasm ready for the intellect, it produces the image. Suarez sees herein only three ways of expressing one and the same thing, the production of the image. To derive the image from a phantasm and from individuating notes are different things. The latter expression is incorrect.

Division. Three parts.

I. Need of image as determining principle.
II. Image, joint result of phantasm and working intellect.
III. Image and receiving intellect combine as partial subordinate efficient causes to produce idea.

PROOFS I, II, III

I. 1°. The need of the image is rooted in the twofold fact that the mind views all objects with indifference; and that, to know, the mind must assume the relation of resemblance with its object. Hence our argument.

To apprehend a set object, the mind must lay aside its indifference to all objects, and restrict its attention to this particular object. This can be effected only by intrinsic union of the mind with its object, or, failing that, with some likeness representative of the object, and fitted to enter the mind. Intrinsic union of mind and object is impossible. One is spiritual; the other, material. Therefore union of mind with the object's likeness is the one way left; and this likeness, the only likeness fitted to enter the mind, is what we call the imprinted intelligible image. Ergo the intellect, to understand, has need generally of the imprinted intelligible image as a determining principle.

N.B. The material phantasm cannot unite with the mind to remove its attitude of indifference, either as a mere condition, or a form, or a cause immediately with the mind effective of the idea. Therefore all its activity is restricted to coöperation with the mind in the production of a principle, able by intrinsic union to help the mind elicit the idea. And this combined effort of phantasm and mind results precisely in what we termed the imprinted intelligible image. Mere presence of the phantasm as a condition could never intrinsically affect the mind's attitude of indifference. Witness magnet and wood. The phantasm could never enter the mind as a form, because its proper seat is the whole man, the composite made up of body and soul; whereas the mind dwells altogether in the soul. The phantasm is, besides, a quantitative accident, and cannot be form to a simple substance like the mind; it is an individual and material thing, whereas the mind apprehends things universal and spiritual. The naked phantasm cannot work in conjunction with the mind, because its material quality bars it from intrinsic union with the mind. Phantasm and mind not like two horses, but like pen and hand.

2°. The need of this image can likewise be gathered from

comparison with sensation. The senses, to perceive, need imprinted sensile images of their objects. In a parallel way, the mind, to understand, ought to have imprinted intelligible images of its objects.

N.B. The two images, the imprinted and the resultant or developed, are means by which the mind knows its object, but after different manners. The imprinted is effective merely, the resultant or developed is formal as well as effective.

II. The working intellect and the phantasm are the image's, *a.* efficient causes, *b.* partial, *c.* subordinate, a single complete principle of activity.

a. Efficient causes. They are principles producing another existence by the real and physical exertion of their powers.

b. Partial. Neither is equal to the whole effect. The image gets its spirituality from the working intellect; its power to represent, from the phantasm. The illumination or elevation derived from intellect to phantasm is extrinsic, and leaves the phantasm wholly the same in itself. It remains always quite material. A parallel instance is the case of two boys, unable of themselves to haul a boat, and equal to the task when helped by four others. The same two boys are now partial causes of the whole effect, and undergo no change whatever. An engine could lend them the same assistance, and the two boys would still be partial causes, without becoming engines. Between the phantasm and working intellect there is, of course, want of proportion as far as physical entity is concerned; but proportion between them in point of power and causality is present, and that is enough. Proportion of entity is wanting between the two boys and the engine, but that prevents nobody from calling the boys and the engine causes of the effect. To work together, they must unite, not indeed in being or entity, but in power, like the boys and the engine.

c. Subordinate. The phantasm and working intellect are of different rank and nature; the phantasm contributes to the image its representative quality, the intellect its spirituality; in such a way that one without the other can do nothing, neither ever becoming able under any supposition to produce the whole effect. One is principal, the other instrumental; like the penman and his pen, the sculptor and his chisel.

III. *a.* The receiving intellect is partial cause of the idea. *b.* The image is partial cause of the idea.

a. A vital act must proceed from a vital principle or cause. But ideas are vital acts, and the intellect is vital principle or cause. Ergo ideas proceed from the intellect.

N.B. If the image were sole cause, the idea would be produced in the intellect but not by it.

b. When of two principles one completes the other in the order of efficiency, the first assumes the quality of partial efficient cause. But the image completes the receiving intellect in the order of efficiency. Ergo the image is partial efficient cause of the idea.

N.B. The image contributes determinateness to the receiving intellect, it is the phantasm spiritualized.

a. and *b.* An idea is the vital expression of a set object. Its vitality comes from the receiving intellect, its expressiveness of a set object comes from the image. Ergo, because the whole act is vital and at the same time expressive of the object, the whole act proceeds from one and other principle. They are, besides, of a different rank and nature; and one without the other is unequal to the effect, or idea.

N.B. Of the two principles, the mind is the more important, because origin of the idea's vitality. In point of specification the image is the more important, because origin of the idea's determinateness. The image can be called the mind's form, or formal cause of the idea, inasmuch as it determines the mind and gives specific value to the idea; and the imprinted image is efficient cause of the idea, inasmuch as it actively coöperates with the mind, after making it immediately ready for the act. Therefore, thought is a new act, distinct from the first image, its production and its reception. The developed image is in the intellect in a vital way, and the whole act arises from the intellect, and remains in the intellect.

Two Assertions. *a. b.*

a. 1. Our ideas of individual material things are particular and proper, not general and common.

2. Their imprinted intelligible images are likewise particular and proper.

S.Q. Cajetan denies the whole statement, asserting that the mind first forms universals, and passes from them to particular individuals by a process of argumentation. St. Thomas denies the second part, asserting that the mind first knows universals, and then by a species of reflection on, or return to, the phantasm, knows clearly and distinctly particular individuals. In other words, we have developed images of particulars, imprinted images of universals alone.

TERMS

Ideas are particular and proper, when the notes they embrace belong to one set object and to no other, and when they clearly separate this set object from every other like it, e. g. Peter. They are general and common when they are universals, e. g. man. When proper means definite and distinct, when common means confused and indefinite, our ideas of particulars are rather common than proper. Constituent notes are less clear in particulars than in universals.

PROOFS

a. 1°. In the judgment, Peter is a man, one term is particular; the other, universal. To frame judgment, we must have like ideas of both. Ergo particular and proper.

2°. Developed image and imprinted image ought to be of the same order. If one is particular, the other ought to be particular and proper. Developed images are particular and proper. Ergo imprinted images ought to be particular and proper.

N.B. A thing's individuality is not constituted by its matter, but by its entire reality. The individual stripped of its matter, still remains an individual.

b. Knowledge of individual particular objects precedes knowledge of universals.

1°. First images are basis of first knowledge. Images of individual particular objects are the first we receive. Ergo knowledge of individual particular objects precedes knowledge of universals, e. g. this body before body; this sound before sound.

2°. Particular and proper ideas can be foundation for universals, not vice-versa. Ergo.

3°. Children first get idea of this red thing, then successively they get ideas of thing, quality, color, red.

4°. Experience is proof that we first know individual particular objects.

To Reconcile Seeming Differences Between the Scholastics

Suarez refuses efficient causality to the phantasm in the production of the image, confining it to the working intellect. He makes the phantasm matter for the image, or incentive for the intellect, or model cause. He calls the production of the image no vital and immanent, but a transient act. Hence the working intellect is not cognoscitive, but merely preparative. His reason is parity with the will. The will is the whole cause of its operation, though intellectual knowledge necessarily precedes. In like manner the working intellect ought to be whole cause of the image, though the phantasm necessarily precedes. Opponents to Suarez try to show that the phantasm would in that case be deprived of all causality in the production of the images; but to my mind they fail to make clear how model causality would be absent. Such causality is always extrinsic and calls for no intimate or intrinsic union with the efficient cause. We maintain against Suarez that the phantasm exerts what efficient causality belongs to the instrument, the pen in the case of writing, the chisel in the case of a statue. For such causality merely extrinsic union between the principal agent and instrument is needed, and of this the material phantasm is capable. The production of the first image is no vital or immanent act in strict sense, because, though its term or result dwells in the intellect, it proceeds from a partial principle outside of the intellect. On the contrary, the production of the second image or idea is a vital act, because it proceeds in its entirety from the intellect, equipped, of course, and intrinsically equipped with the first image; and because it remains in the intellect. The material nature of the phantasm bars intimate union with the working intellect, and as a mere instrument it demands only extrinsic union. The spiritual nature of the first image fits it for intrinsic union with the receiving intellect, and renders the idea a vital or immanent act. The image cannot be called an instrument, as compared with the receiving intellect. The two are equally principal. The phantasm is and must be called an instrument as compared with the working intellect.

Opinion of St. Thomas

Two reasons why phantasm cannot immediately combine with receiving intellect to produce ideas. 1. Phantasm is likeness of individual thing. 2. It exists in a body-organ and is organic. Ergo it cannot pass to receiving intellect, which represents universal, and is immaterial.

N.B. Sensile image can pass to eye because both represent individual things and are organic.

Illumination of Phantasm

Phantasms are made intelligible by working intellect, as colors are made visible by light.

N.B. Two opinions about color and light, 1°. Light gives color the power to excite vision. 2°. Light merely clarifies the medium air.

Light makes color actually visible, the working intellect makes the phantasm actually knowable. Color, made actually visible by light, impresses its likeness on the retina; the phantasm, made actually knowable by the working intellect, impresses its likeness on the receiving intellect. Color in the presence of light becomes actually visible, to the extent that it becomes able to excite vision, not to the extent that it is actually seen. The phantasm is made actually knowable by the working intellect, to the extent that it becomes able to excite the receiving intellect, not to the extent that it is actually known.

The two kinds of illumination for phantasm are root-illumination and formal illumination. Root-illumination is derived from intellectual soul. Because sensation in man is more potent than in brutes, phantasm is more potent in man and better fitted to produce image. Formal comes from fact that working intellect enters into intimate union with phantasm, and raises it as principal raises instrumental. Because immaterial, its union with phantasm is restricted to latter's universal aspect, neglecting its material surroundings. Hence a twofold abstraction,

1. formal, 2. causal. One rids the phantasm of material surroundings, and views it in the light of a universal, making it, as far as view is concerned, homogeneous with the receiving intellect, or immaterial. The other views the phantasm as material or stuff for the cause of intellectual knowledge or thought. The working intellect plays the part of formal cause; the phantasm, the part of material cause. The image is spiritual on the side of the working intellect; it is representative of the object on the side of the phantasm. The phantasm therefore contributes efficiency and determinateness to the working intellect in the production of the image. The illumination and the abstraction attributed to the working intellect are one and the same act. Light at the same time manifests color in the object and abstracts from its sweetness and other qualities, being of no service to impress them on the palate or other senses.

Opinions of Mastrius, Conimbricenses and Others

The working intellect acts not on the phantasm, but with it. The phantasm undergoes no intrinsic change or elevation; but the addition of outside light from the working intellect raises it to the dignity of participation as an efficient cause in the production of the image. The working intellect is no complete and whole cause of the image; the phantasm coöperates with it in the rôle of a less principal cause. The image in point of being is spiritual, and this quality it gets from the working intellect; in point of power to represent, it pictures the object, and this it gets from the phantasm. Matter cannot act on spirit as a complete and whole cause, or even as a more principal cause; but it can act on spirit as a partial or less principal cause. The phantasm becomes no instrument, in the hands of the working intellect, with intrinsic elevation like that of the pen in the writer's hand. It simply remains a less principal cause, acting in conjunction with the working intellect, like the boy aided by four others in hauling a boat that calls for the strength of five. The boy's power is not intrinsically modified, it is merely helped from the outside. The two together, phantasm and intellect, constitute a single whole and complete cause; one contributing to the image its spirituality; the other, its representative value. The Conimbricenses say that the phantasm, in spite of its material nature, is made fitter and more able by extrinsic union with the working intellect to produce beyond its natural capacity a spiritual effect. With them the illumination of the phantasm is not root-illumination, as Capreolus thinks; nor formal, as Cajetan thinks; but efficient. They are far from meaning that the working intellect intrinsically modifies the phantasm by pouring new light into it. But, like a light shining from the outside, it raises it by a share in its own radiance to the dignity of participation as a partial cause in the effective production of the image. The working intellect is called an outside light, not to deny it the union in force between the two partial causes, but to deny anything like intrinsic elevation, resulting to the phantasm from a share in the working intellect's own being or reality. They vindicate efficient causality to the phantasm for two reasons, to secure determinateness, and to account for the element of representation in the image. They reject model causality on the ground that it is rather passive than active; whereas the causality of the phantasm is essentially active. The working intellect does not produce the image from the phantasm, as the artist or sculptor produces his painting or statue, with an eye on his model.

Opinions of Cajetan, Capreolus and Scotus

These writers agree with us in ascribing efficient causality to the phantasm. Cajetan and Capreolus make the phantasm an instrumental cause; Scotus with us makes it a partial cause, uniting with the intellect to form the complete and whole cause of the image. Each of the two opinions is highly probable. Instrument, however, must be taken in its wider sense; and must be made to mean whatever lends assistance to another in the production of an effect. The phantasm is no instrument in strict and proper sense, because it derives no intrinsic elevation from the working intellect. When two such causes are heterogeneous, like the phantasm and working intellect, one cannot of itself produce an effect of the same nature as the effect ascribed to both. The parity of two lamps and one lamp producing light, fails in this that the partial causes are homogeneous.

P.S. Suarez thus explains the whole process of thought. With the eyes we see Peter; this sensile image is transferred to the imagination, where it becomes a phantasm; the working intellect in union with the phantasm produces the individual particular imprinted intelligible image of Peter, and the receiving intellect in union with this last produces the idea of Peter, who is an individual particular object. Then the receiving intellect by a second effort, prescinding or abstractive in nature, without any new image, omits all the individuating attributes of Peter, without a care for his individual differences with other men, forms an idea of his specific nature, his quality of man, and this idea is what we call the direct universal. At last by a third effort, after employing the same process with regard to several men, by a method comparative in nature, this quality of man in Peter is conceived as a quality common to a multitude of individuals, and in this way is conceived what we call the reflex universal.

PRINCIPLES

A. The greater contains the less. Ergo, the intellect by itself is equal to the task of producing the image.

Answer. In its own order, I grant; in another order, I deny. The intellect cannot by itself understand, neither can it produce the image. The phantasm is needed not in the cognoscitive order, but in the order of determinateness and representation. Four quarts of wine do not contain three quarts of water. It might be true of milk.

B. No proportion between phantasm and working intellect. Ergo.

Answer. In point of being, I grant; in point of causality or power, I deny. The phantasm is not formally and intrinsically united with the intellect.

C. An active is superior to a passive agent. Phantasm is active, intellect is passive.

Answer. In question of two whole and complete causes, I grant; in question of two partial causes, I deny. Besides, the agens is active as well as passive.

D. Matter cannot act on spirit. Ergo.

Answer. As whole cause or more principal, I grant; as partial or less principal, I deny.

E. Image is made out of phantasm. Ergo, material cause.

Answer. As virtually containing the image, I grant; as stuff of image, I deny.

F. The effect follows the weaker of the two causes.

Answer. In syllogisms, I grant; outside of syllogisms, I deny. The saying holds good for the conclusion in a syllogism. In this present case the effect follows both causes, getting spirituality from the working intellect, and representative power from the phantasm.

G. Image cannot be explained, unless phantasm receives something from intellect.

Answer. Example of boys hauling boat with engine explains things.

THESIS VIII

There exists in man a rational appetite or will, which can desire every good proposed by the intellect, and nothing but good. All the objects of its actual desires must in some measure assume a relation of fitness with the subject.

Maher, pp. 378–425; 208–228. *Jouin*, pp. 171–180.

Division. Our thesis contains four parts. I. Man has a will. II. The will has for object every good. III. The will never has evil for object. IV. Every object of man's wishes must redound to the wisher's interests.

QUESTION

All morality resides in the will, and a thorough knowledge of Ethics is impossible without an equally thorough knowledge of the nature of the human will. Freedom of will is an all important factor in the discussion; but experience is so loud in its declaration of this natural dogma that we can for the present leave it untouched. It is a large question, and will get proper attention in next thesis. Here we contend that man has a will, that good is the only object capable of setting its activity in motion, and that an element of selfishness is naturally, and, therefore, necessarily bound up in every human desire.

TERMS

Rational appetite or will is a spiritual, inorganic faculty of the soul, capable of seeking good by acts elicited under the direction of the intellect. It is opposed to sensitive appetite, common to man and beast, dealing with merely material or sensible goods. The most apparent difference between these two faculties is furnished forth in the freedom inherent in one, alien to the other. There are, of course, other differences more important and more characteristic; but since they depend for illustration on objects not common to man and beast, a common foundation for comparison is wanting and contrast loses. But, supposing the objects of appetite in some definite instance the same, freedom in the case of man, necessity in the case of brutes, become distinguishing characteristics. Thus, a hungry horse when confronted with oats, and equipped with all the usual requirements for the enjoyment of a good meal, cannot refrain from eating. A man on the very verge of starvation, can, in the midst of plenty and in spite of most vehement desire and utmost relish, shut his lips tight, and persistently refuse to touch food. The reason is plain. A horse's highest faculty of desire is sensitive appetite, a necessary agent, which in the presence of certain conditions must act. Man has, in addition to this sensitive appetite, a spiritual faculty of desire called will, a free agent forced to act by no combination of circumstances, by no array of outward conditions. The will in man is absolute mistress of all the sensitive appetite's motions, and can on all occasions command them authoritatively. The will can, therefore, say nay to whatever sensitive instincts threaten harm to man's higher good. It can for purposes of virtue order fasting, though the body would be much benefited by feasting. It can, for purposes of fame, keep out of bed whole nights at a time men bent on winning an election or solving some deep intellectual problem. But, like other masters, the will can, if so inclined, surrender its supremacy, and follow the behests of lower appetites. To escape a quarrel with the senses, it can eat, drink, and make merry, even to the death of the soul. It can yield to sleep, that lands the sleeper in a hospital or the morgue.

Every good. Like the two other transcendental qualities of being, one and true, good admits of no essential definition. The three might be called being without division, being with mind-conformity, being with fitness; but indivision, conformity, and fitness are themselves being; and what ought to be the specific difference is contained in the genus. *Good can be best described as what a thing possesses in virtue of its perfection, completeness or finish.*

Aristotle offers this other description, "Good is what everything seeks." The first assigns the real cause of a thing's goodness. A thing is good, not because everything seeks it, but because it is perfect, complete or finished. Quite the contrary, one thing is sought by another because it is good. Transcendental goodness in foundation, is a thing's being or perfection; formally, it is the same, with the quality of fitness or desirableness added. Perfection is nothing more than finish. Thus, a work is said to be perfected when finished; God's attributes are said to be perfections, because they are the ne plus ultra in their several spheres. God's wisdom is a perfection, because it is as capacious as wisdom can well be, when pushed to its limit. Our wisdom is perfect, when it is as far-reaching as man can ambition. Every class of beings has its own grade of perfection, and our wisdom can as truly be called a perfection as God's. However, only God's wisdom can be called absolute perfection. The degrees of perfection conceivable are without number. A thing is said to be first finished or made, when it passes from the state of possibility to that of actuality. A clock is said to be finished or completed, when from having been a clock in possibility it becomes a clock in fact. After its completion a being can acquire other and other perfections. Hence the first obvious division of good things; good in some respects, and good in every respect. God alone is absolutely good; but our thesis holds true, if every being is good in some particular or other. Another division of goods:

Good	1. Real	3. Becoming
	2. Apparent	4. Agreeable
		5. Useful

Explanation of Diagram: *1.* Good in itself, that which is in reality and truth the good it is thought to be, and is suited to the desires most in harmony with the nature that seeks it. Such desires have their origin in the specific portion of a being.

2. Evil in itself; good in the mind; apprehended as good; that which is not the good it is thought to be, because it is suited to desires less in harmony with a nature. Such desires have their origin in the generic portion of a being. The specific portion of man is rationality, his generic portion is animality. Desires originating in his reason, his spiritual desires, aim at his only true good; desires originating in his body, the

seat of animality, his carnal desires, have only apparent good for object, and are often directly opposed to his real good. Apparent good is real good, when reason rules. Real good opposed to reason becomes apparent.

3. Very like real good, inasmuch as it is something befitting the whole man, and is loved for itself. And yet hardly any good is so purely becoming as not to admit modifications, partaking of the nature of the useful and the agreeable, e. g. virtue.

4. Befitting man as a whole, and loved not precisely because of itself, but because of the pleasure attendant on its possession. It often partakes of the nature of an apparent good, inasmuch as it ministers to only what is generic in man, and opposes reason, e. g. trip to the country.

5. Sought not at all for itself, but because it serves as a stepping-stone to some other good. It would not be missed, if only the good it helps to procure could be obtained without its assistance, e. g. medicine.

N.B. Nearly every good in nature is a mixture of the three, and is one or other according to the view taken of it.

Other examples are light for plants; moisture for roots; straws for the swallow; downward motion for a stone, rest for the same, occupation of proper place.

Proposed by the intellect. The will is a blind faculty and needs guidance. Though condemned to inactivity till it receives a message from the mind, it invariably shapes its own course, and reserves to itself the right to accept or reject the advice of its friend the intellect.

Nothing but good. Since everything positive is good, the capacity of human desire is without limit. Evil is a negation, and sin itself physically considered, or viewed as a positive something, is good. Evil is the denial of good. More properly, it consists in the absence of some good that a being should have or own. Hence want of sight is no evil in a stone or a tree; but it is an evil in a horse or a man. Something good always serves as a foundation for evil. In other words, there is nothing in the universe wholly and solely bad. Lazy pupils furnish the leaves of the trees with their food in the shape of nitrogen. Whatever is, is good; good and being are convertible.

PROOFS I, II, III, IV

I. 1°. Man often longs for objects, which are beyond the sphere of sensitive appetite. Ergo, besides sensitive appetite, man must be equipped with some superior faculty of desire, spiritual and rational, a will.

With regard to the Antecedent. Virtue, eternal life, God, honor are such objects.

With regard to the Consequent. No effect can be without its proportionate cause.

2°. God has implanted in every creature a tendency or motion towards self-perfection in strict accord with that creature's nature. But man's nature is supra-sensitive, intellectual, rational. Ergo, the faculty in man corresponding to this tendency or motion is supra-sensitive, rational, a will.

II. 1°. Experience is witness that no conceivable good escapes the attention of man. Ergo.

2°. The energy of the will has for measure the energy of the intellect. But the intellect is capable of knowing all entity, all being, all good. Ergo, the will can desire every good.

III. No faculty can embrace a thing outside the sphere of its formal object. But evil, the opposite of good, is outside the formal object of the will. Ergo, the will cannot desire evil, i. e. it can desire nothing but good.

With regard to the Minor. Evil, as such, is nothing. Evil, as such, is absence of good; and good proposed by the intellect is the will's formal object.

IV. 1°. The good we seek, we want for ourselves or others. If for ourselves, our statement stands. If for others, then, because these others are some way connected with us, their good is in a measure our advantage; or we find in the very act of wishing some feature of self-profit, whether it be usefulness, or pleasure, or fitness. Ergo.

N.B. From acts of benevolence the quality of fitness can never be absent.

2°. Every movement of the will is a striving towards some object, in which the will seeks rest; and no agent looks for rest in a good thing absolutely without the relation of fitness for himself. Ergo.

PRINCIPLES

A. The last part of our thesis is at seeming variance with what theology teaches concerning perfect love of God. Perfect love of God is love of such sort as thoroughly excludes all motives of selfishness, and tends towards God for His sake alone. Imperfect love has for basis and support, not the infinite perfections of God, but some profit we expect to derive from the act, e. g. eternal happiness in Heaven, escape from the pains of hell. It would thus seem that, because a man's own interests cannot be absent from any movement of his will, perfect love of God, which of its very nature banishes all thought of self, becomes impossible. But a little reflection removes the difficulty. Nothing, certainly, is more in harmony with the dignity of human nature than perfect love of God; and every act of the kind, whether the agent adverts to the fact or not, is a consummate perfection. Therefore, at the very instant of perfect love man necessarily assumes a new dignity, and adds to his wealth of perfections. All this, too, without once making his own profit the ground for positing his act of love. Of course, if he changes his motive, and makes the fitness of the act the reason for his acting, he falls away at once from perfect love. In other words, self-profit is a condition necessarily involved in even perfect love of God. It never rises to the dignity of a motive. Or, as theologians express it, self-profit is the ontological root of even perfect love, it is not perfect love's motive-root. The distinction means simply this, that, independently of the lover's intention, the element of self-profit is mixed up with every object able to elicit emotions of love. This element is wrapped up in the very being of the object in question, and cannot be separated from it. But nothing prevents the lover from neglecting in his calculations this inborn element, and choosing for motive whatever consideration he sees fit to adopt. This consideration, to constitute an act of perfect love, must be God alone, or God's infinite perfections.

B. An elicited act proceeds from the will solely, it begins and ends in the will. An ordered act proceeds from the will in conjunction with another faculty; it begins in the will and ends with, e. g. the intellect, the senses, or the power of motion. A mere wish is an elicited act; the raising of the hand is an ordered act.

C. The intellect, the end, and the sensitive appetite act on the will. The intellect exerts a moral influence on the will by way of persuasion, inasmuch as a formal judgment of the mind is a prerequisite for deliberate and free acts of the will. In other words, the intellect sets the will in motion by proposing to it something desirable. The end exerts figurative, not a physical, influence; inasmuch as it attracts the will by its desirableness. Its effect is wholly confined to the intentional order, not the order of execution. The sensitive appetite exerts merely indirect influence on the will; inasmuch as it vindicates to some object an appearance of fitness, and, by concentrating the attention on the good sought, affects the mind's judgment, and through its agency the will.

D. Apart from the soul's vegetative powers, the will can issue orders to all the soul's forces. It wields over the sensitive appetite the authority of a king over his subjects, not that of a master over his slave. It rouses the mind to attention, and to assent in judgments not immediately evident.

E. The manner of desire is the characteristic that chiefly distinguishes appetites, not their objects. Rational appetite determines itself, shapes its own course. Sensitive appetite is determined from without, is guided by another. The objects of the two appetites may be identical, the manner of desire is in each case different.

THESIS IX

Man's will enjoys freedom of choice, and no previous judgment holds it to a set decision. Fatalism, therefore, and Determinism are absurd.

Rickaby. Free Will and Four English Philosophers.

QUESTION

We stand for free will. Our opponents stand for Fatalism or Determinism. The Calvinists or Presbyterians as a body belong to this class, because of their belief in predestination. Determinists pretend to differ from fatalists, but the difference is small.

TERMS

Will is rational appetite, a spiritual, inorganic faculty, appetitive of good at the instigation of the intellect. It seeks good, shuns evil; and its various operations are grouped under the nine names already attributed to the manifestation of passion or sensitive appetite, as species of the two generic emotions, love and hate. They are desire, delight, hope, despair; abhorrence, displeasure, fear, courage; and anger. Though their names are the same, the operations are quite different. Love and desire in the will are quite other than love and desire in the appetite; and the kind of knowledge basing the emotions is the radical measure of their difference. They are as far apart in nature and perfection as intellect and sense. In man sense and intellect work together in mutual harmony, and the two appetites, superior and inferior, will and appetite, so easily merge that it is a task to make separate study of them in our consciousness. Suffice it to say that the passions or manifestations of sensitive appetite betray themselves in body-changes, and turn invariably on material, concrete and particular goods; while the manifestations of will, our wishes, restrict themselves to the soul and regularly turn on spiritual, abstract and universal goods. When particular goods occupy the will's attention, they are viewed in the light of universals; and we were at some pains to make this point clear in our Ethics, Thesis V. We could perhaps with profit label emotions of the will in a way calculated to keep them distinct from the passions; and with all modesty we venture these several names, wish, enjoyment, longing, discouragement; aversion, sadness, dread, fortitude and rage. It might be better still to call the passions desire, delight, longing, despair; abhorrence, sadness, dread, courage; and rage; reserving for movements of the will wish, joy, hope, discouragement; aversion, displeasure, fear, fortitude; and anger. Sense precedes intellect in the field of knowledge, and in the field of desire appetite is before will. Previous delight would seem to be an indispensable requisite for desire. The child first experiences good resident in color, sound, food or whatever else; delight results, and at some long or short interval after the experience closes, some incident awakens a phantasm of the now absent good, and desire ensues. In a parallel way, intellectual knowledge of some absent blessing can urge the will to wish its possession. In last analysis, every wish involves a triple process, thought of good; appreciation of its goodness; and tension, attraction, impulse towards it. Sense, the regulator of passion, is of very wide extent, and practically without limit. Utilitarians are wrong, when they maintain that all our wishes are towards pleasure and away from pain. The will's formal object is good; and good is threefold, becoming, agreeable and useful; honestum, delectabile and utile. Becoming good can stir the will as well as agreeable good; and, when that is the case, our wishes are not towards pleasure and away from pain. Many of our desires are unselfish, and primarily trample our personal pleasure. We can choose right for its own sake against the maximum of pleasure. The Hedonistic paradox vouches for the same truth; deliberate pursuit of pleasure is suicidal, pleasure kills pleasure.

Choice. Choice supposes a conflict of desires. The stronger desire ought to win, though free will can, up to the last moment, keep it from victory. The strength or weakness of a desire is measured by the force of its motives; and every motive is a mixture of these several elements, subjective consciousness of the object's goodness, its own objective goodness, character of the man, and degree of attention or absorption given to object. Many of our acts are spontaneous, and void of deliberation, e. g. dressing, eating, walking, talking. In acts of the kind choice plays little or no part; and they are, as a rule, morally right or wrong indirectly and in cause. At other times we are beset by different motives, urging different courses of conduct; and we simply must choose. Some of these motives are moral obligation, worldly advantage, pleasure. Deliberation then has place. We weigh things, balance them, and often the process covers only an inappreciable amount of time. Choice or decision follows; and this act is constituted by the acceptance of some suggested course, or its rejection. Psychologists distinguish four different types of choice or selection, and they admit of easy understanding. Reasonable decision has clear balance on one side. Impetuous decision is impatient of suspense. Acquiescent follows present inclination, line of least resistance. Anti-impulsive calls for painful and prolonged endeavor; it is like driving a thorn into one's own flesh. James, vol. 2, p. 534. All four kinds are sure signs of freedom, the fourth kind is unimpeachable evidence. Volition is another name for choice, and quite a different thing from mere desire. Desire may embrace two contending courses of action, while volition necessarily embraces one and rejects the other. Some descriptions of common terms. Instinct means unconsciously purposive impulse. Impulse means tendency towards good obscurely felt; it is feeling-prompted movement. Desire implies tension, yearning towards absent good. Motive is whatever attracts the will. Intention is end energizing the will. Choice is selection of means. Purpose signifies deliberately formed intention with regard to a series of future acts. Wish is mere desire without effort or intention.

Choice is a manifestation of self-control, a very important factor in morality; and this control is physical, prudential or moral. Physical is exerted when we keep down our temper, keep down manifestations of it. Prudential is control of thought. It may be direct or indirect. Direct, when one says, I will not be angry. This is a weak means, because it fixes attention on the feeling we want to escape. Indirect, when we transfer our attention to some other matter; when we make a determined effort to think of something else. Children should be trained to self-control. They are helped to self-restraint by recollection of a past prohibition or painful experience. Hence, spare the rod, and spoil the child. Hence judicious expression of approval or disapproval is a great need. Self-control comes after physical appetite, or instincts and desires. It develops with habits, which are acquired aptitudes for particular modes of action. With Carpenter the physiological basis of habits is growth of organism to mode in which exercised. He makes their psychological basis association by contiguity. Habit is a second nature or bent. Some rules for habits. Bain offers this, Make a vigorous start, and admit no exception till habit is rooted. James has this: Make your nerves an ally, not an enemy. Seize first chance to keep resolution. Add a little gratuitous exercise every day. Self-denial is the only means to strengthen will. Order is a great help. School-life and discipline of games contribute much to same result. This self control is needed for individual and state; it is the moral element in education; there can be no morality without religion. Character is a combination of habits and temperament; it is part nurture, and part nature. Characters are strong, obstinate and vacillating or weak. Temperaments are choleric or energetic, sanguine or vivacious, phlegmatic or somnolent, melancholic or introspective.

Fatalism. For a fair exponent of Fatalism we choose Jonathan Edwards. He was born at Windsor on the banks of the Connecticut in 1703. At thirteen he entered Yale, when seventeen graduated, and at the early age of nineteen was a preacher in New York. He labored afterwards in and about Boston, wrote much of a metaphysical, political and religious nature, was called to the presidency of Princeton University in January, 1758, and two months later yielded to a fatal attack of smallpox. He was a lovable character, and a glance at his dead portrait is sufficient proof that to know him was to revere him. Friends, allowing their affection to run away with their good sense, thoughtlessly lavish on him such titles as the greatest theologian that lived in the Christian ages, the Metaphysician without a rival, the wisest and the best of mankind. There is no denying that he was a pure and upright man, but to say that he knew as much theology as some of to-day's obscure workers is an exaggerated untruth. His knowledge of metaphysics was painfully limited, and shockingly at fault on questions that demanded but a small amount of penetration. An infatuated reviewer hazards the remark that his defense of Calvinistic divinity remains unanswered and unanswerable. He triumphantly goes on: "The subject since then has hardly been one of controversy, though it has been occasionally talked about. Scholars have no need to be informed that Edwards never entertained any such doctrines as the word Fatalism describes." Some of the assertions made in Edwards' own work prove this brag arrant nonsense. We quote at length, "We say with propriety that a bird let loose has power and Liberty to fly. But one thing more I would observe concerning what is vulgarly called Liberty; namely, that power and opportunity for one to do and conduct as he will, or according to his choice, is all that is meant by it, without taking into the meaning of the word anything of the cause or original of that choice; or at all considering how the person came to have such a volition; whether it was caused by some external motive, or internal habitual bias; whether it was determined by some internal antecedent volition, or whether it happened without a cause; whether it was necessarily connected with something foregoing, or not connected. Let the person come by his volition or choice how he will; yet if he is able, and there is nothing in the way, to hinder his pursuing and executing his will, the man is fully and perfectly free, according to the common and primary notion of freedom. But the word as used by Arminians, and Pelagians, and others, who oppose the Calvinists, has an entirely different signification. These several things belong to their notion of Liberty. 1st. That it consists in a self-determining power of the will, or a certain sovereignty the will has over itself and its own acts, whereby it determines its own volitions, so as not to be dependent in its determinations on any cause without itself, nor determined by anything prior to its own acts. 2nd. Indifference belongs to Liberty in their notion of it, or that the mind previous to the act of volition be in equilibrio. 3rd. Contingence is another thing that belongs and is essential to it, not in the common acceptance of the word, as that has been already explained, but as opposed to all necessity or any fixed and certain connection with some previous ground or reason of its existence. They suppose the essence of Liberty so much to consist in these things, that, unless the will of man be free in that sense, he has no real freedom, howmuchsoever he may be at Liberty to act according to his will. The brute creatures are not moral agents, because they do not act from choice guided by understanding, or with a capacity of reasoning and reflecting, but only from instinct." These are a few of Edwards' utterances concerning the will; and the fear they betray about entering deeply into the question, and their insistence on ideas common to the uneducated crowd, are signs of a surface-knowledge, afraid of the light. Fatalism is a child of Satan, and like Satan it loves the dark. We, who form part of the multitude styled by Calvinists Arminians, feel confident enough of our position to invite scrutiny, and descend to the minutest possible details. These Arminians were a sect among Calvinists, who rejected Calvin's doctrine of predestination. They got their name from a Dutch professor, Jacobus Arminius, who headed the sect, called Remonstrants.

The author, no doubt, means well; and much of his inaccuracy is due to the feebleness, with which he takes hold of his subject, and the dread he has of penetrating beyond mere appearances. Fatalism is consistent with the freedom of a bird, not with the freedom of a man; it is consistent with immunity from violence, not with immunity from necessity. In the case of a bird freedom is used figuratively. Birds are free only by analogy. Liberty or freedom is a property of the will, in much the same way as laughter is a property of the man. Choice, taken as a power, may be identified with liberty and freedom; taken as an act, it is the final result or effect of the will's operation. The will itself is best defined as rational appetite, that faculty spiritual and inorganic, which by acts elicited under the guidance of the intellect seeks after good. Edwards is impatient at our leading into the discussion notions of cause of volition, indifference of will, and the like. In his shallowness he fails to see that liberty cannot be half understood, unless the nature of the will and of its operations is beforehand mastered. Many causes can be ascribed to each movement of the will. Thus, the intellect exerts on the will an influence peculiar to moral causes, that of persuasion; or, according to St. Thomas, the intellect sets the will going, only in as much as it proposes to the same a thing desirable. The end sought exercises an influence, best described as attraction or beckoning towards. The sensitive appetite, common to man and beast, is on occasions no small factor, when the will is about to put an act. These various causes play an important part in man's human doings; but when the question of liberty or freedom is uppermost, they fall back before what we designate the determining cause of the will's choice.

If I understand Edwards and his brother Calvinists aright, God, and God alone, is such determining cause. It must be remembered that God is said to be the first cause universally, whether guiding cause, drawing cause, or determining cause. For from Him, the uncreated cause, all these created causes derive their full efficacy, and on Him they depend for all their validity. But He is no more the second determining cause than He is our intellect and our will; He is no more the cause of my free choice than He is of the building on which the workmen are now engaged. Man's will is itself the only determining cause, consistent with human liberty. No created good, as experience teaches, is such cause; no uncreated good is such, unless we bid adieu to liberty, and agree to reckon man a necessary agent, with only that shadow of choice, which consists in invariably doing what another, even though that other be God, determines on having done. Nor need this species of self-causation frighten the reverent. It does not make of the will, or of the act of the will, a self-existent being. It simply makes of the will, which was primarily made by God, a self-determining cause. It does not annihilate the influence exerted by other causes, such as God, the intellect, the end and such like; but it vindicates to the will the awful power of ultimately shaping its own choice.

Now that the faculty, whose property is much-disputed liberty, is sufficiently familiar, we shall labor to clear up difficulties liable to arise from this other source. Liberty in its simplest acceptation means, not precisely power that any one has to do as he pleases, but rather freedom or immunity from something. Liberate, deliver and liberty are all words from the same Latin stock. Liberty is not a power or a faculty, it is a property of some power or faculty, called the will. Liberty is not choice. It precedes choice, and for particular instances ceases when choice begins to exist. Liberty, too, has many aspects. It may be what philosophers are pleased to call immunity from force or immunity from necessity. The former is immunity from external violence, the only kind known to the bird mentioned by Edwards. The latter is immunity from an inner force, and to this kind birds and everything less than man are utter strangers. Instinct dominates and determines all their activity. Immunity from necessity can be threefold, that of contradiction, that of contrariety and that of specification. The first is in play when the will chooses, for instance, between loving and not loving; the second, when it chooses between loving and hating; the third, when it chooses between walking and studying.

But the most striking peculiarity of all in man's liberty, is that state of absolute indifference, in which it must continue up to the very moment of its choice. It is an active, not a passive indifference; and consists in the circumstance, that, though every conceivable condition in the shape of ability, inducement, inclination and the like, be present and fulfilled, the will is still able to allow its ability to lie idle, to close its eyes to the inducements, and deny its inclinations. Expressed otherwise, this indifference is contained in the power inherent in the will to adopt one of several alternatives offered, whether the alternative adopted be more in accordance with common-sense or not, whether it has more motives in its favor or not, whether it is in the very opinion of the chooser destined to injure or benefit him. Leibnitz and a few other philosophers are of opinion that it is impossible for the human will to choose an object or a line of conduct, which is calculated in the mind of the chooser to prove damaging in the event. But experience is argument enough to upset every such theory. A man's will may very decidedly lean towards something, the man may know in his heart that such and such a decision alone will meet with reason's approval, he may count as sure his eternal damnation in the case of a refusal; and yet, up to the very moment of choosing, his will, though biassed by these different reflections and emotions, nevertheless, ultimately determined by itself solely, can reject the something to which his eternal salvation is attached. If God deprived man of this dread power, man would not be a free being; and man's service would be worth about as much as that of brute beasts, and as little deserving of eternal reward. God can suggest motives, His saving grace can do a vast deal towards guiding His servants aright; but at the close of all, man has his destiny in his own hands. Fatalism affects man's daily life more closely and ruinously than other false systems encountered in philosophy. A fatalist, whether he considers himself doomed to felicity or perdition, is a wretched character, indeed; and in either event is open to tremendous moral dangers. If satisfied that Heaven depends not on his efforts, but on God's kindness, a door is thrown open to all sorts of excesses and license. If satisfied that in spite of all his honest efforts he is to associate throughout eternity with criminals, the only alternative is, of course, to give his passions full fling, and make this earth his Heaven.

Determinism. Fatalism or Determinism is the doctrine we combat in this thesis. Mill endeavors to distinguish between Fatalism, which he repudiates, and Determinism, which he advocates. In Fatalism our conduct is fixed by fate or external circumstances, in a way independent of our feelings and wishes. In Determinism our conduct is fixed by our feelings or wishes, and these in turn are fixed by our character. The determinist can try to shape his own or another's conduct by appeals to feelings, though the attempt is mere sham. The fatalist must abandon every such attempt. Determinism is a soft Fatalism, which claims the name of freedom. Fatalism is too gross a theory to appeal to modern refinement, freedom of will proves too much a source of annoyance to the irreligious. Determinism would seem to have been hit upon as a happy means of escape from the reproach of silliness and remorse of conscience. Determinism differs too little from Fatalism to deserve a new name. It is but another phase of a theory old as Sophocles and his story of Œdipus. With the ancients, man had no control over his destiny. Some outside force, like the divinity, fate, chance, Nemesis, arranged at its own pleasure every detail in a man's life; and, as occasions arose, man without any choice in the matter simply followed this fixed schedule. He might be eminently virtuous, or eminently wicked; but personal endeavor counted for just nothing in his life's history. No matter what effort he made to escape the perpetration of murder, at the hour and on the day decreed by fate, he found himself betrayed into the act, and was all wonder at the occurrence, as inevitable as it was unforeseen. And fate consulted only its own plans in formulating its decrees. Its victim's honesty or wickedness was never taken into account. Foreknowledge of his future dispositions never operated with fate to save him from crime; and its helpless victim, when the crisis came, thought himself a hero, only to discover suddenly that he was a parricide, or an adulterer of the vilest type. The predestination of the reformers is this Fatalism of the ancients, transferred to modern times. With them, God is fate; and man has about as much to do with his salvation or damnation as he has to do with the shape of his nose. These false teachers,

> "Complacent fold their scarlet hands,
> And Heavenward roll their rheumy eyes
> To thank the god, pound-penny wise,
> Who freedom tied with iron bands;
> "Then bade his slaves work out their fate,
> And choose, where choice is out of reach;
> Predestining beforehand each
> To everlasting love or hate"

We believe with Fatalists that some certain men are predestined to Heaven, some certain others to hell; but always with dependence on the free exercise of their will. As a matter of fact, every man born into the world is going to die a saint or a sinner; his last moment is going to find him in the state of grace or in the state of sin. In every emergency of life, from the cradle to the grave, he is most assuredly going to make definite choice between two or more fixed lines of conduct; he is going to infallibly yield to or resist temptation; and God's wisdom would be an imperfect thing, unless He knew from all eternity what was going to be the outcome of the struggle in each individual case. But we are no Fatalists. God's foreknowledge of things is far from interfering with, or destroying, man's free will. God does not first decree things, and then make man's conduct measure up to, or fit in with His decrees. He first foresees the free and untrammeled conduct of men, and then, without exerting the pressure of a hair on their freedom, He makes His decrees measure up to or fit with men's conduct. Men may profess to see a species of iron cruelty in the arrangement; but, whether cruel or not, there was no alternative for God, in the event that He wanted to create men free, and safeguard His other attributes. The cruelty of Fatalism is immeasurably more abominable and despotic; absolutely subversive of morality; provocative, at the same time, of overweening presumption and abysmal despair, of sottish laziness and ungenerous cowardice. It is no cruelty in God to let free agents work out their destiny for weal or woe along the lines of their own nature; and God is not to blame for man's abuses. In another order He could hinder these abuses, but not in the present; and this self-imposed helplessness is no imperfection in God.

Determinism is a refinement of Fatalism; invented, to save its parent from the shame attaching to idiocy; and encouraging blind adherents to persevere in their folly, with the thin assurance that, in spite of fate, they still are free. A man's conduct, they say, is determined by a mixture of internal and external agencies, making up his character. Character, we have seen, is the result of inherited constitution and personal acts, culminating in habits. Of these two factors in character, habit is far and away the more important; and, because it is the element we determine or manufacture for ourselves, it is foundation for the conviction that character is the man, and that a man is what he makes himself. The constitution we inherit from our parents is, in substance, quite beyond our control. It may create trouble for us in the moral order, it may pave the way of virtue with roses, and exempt us from struggles, that are nothing short of an inheritance to others. But we know our limitations; our constitution and tendencies are no secrets to ourselves; and, as it is our duty to fight every wrong inclination, even when inherited; and, as it would be superlatively cruel and absurd to think that every such battle means sure defeat, we must carry about with us a power able to correct even our constitution, to follow its behests when they are right, and manfully, heroically spurn them aside when they are wrong. Therefore, even from the viewpoint of constitution, man's will is not determined but free. Moral evil consists not so much in having wrong tendencies, tastes and inclinations, as in yielding to them, and supinely allowing them to sway our whole conduct. Temptation is no wrong, consent to it constitutes all the blame; and in Determinism consent and temptation are identical, when defeat is the outcome, because dissent in that case is out of the question.

Habits are the other feature of character, and Determinism would have us think that habits determine us, in emergencies of choice, to this or that line of conduct. Whatever influence habit exercises over our free-will, and we are far from attributing to habit any decisive or determining influence, that influence is rooted in movements the will elicited, when the will admitted the separate acts constituting the habit. The resultant of habit may be an indeliberate act, put without choice or effort; but the habit itself is resultant of free and deliberate acts, whether they be few or many. Thus it happens that every indeliberate act, due to habit, is free, at least in cause; while every deliberate human act is free in itself and by very nature.

Along with natural disposition and acquired habits, our opponents mass together a multitude of external conditions, influences, and motives as determining causes of our conduct. We stand ready to grant that these several elements enter largely into the economy of free-will as persuaders, counselors, weights in its adoption of a policy; but we emphatically deny that they necessarily constrain the will, or irresistibly hold it to either of any two alternatives. They may urge the will, advise it, bring pressure to bear on it; but the will itself remains always master of the situation, and never loses its power to refuse to be persuaded, to reject even the wisest advice, and resist every species of outside pressure, even to its own loss and discomfiture. And this is exactly what we mean by free will. It is stronger than disposition, stronger than habit, stronger than whatever combination of environment, education, and motives. It can prefer folly to wisdom, vice to virtue, pain to pleasure, loss to gain, hell to Heaven; conscious, all the while, that it is trampling under foot better instincts, degrading its owner's dignity, sacrificing the greater for the less, and accumulating a rich store of bitter remorse and piercing regret.

Professor James on the whole stands for freedom of will. But he hesitates. He makes his position a matter of choice, and flatters determinists with the acknowledgment that psychology is unable to solve the problem, and definitely decide one way or the other. His psychology may be unequal to the task;

and the circumstance ought to have, at least, tempted him to revise his work, and diligently search it for flaws. The system of psychology, unable to explain so patent a fact as free will, must be radically wrong and imperfect. He prefers to leave the question of free will altogether out of his account; because, he says, if it exists, it can only be to hold some one ideal object a little longer or a little more intensely before the mind, and so make more effective one of two alternatives, which present themselves as genuine possibles. He makes choice the outcome of attention, and seems blind to the circumstance, that we can in an instant admit one of two alternatives, after giving whole hours to the consideration of its opposite. Dynamically, he makes free choice an operation amongst those physiological infinitesimals, which calculation must forever neglect. Here he may be scattering that mind-dust, of which he speaks in another chapter; and, whether or no, he is throwing the dust of obscurity into the eyes of his readers. Choice is a matter to be decided by psychology, not by physiology; unless we want to surrender our trade and all turn materialists. And choice in psychology is no operation among infinitesimals, but among definite agencies, written in as large characters as a Hippodrome sign, and closer to the man than his nose.

James thus analyzes Determinism and Fatalism. Fatalism affirms the impotence of free effort; Determinism, its unthinkability. The latter admits the name, acknowledges effort which seems to breast the tide, but claims the effort as a portion of the tide. Variations or exertions of free effort are in this system mathematically fixed functions of the ideas themselves; and these, in turn, are the tide. This tide-theory fits in with James' own fancy; because, in his doctrine concerning the origin of our ideas, he is a rank associationist. He and his fellow-conspirators against sound philosophy forget that, even if flow of thought be conceived as a tide, the cause of the tide still awaits explanation; and that is where his theory fails, and where our theory succeeds. The cause of the tide is the intellect, a spiritual and inorganic faculty of an immortal soul, which James and men of his ilk hate to admit. The cause of choice or selection is the will, another spiritual and inorganic faculty of the same immortal soul; and to refuse to acknowledge an intellect, is to refuse to acknowledge a will.

The explanation of free effort offered by Professor Lipps likewise appeals to his favor. This learned professor wants to explain the very simple phenomenon of self-determination, and pompously explains just nothing. When opportunity to choose arises, two masses of ideas contend for our consent; one larger, the other smaller. The larger invariably and irresistibly wins; and yet we are said to determine ourselves, because the more abundant mass is conceived as ourselves, while the less abundant mass is conceived as the resistance. Which would all be very beautiful, if ideas were in the will and not in the intellect. The truth of the thing is that the will determines itself at the instigation of the intellect. The will is the cause of our wishes, as the intellect is the cause of our ideas. Ideas have about as much to do with our wishes as outside objects have to do with our ideas; with this difference, that the will enjoys freedom, to which the intellect is a stranger.

And this brings us to the dishonest estimates of Scholastic doctrine seriously put forward by our opponents. James calls them caricatures of the kind of supposition free will demands. Men like John Fiske are nothing short of dishonest, when they tell their readers that in our system volitions arise without cause and are ascribed to blind chance. For their instruction, we repeat that mind or self is the cause of our volitions, and that chance plays no part whatever in the transaction. It is equally unjust and untrue to say that volition with us is motiveless. Volition with us is not wthout motives, but between them. We adopt the examples Fiske himself proposes. We can suspect an enemy of murder, because, while disposition is not a determining, it is still a weighty motive. Hence we give the enemy a fair trial, and proceed with due caution. And this is a wise provision of law, for we often discover that some former friend really perpetrated the deed. As Mr. Fiske sees things, the enemy would have no choice in the matter but to kill; and we should ourselves be murderers, if we hanged the man who killed another from resistless impulse. It is not good law to punish the insane. When a man hurls himself from a high window, the first impulse is to account him insane; because, though the instinct of self-preservation is not a determining motive, it is nevertheless a weighty motive, and the suicide's choice seems so absolutely devoid of reason that we charitably suppose him stripped of that faculty. And yet men have thrown themselves from high windows without being insane; and if they survived the shock, they were arrested and hauled to court for trial, and on no few occasions punished with imprisonment. Were Mr. Fiske their judge, he could not in conscience pass sentence of condemnation on attempted suicides, because in his theory the poor fellows did simply what they could not help doing. We can, as well as he, frame a theory of human actions; but with us the theory will be always subject to correction, with him it will be always infallible. Therefore, all the man's rhetoric about the mother strangling her first-born, the miser casting his gold into the sea, the sculptor breaking in pieces his statue, goes for naught; unless it goes to prove what we readily grant, that the will in free choice is always influenced, though never determined by motives. His conception of history is as wrong as his philosophy. History is a record of facts, not a compilation of men's motives, environments and dispositions. Free agents are able to cut loose from motives, environments and dispositions; and to suppose that they unvaryingly act in accord with them, is to make a grievous mistake, and substitute idle and uncertain speculation for the truth. It is to measure facts by theories, gather a man's wisdom from the size of hat he wears, and multiply the absurdities that make modern science man's greatest shame as well as his crowning glory.

Freedom of choice. Freedom is immunity from something, and is of three kinds, freedom of nature, freedom from sin, and freedom from woe. St. Paul thus beautifully describes all three. "Having no necessity, but having power of his own will," I Cor. vii, 37. "Being freed from sin, we have been made servants of justice." Rom. vi, 18. "Delivered from the servitude of corruption into the liberty of the glory of the children of God." Rom. viii, 21. We have to do with the freedom of nature; and it is of two kinds, immunity from extrinsic violence, and immunity from intrinsic violence; or from force, and from necessity. Immunity from force makes an act spontaneous or voluntary, and is common to minerals, plants and brutes with men. The word spontaneous is applicable to whatsoever beings; to fire and plants, as well as to man. The word voluntary in its strict sense applies to man alone, though in a wider sense it can be said of brutes. Usually, spontaneous is reserved for acts of the sensitive appetite; voluntary, for acts of the rational appetite or will. Seeing and walking are said to be voluntary in a mediate way, because of a command issued by the will.

Immunity from necessity is man's peculiar possession; and is called freedom of indifference, freedom of choice, and free will. It is threefold, that of contradiction, that of contrariety, and that of specification. It can be best described as that quality, in virtue of which the will can, when every needed prerequisite for action is present and fulfilled, elicit an act or refrain from doing so, elicit a good act or a bad act, elicit any one of several specifically different acts. Freedom is neither an act nor a habit, but a quality of the will. Its indifference is towards the act called second, not the act called nearest first or remotest first. The will is in actu primo proximo to choice or election, called actus secundus, when every prerequisite, intrinsic and extrinsic, for action is present and fulfilled.

This indifference of the will must be objective and subjective, both passive and active. Objective is on the part of the object, and is verified when the good in question is of such a nature that it can be either embraced or rejected. Objective is needed, because freedom can turn on only such an object; it is not enough, because it affects only the judgment, and freedom is a matter of will, not of intellect. Subjective is on the part of the will, and consists in the circumstance that the will is prepared and ready to act or be acted on; the indifference being active and passive respectively. Subjective passive is needed, because the act as immanent must be received in the will; it is not enough, because otherwise bodies with respect to accidents, and prime matter would be free. Subjective active indifference is needed in two senses, separate from nearest first act and conjoined with nearest first act; in separate sense, because even without the needed prerequisites the will must be in root capable to choose. This indifference in separate sense is not enough, because otherwise the intellect would be free, inasmuch as it is indifferent before the phantasm coöperates. In conjoined sense, because it is the one thing wanting, when all else is supplied; it is enough, because to act follows. Freedom is likewise divided into physical and moral. Physical is freedom from violence, whether extrinsic or intrinsic. Moral is freedom from law, or the right to choose between opposites without damage to any prescription of morality.

Previous judgment. The will acts at the instigation of the intellect. Good is its object, and intellect is what distinguishes good from evil. The intellect, therefore, discovers good to the will; and when that good is less than God intuitively seen, the will has power to embrace or reject it. Judgments preceding work of the will are conceived as of two kinds, speculative and practical. The first is worded this way, "This object is open to choice or rejection." The second is worded this way, "This object ought to be chosen, if you want to be prudent; it may be rejected, if you want to be imprudent." The judgment, "I choose this," is not previous, but consequent to work of the will; and announces the will's decision, resulting from the free and untrammeled use of its own native activity. A whole army of judgments, speculative and practical, may precede the will's choice. They may influence the will by urging, advising, proposing motives; but they never determine the same in such fashion that any one of several alternatives becomes impossible. That impossibility arises only after the will has made definite choice, and it constitutes what we call consequent, not antecedent necessity.

The Thomists would seem to attribute to their practical judgment a constraining force, destructive of freedom. But, as good Catholics, they cannot run counter to a dogma of faith; and free will is such a dogma. Therefore, they have recourse to the rather weak explanation that their practical judgment is itself free, and man's choice has its freedom from this circumstance. It might be better to reject every species of practical judgment, with an appearance even of Determinism, and say that the only previous judgment required is speculative. It is hard to see how freedom can stand with the judgment, "This must be done," for prerequisite; and it is harder still to see how any such imperative judgment squares with the truth, when any two finite goods are proposed as alternatives for choice. Such a judgment would be a lie pure and simple, as we know from experience. It is the business of the intellect to furnish light to the will, not to determine it. Praemotio physica is another Thomistic theory at seeming variance with the truth; but we choose to postpone its discussion to Natural Theology. It bears on God's coöperation with His creatures, and was seemingly invented to safeguard His eternal decrees, His dominion, and wisdom. Let it be enough for the present to remark that without any praemotio physica, or interference with man's free will, God's coöperation, decrees and wisdom can be otherwise kept safe from danger. Foreknowledge of man's free acts guides God in His decrees, and man's free acts precede God's knowledge, not of course in the order of time, but in the order of nature.

Division — Two parts. I. Man's will enjoys freedom of choice.
II. No previous judgment determines the will.

PROOFS, I, II

I. Free will is a fact, and no amount of bad philosophy can reason away facts. It can confuse people, but not convince them.

1. The fact of consciousness. The deeds we daily do are in our power, ourselves for witnesses. At our own good pleasure we do this, and we do that, and we do their opposite; and, while actually engaged in the performance of some particular work, we feel altogether free; we feel in such sort masters of ourselves that we could equally well act otherwise, if disposed to incur the reproach of imprudence and blame; and all this without a change in circumstances, without a change in our motives.

2. The fact of common agreement among men. Even Determinists in practical every-day life shape their conduct in strict accord with our theory. They talk Determinism, to act Free-will. They ascribe objective value to all these several ethical notions, imputability, responsibility, virtue, vice, justice, injustice, merit, blame, right, duty. They advise and exhort their friends. They lay down rules, enact laws, proffer counsel, draw up petitions, assign rewards, and inflict penalties. In Determinism, environment, character, and habits inexorably fix a man's conduct; all three are out of his control; he does simply what he cannot help doing; and in this sorry event these several ethical notions are absolutely without meaning or substance. This universal consent of mankind with a bearing on the reality of free-will is no mere theoretical tenet, like the earth's movement around the sun, but an eminently practical dogma, of vital importance in men's affairs, and the very basis of civil and political society.

3. The metaphysical fact of relationship between intellect and will. We will as we know. Determinism goes to the absurd lengths of binding the will to necessarily embrace what the mind clearly tells the will need not be embraced. In other words, Determinism is a huge lie, open discord between the objective and subjective. Objective indifference, we have seen, is a reality vouched for by the mind. Every good with which we are acquainted, God Himself not excepted, sails into our notice as a mixture of attractive and repellent qualities, wears in our eyes the double aspect of good and evil. The subjective element, corresponding to this objective indifference, is in Determinism iron necessity, the unfailing and uniform impossibility of escape from what has repellent features. It is highly unnatural to constrain God's noblest creature to embrace without fail a fixed good, that he here and now knows to be altogether unnecessary.

II. Practical judgment, as understood by Thomists, would seem to destroy free will. That faculty is not formally free which is no longer indifferent, no longer vested with ownership in its act, when once every prerequisite for the act is verified.

But such a faculty is the will, when, in the theory of our opponents, the last practical judgment is uttered. Ergo, in the theory of our opponents the will is not free.

With regard to the Minor. This practical judgment is a prerequisite for the act; because without it, they contend, the will can elicit no act, and with it the will is no longer indifferent to several alternatives, but necessarily restricted and determined to one.

N.B. The act of the will, they say, is not absolutely, but only conditionally determined; it is mediately free, inasmuch as the will allows itself to be swayed by the motives provoking the practical judgment. This subterfuge is nothing worth, because the will would in this event be swayed either by chance or by a second practical judgment. Chance is no cause at all, and this second practical judgment would call for a third, and a fourth, and a fifth without end. Again, they say this practical judgment has its origin in a certain predilection of the will. If this predilection is one of the prerequisites for the act of choice, the will is no longer free, but determined. If it is not, the will is free; but no last practical judgment is needed among the prerequisites.

P.S. Additional proofs of free will from Maher, pp. 398–425.

ETHICAL — PSYCHOLOGICAL — METAPHYSICAL

Ethical Argument. 1. Obligation. If I am bound to abstain from an evil deed, it must be really possible for me that this deed shall not occur. And the obligation is plain. "Right conduct is not merely a beautiful ideal, which attracts me. It commands me with an absolute authority. It obliges me unconditionally." Noel. In the Determinist theory no other choice than that actually elected was really possible to the sinner throughout his life, and the present criminal choice is inexorably determined by the equally inevitable choices that went before.

2. Remorse and repentance. These emotions are possible only in case of acts I freely did, acts that were mine, acts I could have avoided. No remorse or repentance accompanies harm done through no fault of mine, but by accident, harm not in my power. Determinism makes both classes of acts equally the inevitable outcome of my nature and circumstances. With it, crime is as unavoidable as an earthquake.

3. Merit and desert. We deserve reward or punishment only by acts that are free. Other acts deserve neither. Witness the "I could not help it," of the child about to be punished. In Determinism, punishment is purely preventive, not retributive. Praise and blame are not just rewards for self-sacrifice, but judicious incentives for future services. Like the old saying, "gratitude is a delicate sense of favors to come."

4. Responsibility. I might fasten a plague on the whole city, administer poison to father and mother, and yet not be responsible, or morally guilty, or justly punishable; because it was not my free act, because I could not help it. Maniacs and somnambulists are judged unaccountable for same reason.

Three things constitute responsibility, binding authority, knowledge of this authority's will, and power to perform or abstain from the act; in fewer words, duty, knowledge of duty, and freedom.

5. *Justice* means volition according to law. In Determinism, all volitions are as much according to law as the ebbing tide. Moral law is physical law; and whatever is, is right.

N.B. Determinism distorts moral conceptions. It gives new meanings to notions as old as the world. Right science accepts facts as they are, examines without manufacturing them, interprets without transforming them.

Psychological argument, from consciousness, or introspective analysis of our own volitions.

1. *Attention.* I myself guide the course of my own thoughts. This phenomenon is clear in recalling a forgotten fact, or in guessing a riddle. Alexander alleges the example of two weights pulling as twelve and eight. Endow these weights with active power of selective attention, and twelve can become five, eight can become twenty.

2. *Deliberation.* There may be question of investing my money or selecting a servant. Deliberation is plainly an exercise of free volition. I freely recall and detain the reason or motive before my consciousness. I have had experience of the opposite kind, passive oscillation of rival impulses, and can therefore compare.

3. *Choice or decision.* This is the culmination of freedom. I may be tempted to excuse a fault by a lie, to commit some small dishonesty. The evil thought may be present before advertence; then its sinfulness appears, and the struggle begins. I decide to consent or resist. The act of decision is mine; it is free, not determined by habit or motive; and this very circumstance is ground for remorse or congratulation.

4. *Resistance to persistent temptation.* This is activity along the line of greatest resistance, volition against the preponderating impulse or motive. Motive of virtue attracts without making my course the pleasanter.

N. B. Spinoza objects, saying that men deceive themselves in thinking that they are free, because they know not the cause of their actions. A different act is conceivable, and this they confuse with possibility. *Answer:* We know self to be the cause, and the possibility of the act is conceived as a hypothetical reality easily reducible, and too often reduced, to an absolute reality.

Metaphysical argument, from imperfection of created goods. Every good on earth is a mixture of good and evil. Will is determined by adequate object alone, perfect good, God intuitively seen. Element of good is attractive; element of evil, repellent. What of its very nature repels, cannot irresistibly attract.

N.B. Free will upsets Materialism, and this is the rock of offense. It calls for a spiritual faculty, superior to matter, not completely controlled by physical organisms. If the will is free, man is more than an organized frame.

PRINCIPLES

A. Psychological — B. Metaphysical — C. Physiology, Physics, Statistics.

A. Psychological. 1. Abusive lies. Bain says, free will is a power that comes from nothing, has no beginning, follows no rule, respects no time or occasion, operates without impartiality. *Maudsley* says, free will is an unmeaning contradiction in terms, an inconceivability in fact. *Stout* calls it a Jack-in-the-box, it springs into being of itself, as if it were fired out of a pistol. *Answer:* Lies need no answer. Choice in Determinism resembles the pistol-bullet. It is about as free, meritorious, and blameworthy. Recall the Brockton murder described by James.

2. Introspection tells us that we are always determined by motives, unable as we are to resist strongest or most pleasurable. *Answer:* Introspection tells us the contrary. Involuntary acts are determined by character and motives, and they are numerous. Deliberate acts are influenced, but not determined by them.

3. The strongest motive always prevails. *Answer:* The strongest, meaning the ultimately prevalent, I grant; and that is tautology, or by consequent necessity. The strongest, meaning the most pleasurable, I deny; or by antecedent necessity.

4. Free will is liberty to desire or not desire. Impossible. Ergo. *Answer:* This is an unfair description. Lewes is fairer. Desire is ambiguous. It can mean consciousness of want, and rejection of, or consent to feeling. Free will is desire in second, not in first sense.

5. Our neighbors are always determined by character and motives. Social life is impossible without forecasts. Men's conduct is as measurable as the movements of a planet. *Answer:* Such forecasts deal with external acts, and many such are indeliberate. The will is influenced, though not inexorably determined, by character and motives in even deliberate acts. Only the virtuous resist the solicitations of pleasure. Mental association somewhat accounts for these forecasts. Character and motives are the only factors in others known to us, their wills are hidden. Reflection enables us to praise or blame, and therefore ascribe moral acts to free will.

6. Self or the Ego is a mere aggregate or series of states without anything permanent. *Answer:* I deny. Self is permanent subject, enduring one and same in varied changes.

7. *Spencer* denies a permanent self or Ego. *Answer:* So much the worse for Spencer. Consciousness is evidence. Memory and reflection are evidence. Consciousness of a permanent self cannot certainly prove it transitory.

B. Metaphysical. 1. Nothing exists without a cause. Ergo no free will. *Answer:* Self, the Ego, the will, is cause of choice.

2. Free will is against the law of causation. *Answer:* This objection mixes two things, nothing without a cause, and uniformity of nature. Uniformity in physical order is different from uniformity in sphere of the mind. The law is not yet completely established in physical nature. In sphere of the mind exceptions are innumerable.

C. Physiology, Physics and Statistics.

1. Uniformity is rigid among corporeal changes. Ergo equally rigid in mental correlates. *Answer:* Mind depends on body, but its acts are not determined and conditioned by body. Ladd says, "Physiology neither disproves nor verifies the postulate of free will."

2. Physics, and Conservation of Energy. *Answer:* This law would prove that no bodily movement was ever influenced by a mental act; and this is against experience.

3. Statistics. Buckle says, "Suicide is the product of general conditions in society. The felon only carries into effect what is a necessary consequence of preceding circumstances, and all this is proved by statistics." *Answer:* Free will is compatible with general uniformity in even individual conduct, because indeliberate acts are outcome of character and motives; because a man cannot act without motives, and the commonest motives are pleasure, interest, and duty; because motives influence without determining. Statistics are for the community, not for an individual. No two of all the suicides were precisely alike in antecedents. If it could be shown that three hundred precisely similar sheaves of motives actuated three hundred suicides, something would perhaps be accomplished.

D. Theology. God's foreknowledge would be uncertain. *Answer:* There is no future or past with God, all is present. He foresees free acts without determining them. God's vision does not affect our freedom. Recall Dante's boat and the man on shore.

E. Psychology would be impossible as a science. There would be nothing uniform, no law in theory of free will. *Answer:* Psychology has abundance of other material for laws. The interference of free will is ethically momentous, psychologically small. Besides, free will knows conditions, and is not altogether lawless.

(*F*) *Hobbes,*—(*G*) *Hume,*—(*H*) *Mill,* are all opposed, with Locke, to free will. *From Rickaby, S. J.,* "Free Will and Four English Philosophers."

F. Hobbes. 1. It is no dishonor to God, to say that He can so order the world as sin may be necessarily caused thereby in a man. Power irresistible justifies all actions. Ergo, God can force a man to sin, and then punish him without being unjust. *Answer:* Mill has to say on this god of Hobbes. "I will call no being good, who is not what I mean when I apply that epithet to my fellow creatures; and if such a being can sentence me to hell for not calling him so, to hell I will go."

2. Laws prohibiting necessary acts are not unjust. All law is just, because the subject consents. Theft, though necessary, can be punished to deter others. Necessary acts of theft are noxious, and we justly destroy all that is noxious, both beasts and men. *Answer:* There is a difference between punishing and blaming. We blame men as well as punish them.

3. Consultation precedes choice, and therefore consultation is not in vain. *Answer:* But the consultation of Hobbes was determined by antecedent circumstances, reaching farther back than the birth of the consultor. Hobbes sees danger in this doctrine. Hence his request to the Marquis of Newcastle and the Bishop of Londonderry to keep private what he writes here.

4. Praise and dispraise depend not on the necessity of the action. We praise what is good, and dispraise what is evil. Necessary acts can be good or evil. *Answer:* Praise touches excellences proper to thing's nature. Inanimate things are praised for their beauty and usefulness; plants and brutes, for full growth; men, for stature, strength, beauty, quick wit, command. Man is alone praiseworthy, when he exercises free will.

5. Piety means two things, to honor God in our hearts, thinking mightily of His power, and to signify that honor by words and acts. Necessity allows of both. *Answer:* Power is the quality in God best known to beginners. After power, comes justice. The tyro fears, the proficient hopes, the expert loves. The god of Hobbes is not good, he is only omnipotent.

6. The prayer is decreed together in the same decree, wherein the blessing is decreed. *Answer:* The prayer is foreseen in the decree, wherein the blessing is decreed. Prayer is the acknowledgment of God's dominion, but it is for that very reason free. Forced acknowledgment is no homage.

7. Sin can be voluntary, and yet necessary. *Answer:* Necessary sin is no contradiction. It has place in hell. Love in Heaven is voluntary and necessary. Love of an object, that completely satisfies, is necessary and voluntary. A toy satisfies the child; God, a seraph. Man occupies a middle position; nothing on earth completely satisfies him. Ergo, voluntary in man means free. Read Ecclesiasticus xv, 11.

8. Necessity is not compulsion, as is plain in the case of a sailor throwing his cargo into the sea. Love, revenge, lust are free from compulsion, but are necessary acts. *Answer:* Aristotle thus defines compulsion, "violence from without, the party compelled contributing nothing of his own." Goods cast into the sea are no fair example of compulsion. A deed done by compulsion of fear is not necessitated. Passion weakens freedom, and fear is strongest of the passions. The popular impression that fear compels, is grounded in the fact that other passions are home-products, while fear is an importation from outside.

9. The last dictate of the understanding necessitates the act, as the last feather breaks the horse's back. *Answer:* Here is the process. Speculative judgment comes first, This is open to choice, so is that. Hypothetical practical judgment follows, This ought to be chosen, if I want to be prudent; and that can be chosen, if I want to be imprudent. Absolute practical judgment closes the process, I choose this, and I want to be prudent; or I choose that, and I want to be imprudent. The absolute practical judgment is but a mental expression of the willed act, and is altogether consequent to the will's determination. The hypothetical practical judgment precedes the will's act, and leaves everything undetermined. Hence our distinction. The last judgment of the mind determines the will, the last speculative judgment, I deny. The last practical judgment, I distinguish. The last hypothetical, I deny. The last absolute, I distinguish again. With antecedent necessity, I deny. With consequent necessity, I grant. We cannot actually choose a thing, and remain free to choose its alternative. But the necessity we impose on ourselves is consequent, not antecedent to our actual choice.

10. Water has liberty to descend, because there is no impediment in the nature of water. Its inability to ascend is not want of liberty, but want of power. In the same way man has liberty, even when necessitated; because there is no impediment in his nature. His inability to choose an alternative is not want of liberty, but want of power. *Answer:* Water and brutes are free metaphorically. Things are said to be free, when allowed to act according to their nature. Natures are different, and ought to be of different powers. Man ought to be free in one way; water and brutes, in another. Hobbes makes them all free in the same way. Like Edwards, Hobbes knows only one kind of freedom, that from force or violence. He knows nothing about freedom from necessity. Intrinsically, water is just as free to ascend as it is to descend. All the difference is extrinsic. Water has no real freedom at all. Freedom means choice, and water never chooses. Somebody chooses for it. Somebody removes the impediment, and it flows. Somebody sets an impediment in its path, and it stops flowing.

An up-slope is an impediment, a down-slope is its removal; and the water never makes either. Water seems to be free, just as the meadow seems to smile, or the medicine seems to be healthy. All metaphors are as close approaches to the truth. Man's proper freedom is from within, not from without. He enjoys the inferior kind of freedom common to rivers and birds. We call it freedom from force or violence. But his rational nature calls for a higher kind, denominated freedom from intrinsic constraint or necessity. Something in water makes flowing necessary, when impediments are removed. Nothing in man makes it necessary for him, in whatever emergency, to choose one alternative rather than another. Nothing outside of man can constrain his will, though many outside impediments can constrain his other faculties; and while his will is never under restraint, the man himself can be said to be in that condition.

11. I conceive that nothing taketh beginning from itself, but from the action of some other immediate agent without itself. The cause of will is not the will itself, but something else not in its own disposing. *Answer:* Spontaneous volitions are traceable to necessary causes, reflex volitions ordinarily are not. This is but a repetition of the aged Scholastic difficulty, Omnia mota moventur ab alio, everything moved is moved by another, whatever has motion is moved by another. And the answer is easy. There is a difference between moving and necessitating. Hobbes has to prove, not that the will is moved, but that it is necessitated by another. Many outside things move the will. The intellect moves it by proposing good, and this is terminative motion. God moves it by concurrence or coöperation. But, when an agent, like the will, enjoys active indifference, nothing outside moves it determinately and physically, but only morally and in the order of thought.

12. A sufficient cause is a necessary cause. Every alternative actually chosen is by the very fact a sufficient, and, therefore, a necessary cause. Ergo, no free will. *Answer:* An object that has drawbacks is no sufficient cause for a necessary volition. If a volition follows, it will be not necessitated but free. There is sufficient cause for a free volition, not sufficient cause for a necessary volition.

13. It is necessary that to-morrow it shall rain or not rain. If it be not necessary it shall, it is necessary it shall not rain.

Answer: Either is true determinately, I deny; — indeterminately, I grant. Hobbes answers, necessity remains, though we know it not. Take this example. It is necessary that to-morrow Philip shall sin or not sin. Hobbes cannot show that sin in Philip to-morrow is either a necessity or an impossibility antecedent to his exercise of free will, but only consequent on same; and we admit consequent necessity or determination. He mixes two things, the assertion of Philip's sinning to-morrow necessarily involves the denial of his not sinning, and the assertion of Philip's sinning to-morrow involves the denial of his necessarily not sinning.

G. Hume. 1. The exceeding multitude and variety of the antecedents to volition, alone prevent us from determining accurately in all cases the result, which uniformly and necessarily follows. *Answer:* Freedom of will is not based on the impossibility of predicting a man's conduct. It is quite as impossible to predict the weather, and nobody on this account calls the weather free. The basic argument for free will is consciousness of the fact; and this is strengthened by others, in which impossibility of prediction forms no part. The conduct of a man cannot be predicted with anything like absolute certainty; and free will is the chief cause, not antecedents. It is easier to make a guess at the weather. Of course man is amenable to motives, environment, habit and disposition; but these several factors exert no determining influence. They are on so many occasions discounted, that predictions based on their constancy are altogether unreliable. The number of instances sufficing for an induction in the grosser region of matter, is not sufficient in the finer domain of intelligence.

2. Because God is the ultimate author of all our volitions, human actions either have no moral turpitude at all, or they must involve our Creator in the same guilt. *Answer:* Hume solves the difficulty by declaring it a sublime mystery, to pry into which is temerity. To reconcile free will with God's prescience, or to defend absolute decrees and free God from sin, exceeds, he thinks, all the power of philosophy. In our system, the mystery admits of easy solution. God's prescience is consequent to man's exercise of his free will, not indeed in the order of time, but in the order of nature.

H. Mill. 1. Freedom is consistent with divine foreknowledge. Ergo, with human. *Answer:* No parity. God is infinite, man finite. With God, duration is eternity; with man, time. Eternity is nunc stans, time is nunc fluens. There is no past or future with God. What will happen a hundred years hence, is present in the now of God. Men must wait till it happens. St. Augustine reduces the three tenses to one, the present. The present of things past is memory; the present of things present is intuition; the present of things future is expectation.

2. "We know that we are not compelled to obey any particular motive. We feel that, if we wish to prove that we have the power of resisting the motive, we could do so (that wish being, it needs scarcely be observed, a new antecedent); and it would be humiliating to our pride, and paralyzing to our desire of excellence, if we thought otherwise." *Answer:* This looks like our own doctrine. The parenthesis makes it Determinism, because it makes our volitions and actions invariable consequents of our antecedent states of mind. We maintain that our conduct and volitions are consequents of choice, and choice can oppose antecedent states of mind. It can reject what the mind approves, and approve what the mind rejects. Hammered iron is the invariable consequent of antecedent conditions. Crime is not, as can be readily seen in the case of saint and sinner, with the same disposition and the same motives at their disposal. According to Mill, Abel would never do right, if placed with Cain's character in an occasion similar to that in which Cain does wrong.

3. Determinism means that the given cause will be followed by the effect, subject to all possibilities of counteraction by other causes. Necessity, or the doctrine of Hume, in common use stands for the operation of those causes exclusively, which are supposed too powerful to be counteracted at all.

Answer: Hume adds to uniformity of sequence an element of uncounteractableness. But in Mill's philosophy, as in Hume's, whatever is actually uncounteracted is practically and in the concrete uncounteractable; and, therefore, to happen and to happen of necessity are one.

4. Determinism is remote from Fatalism; and yet most Determinists are Fatalists. A Fatalist half believes,— and nobody is a consistent Fatalist,— not only that whatever happens is the infallible result of the causes which produce it, and that is Determinism, but also that there is no use in struggling against it. According to Fatalists, a man's character is formed for him, and not by him. According to Determinists, a man's character is formed in part for him, and in part by him.

Answer: In Determinism we make our own character, if we will; but if we will, comes from no effort of our own, but from circumstances or external causes, which we cannot help. As Mill foolishly puts it, our characters are formed for us in the ultimate resort, by us as intermediate agents.

5. The Free-will doctrine, by keeping in view precisely that portion of the truth, which the word necessity puts out of sight, namely, the power of the mind to coöperate in the formation of its own character, has given to its adherents a practical feeling much nearer the truth than has generally existed in the minds of Necessitarians. Determinism is good for the culture of others; free will, for self-culture.

Answer: Mill would here seem to be a Libertarian. He makes three concessions. We are able to modify our character, if we will; we are masters of our habits and temptations, not they of us; we could resist habit or temptation, even when we yield to it. Perhaps he means, we could, but cannot; could, if circumstances were different; cannot, as they are.

6. What I am able to do is not a subject of consciousness, we are conscious of what is, not of what will or can be. Consciousness is not prophetical.

Answer: I do, I can, I am, are three facets of the same truth. I do, implies I can; I do and I can, imply I am. I can do a thing, does not mean I shall do it. I can, is not prophetic. I can use my endeavor, is a fact of present consciousness. These endeavors will be adequate to the occasion, is an inference from past to future, and is prophetical.

7. I dispute altogether that we are conscious of being able to act in opposition to the strongest present desire or aversion. When we think of ourselves hypothetically as having acted otherwise than we did, we always suppose a difference in the antecedents,— we picture ourselves as having known something that we did not know, or not knowing something that we did know, which is a difference in the external motives; or as having desired or disliked something more or less than we did, which is a difference in the internal motives. Ergo antecedents determine volition.

Answer: Mill here proves himself an absolute Necessitarian, a Fatalist. If a man's aversion to crime is weaker than temptation, he must commit it. If his desire is weaker than his horror, he must abstain from it. And this is Fatalism. Rickaby explains the case by saying that in two alternatives, when one complacency is stronger than the other, the man can wait and do nothing till the other complacency becomes the stronger. After a long or short repetition of this process he eventually selects that one of the two alternatives, to which he last adverted. Mill could well rejoin that the alternative, to which he last adverted, was the stronger of the two, and so determined or necessitated his choice. In this case the circumstance of last advertence would be the determining factor. It might be better to say that though the two alternatives contended simultaneously for notice, and that though one appeared stronger than the other, the man could still choose, and often does choose the weaker. Free will does not necessarily mean the actual, but the possible choice of either. In fact, free will exists no more in this or that particular, when once actual choice has been made. To prove his free will, a man need not necessarily choose the weaker alternative. As a matter of fact, he generally chooses the stronger, but always with an abiding conviction that he could have chosen the weaker.

8. There are two ends, which in the Necessitarian theory are sufficient to justify punishment, the benefit of the offender and the protection of others. *Answer:* There is another feature that renders it altogether unjust, and that is the blame involved in punishment. In addition to pain, punishment involves blame; and this is never imputed to agents unable to help themselves. Mill maintains that we can know that we ought to be punished for our misdeeds without knowing that our wills are free. He affirms that the ordinary notion of justice is altogether a mistake. It is expedient for the greatest happiness of the greatest number, that a man who has been compelled to crime should suffer a penalty able on the next occasion to hold him to virtue, and this is Utilitarianism. In this event, lunatics ought to be punished, as they are open to the agency of fear. But no civilized country has yet descended to that meanness.

9. The true doctrine maintains against Asiatic Fatalism, that of Oedipus, wherein a superior power overrules our desires, and Modified Fatalism, wherein our character is made for us, not by us, that our character is in part amenable to our will.

Answer: This is Roundabout Fatalism. Thus, we can improve our character by our own voluntary exertions, which suppose that there was already something in our character, which led us to improve it, and accounts for our doing so. He derives our volitions from our characters and circumstances, our character from our volitions and circumstances, and our volitions again from our character and circumstances. Unless our character and circumstances cause and determine us to do so, we shall make no voluntary efforts for the improvement of our character.

I. a. Will is moved by greater desire. Ergo.
b. Fear necessitates will. Ergo.
c. Will requires aid of intellect to pass from potency to act. Ergo.
d. Will in first act is still indifferent to will in second act. Ergo.
e. While eliciting an act the will cannot not elicit the act. Ergo.
f. Will acts in virtue of motion received from first cause. Ergo.
g. An act foreknown by God will infallibly take place. Ergo.

Answers: a. Will is moved, attracted, influenced, I grant; determined, necessitated, I deny.

b. Fear exercises greatest stress on will, I grant; fear necessitates, I deny.

N.B. When fear dethrones reason, act is not human; and only human acts are free. When deliberation is absent, act is not human and, of course, not free.

c. Requires intellect to pass from potency to first act, I grant; from potency to second act, I deny. Will in first act is ready to wish, will in second act is actually wishing.

d. Will in first act is indifferent, with merely passive indifference, I deny; with active, I grant.

e. Constraint is antecedent, I deny; constraint is consequent, I grant.

f. This motion of first cause is antecedent and necessitating, I deny; simultaneous and indifferent, I grant.

g. Will infallibly, certainly take place, I grant; will infallibly and with necessity take place, I again distinguish; a necessary act, I grant; a free act, I deny.

J. a. What God foresees will necessarily take place. Ergo.
b. Omission of an act foreseen by God is impossible. Ergo.
c. Free will depends on God's foreknowledge, and this in turn is independent of free will. Ergo.

Answers: a. With logical or consequent necessity, I grant; with physical or antecedent, I again distinguish; in necessary agent, I grant; in free, I deny.

b. Logically or consequently I grant; physically, or antecedently, I again distinguish; in necessary agent, I grant; in free, I deny.

c. Depends on God as spectator, I grant; as determining cause, I deny.

THESIS X

The Truth About Hypnotism

Division

Statement of Question
A. Definition
B. Division I, II, III
C. Hypnotic Sleep
D. Ethics of Hypnotism.
E. Church and Hypnotism.

Maher, pp. 594–603.

QUESTION

Our theme is in point of fact an old one. The name it uses for present disguise is of comparatively recent origin. Error has as many changes of spots as the proverbial leopard, and error's changes are generally no less superficial. We are to-day fighting, in the domains of theology and philosophy, theories done to death centuries ago, and resurrected whole. Hypnotism used to be called Mesmerism, Animal Magnetism, Braidism and other isms too numerous to mention. Mesmer, a German physician (1733–1815), in the course of enquiries into the nature and cure of diseases, thought he discovered in a certain magnetic fluid the vehicle of all the ills to which this flesh is heir; and, acting on his discovery, proceeded to make the world whole through the agency of the wonderful fluid. He was of opinion that every animal, whether man or beast, carries about a stock of this commodity, and that disease is the outcome of a disorder in its distribution, which can easily be set to rights by a few passes of the hand and shakes of the head. There is no denying the fact that certain infirmities, notably those of nervous origin, are eminently susceptible to treatment of this sort. Bread-pills in boarding-colleges have worked wonderful revolutions in the health of boys and girls, and have often saved the victims of a too vivid imagination from early graves. Even so, Mesmer, by instilling large faith into his patients, restored to use many a stiffened limb, and broke up the beginnings of many a serious malady. He himself insisted that everything was due to animal magnetism, the existence of which is to-day roundly denied by the soberer and more eminent students of medicine. Braid was an Englishman, who followed in the footsteps of Mesmer, and met with success so phenomenal that the new remedy became identified with his name.

A. For a definition of hypnotism, I open my Century Dictionary, and find there this accurate description, "An abnormal mental condition, characterized by insensibility to most impressions of sense, with excessive sensibility to some impressions, and an appearance of total unconsciousness. This is true especially of that variety of this condition which is artificially induced, usually by concentrating the attention of the subject upon some object of vision, as a bit of bright glass, or on the operator, who generally aids in producing the result by making a few light passes with his hands. When in this condition, the mental action and volition of the subject are to a large extent under the control of the operator. The state begins in a gradual loss of taste, touch, and the sense of temperature; next, colors are imperfectly distinguished; then, forms grow indistinct; and then the eye is immovable, and nothing is seen. The ear never sleeps in these experiments. The subject believes, and at last does, all that is commanded. Senses fall completely under control of the hypnotizer; and in many cases the interval between normal waking and hypnotic sleep covers only a minute."

The word hypnotism is of Greek parentage, and claims relationship with hypnotizo, the exact equivalent of "to put to sleep." The name is admirably well chosen, as the whole process consists in producing sleep, or lulling all the senses but hearing into unconsciousness. Some very remarkable peculiarities attach to this hypnotic sleep, and render it widely different from nature's sweet restorer. Thus, for instance, all adepts in the art of hypnotizing agree that the ears of the subject under their influence never once lose their acuteness and susceptibility to sound. The other four senses of sight, smell, touch, and taste are all topsy-turvy during the spell, and wholly incapable of discriminating between colors, odors, surfaces, and flavors; but the hearing is wide awake, and detects every whisper. This very circumstance makes it possible for the artist to ply his trade and perform tricks that bewilder the witnesses. For, the senses being the gateways of the mind, the artist through the subject's ear has at least one entrance to the subject's mind; and, once inside, he can there create impressions, that the other senses would, if awake, correct. The hypnotic state can, therefore, be characterized as an incomplete sleep, a doze. It has many points in common with these several phenomena, notably that of delicacy of hearing. It is, like them, interrupted by noise not above the ordinary, or even by deep silence, when some regular chain of sounds preceded. For instance, it has been the experience of many to awake early at night, when slumber is not deep, because a clock in the room suddenly stopped ticking. These same persons, a few hours later, when in the middle of their sleep, would hardly awake, if the world stopped going around. A man under hypnotic influence hears the operator's voice distinctly. He answers in that disconnected sort of language common to dreams. He sees, but so obscurely that he cannot distinguish a horse from a broomstick. He smells and tastes, but cannot distinguish a cabbage from a rose, a potato from an orange.

In this matter of hypnotism, a common every day drunk is an interesting study, and presents many analogies. Thus, when well tightened up, the victim of too much conviviality loses, along with self-respect and gentility, several at least of his five senses. His power of locomotion is so badly beyond control that, try as he will, he cannot make progress, except by tacking; and sometimes his fetches are so wide that he lurches all the way to the car-tracks before steering to the east or west, as the case may be. I have seen them leave the sidewalk altogether, dart through the railing in front of a stranger's residence, continue straight down the area-steps to the basement door, and then turn back only because they found the door locked. People with some experience in this line aver that the houses on either side of the street play a sad trick on the eyes, and seem to lean till they form an arch overhead. They likewise aver that, as soon as they themselves take up a position of rest at a corner, the houses on the opposite side, with their numbers in flaring evidence, seem to pass in mock procession. And all this with such an air of reality that they count it best to wait just where they are, till their house passes along. They confess to snakes, and are frequently detected with their arms thrown lovingly around a cold lamp-post or trolley pole, addressing it as a friend with effusiveness and a copious abundance of tears. I allege these instances, only to prove my contention, that hypnotism is in most cases merely on a level with events in daily life, that, because of their commonness, excite in us no wonder. To understand this the more thoroughly, let us examine in detail some of the startling performances of hypnotism.

B. Division. They can be conveniently ranged in three classes. Let the first embrace such as proceed from deception practiced on the senses. Under the second we can include all such as turn on the obedient deference the subject pays to the commands of the hypnotist. Under the third class we can group marvels that are merely fraudulent appearances, the result of trickery and magic; or, if the realities they are represented to be, outside the sphere of natural agencies, due entirely to the interference of beings of another and a higher order, namely evil spirits or demons.

I. Phenomena of the first and second classes present little or no difficulty to the student of philosophy, at all acquainted with the operations of the senses and the mind's dependence on the senses for its ideas. Thus, the whole process consists simply in this, that the operator, generally a man gifted with a pair of dark flashing eyes, looks fixedly at his victim, and, after a few bewildering movements of the hands, has the subject completely at his mercy. Four of the patient's senses are half asleep and practically useless. His hearing is wide awake, and the performance begins. First, for instance, a potato is thrust into his hand, and he is told with monotonous solemnity that he holds an orange. He is then commanded to eat the orange, and he devours the potato with an air of relish and avidity, thinking all the while that he is really eating an orange. The explanation is easy and simple. The man's sense of touch is numb, and cannot discern the difference between the shape of a potato and that of an orange. His sense of taste is equally numb or drowsy, and cannot distinguish the flavor of a potato from that of an orange. All the while, however, his hearing is wide awake. It never for a moment abandons him; and as it is for the present the only channel through which he receives ideas, he thinks, without any means of correcting the mistake, that everything is just as it is represented by the operator. He thinks that he grasps an orange, that he tastes an orange, that he eats an orange. Numerous other tricks can be practiced on him while the spell lasts. A bundle of rags can be laid in his arms, and, at the suggestion of the operator, he will fondle and toss the same as though it were a real live baby. A rod and line can be put in his hands, and he will sit at the edge of the stage and fish contentedly. Or he will prance about boy-fashion on a broomstick, as though he were riding a cavalry-horse. It is worth noting, in this first series of marvels, that the hypnotist's words are always accompanied by actions. He would be powerless in the four experiments just enumerated, unless he actually slipped a potato into the hand of the subject, laid a bundle of rags on his arm, or furnished him with fishing tackle and a broomstick. I call your attention to this circumstance, as it will afterwards serve to mark off the difference between the mind's activity in the two conditions of dreaming and hypnotism.

II. Passing now to the second class of phenomena, such as turn on the obedience rendered the hypnotist by his subject, we see in them nothing very extraordinary. After inducing sleep, he issues a series of orders that are faithfully executed. He bids the man walk, sit down, dance; and all these different attitudes are assumed in order. He tells the victim that it is warm, and the victim unbuttons his coat for a breeze. He tells him in the next breath that it is cold, and the victim's teeth chatter. He places a piece of hot iron in close proximity to the face and hands of the victim without creating any sensation of pain or discomfort. All this time the victim's temperature, subjectively speaking, undergoes no change. Everything is the result of a catalepsy or partial paralysis, produced by the sleep in which he is wrapped. For my part, I do not wonder that the victim of hypnotism falls into the prescribed attitudes, unbuttons his coat, shivers, and experiences no inconvenience when brought near hot iron. The wonder would be if the contrary happened. While under hypnotic influence, the mind and will of the patient are absolutely at the mercy of the operator, for the very evident reason before advanced. Every sense but that of hearing is practically dead. Touch is of no more value to him than it is to a paralytic. His mind is wholly dependent on his ears for ideas, and whatever statement the operator makes is necessarily accepted as true. Hence, if he says that it is warm, the patient must believe that it is warm, and behave accordingly. If he says that it is cold, there is nothing left for the patient to do but shiver. If he says that a plate of hot iron is cold, the patient has nothing to help him detect the fraud. *The will acts only at the instigation of forms conceived in the mind; and, as the operator holds the key to his victim's mind through the single sense of hearing, his orders are communicated to the will of the victim, and, whether they prescribe walking, sitting or dancing, are immediately executed.* The whole groundwork, therefore, of hypnotism is founded on these two evident principles of Scholastic philosophy. "Nil in intellectu, quod non fuerit prius in sensu," and "Nil volitum nisi praecognitum." They mean in cold English, "Man's mind derives its every idea, in root at least, from the senses," and "Man's wishes derive life and being from his thoughts." The two principles are shadowed forth in our old saying, "What the eye never sees, the heart never craves for."

C. Hypnotic Sleep. It would be here in order to discuss the third class of phenomena, such as speaking or understanding a hitherto unknown tongue, mind-reading, vision through walls and bandages, detection of hidden diseases and marvels of the kind. But, as we have serious doubts about the reality of these phenomena, or admit their reality only on the supposition that they are due to the agency of evil spirits or demons, we prefer to dismiss them for the present with this slight notice. Later we shall have more to say regarding them. We wish to further pursue our investigation into the phenomena of the first and second classes. I have said before, and I now repeat, that the phenomena of the first and second classes are no great marvels of themselves, and admit of easy, natural explanation. But we cannot deny that the hypnotic sleep, which makes them possible, possesses some mystery; and that its production seems, at first sight, something of a miracle. However, experience can be of much valuable service to us here, and we can strip this strange sleep of many of its weird characteristics by viewing it in the light of kindred occurrences, that make all too faint an impression on us because of their frequency. I have already alluded to the stupefying effect of strong drink on a man's senses. Let me call your attention to a few facts in your own experience equally strange. Some preachers have the happy faculty of putting their listeners to sleep. You must know friends, whose heavy conversation is a mild narcotic, producing, first, half suppressed gapes, then humiliating nods, and last of all oblivious drowsiness. Mothers know well the soporific effect of the human voice, when properly modulated; and they lead many an annoying baby to the land of dreams with a lullaby. If you analyze these cases, you will find that sleepiness invariably follows on the constant recurrence of the same tone. The ear tires of monotony, and communicates its disgust to the other senses. The whole man then sinks under the weight of fatigue and seeks rest in sleep. Nor is the ear the only organ thus affected. The eye is just as sensitive to an immovable light, if particularly soft; to a pair of twisted eyeballs gleaming steadily in the dark; and to a series of bright plates or colors passed in rapid succession before it. This, then, is the whole secret of the hypnotist's success. Nature has gifted him with no magic power, no hidden force, no magnetic fluid, no supernatural influences. All such talk is silly nonsense, and the fustian of fakirs. Nature has, perhaps, given him a pair of strikingly dark eyes with a lustrous sparkle, a raven black mustache, the pompous and martial bearing of a drum-major on parade; but beyond this she has bestowed on him no hypnotic abilities denied the meanest of her children. He rolls his lively eyes, he utters a few sonorous words in even stress and with mock solemnity, he makes a few poetically rounded gestures with his shapely hands, and the hoodooed patient obediently falls asleep. From the fact that he singles out definite portions of the hands, and forehead, and ears, designated as the locations of certain sense-nerves, making repeated passes over them, I have no doubt that he produces in the senses of touch, taste, and smell effects of the same nature as those produced by monotony in the sense of hearing, and by quick flashes of light in the sense of vision.

It must likewise be remarked that nearly all his power comes from the patient on whom he practices. If weak willed and anxious to submit to his influence, the hypnotist's task is easy. Many a timid young miss, they say, looks around for a convenient place in which to faint, when made listen to thrilling stories of the hypnotic art, or the darker secrets of fortune-telling. A calm, cool person, with his will in his hands, with complete power over self, master of his every nerve and muscle, aware of hypnotism's hollow pretensions, can be refractory under every attempt, can successfully resist the efforts of all the hypnotists in Christendom. Such a man, however, is a rare bird, and seldom met with at hypnotic seances. The crowd, that usually flocks to entertainments of the sort, is made up of nervous, excitable, fidgety men and women, boys and girls, only too ready to believe that the magician is vested with irresistible forces. And, just as hypnotism is nothing, has nothing, can do nothing, without your consent and assistance, so with your consent and assistance it can make good nearly all its claims at the present day.

Hypnotism is, therefore, a particular kind of sleep, determined by definite physiological causes, without the intervention of any unknown or supernatural agent. A dream presents as many difficulties to the enquiring student as hypnotic sleep. The reason is not far to seek. We are so little impressed by dreams, that we never stop to enquire into their nature and conformation, only because they are in constant attendance on our sleeping hours. Hypnotism arrests our attention, because it falls to the lot of only a chosen few to experience its weird spell. There are, however, differences between the two states of dreaming and hypnotism, as before remarked; and it may be worth our while to here record a few. The impressions received in one state and the other are so vivid and lifelike, that you cannot help believing them realities instead of representations. And yet no impression whatever can be conveyed in hypnotic sleep, unless the operator at the very birth of the impression suggests some definite thought. He must, in other words, place a potato in the patient's hand, a rag-baby in his arms, to successfully deceive. In dreams, on the contrary, no such necessity is apparent. An impression had days, months, years before, and faithfully recorded in the imagination, can give rise to a dream as true to life as the scene that first produced the impression. Sometimes, of course, a dream is the outcome of a present sensation; as, when an arm or limb gets into some uncomfortable position, when the shoulders are pressed heavily by the bedclothes, or when the hand rests suddenly on the hard wood or cold iron of the bedstead. But, generally, our dreams are the growth of old impressions, stored away somewhere in the lumber-room of the imagination. These impressions are kept in equilibrium during the day by the multitude of thoughts, that usually beset us in busy work-time. At night, however, they resume their force, and the dream begins. Though sometimes difficult to trace the connection between past or present sensations and the dream in hand, such a connection always exists. Thus, for instance, you may have been conversing with some friend at a street corner, just as a throbbing locomotive, with flaming headlight, rushed by. That night you dream of a railroad accident; or, mayhap, your fancy converts the locomotive into a lion, with the headlight for eyes of fire, and the puffing for loud roars. If your hand rests on some cold object, you are prone to dream of death, of mermaids. From mermaids you pass to mummies wrapped in antediluvian bandages; from mummies to Egyptian hieroglyphics, and so on without limit. When dreaming, your own brain suggests everything. When under hypnotic influence, you are dependent on the operator for suggestions. If he puts a dish of ammonia under your nose, and tells you that you are smelling a rose, you feel persuaded that you are smelling a rose, though your eyes run with tears.

III. Before passing to the moral aspect of hypnotism, its influence for good and evil, it may be well to insert here, by way of parenthesis, a few remarks about such hypnotic phenomena of the third class as we summarily dismissed earlier in the paper. We said, then, if you remember, that many such phenomena are smart tricks and empty appearances, contending at the same time that others are due entirely to the intervention of evil spirits. With regard to tricks we feel safe in taking this single position. We may not be able to detect and lay bare the inner mysteries of some fraud, hinging on the dexterity of a magician; but we know from antecedent reasons that nature is incapable of such an effort, and that the God of nature would not allow, for the trivial purpose of tickling men's curiosity, so momentous a departure from nature's laws. We conclude, then, that the whole business is a cleverly contrived piece of deception, and that the magician at least knows where the deception begins and leaves off. With regard to evil spirits, I can well afford to be brief. My audience is composed of believers, willing to stake their lives on the truth of God's word as contained in the Bible; and the Bible is clear about the existence of evil spirits, and about their interference in the affairs of men. We, then, as Catholic philosophers, claim that the scale of being in the universe is nicely graded, and that between God and man there is a species of existences superior to man, inferior of course to God. These existences are pure spirits; and, whether buried in hell or glorious in Heaven, are gifted with rare powers of intelligence, more conversant with the secrets of nature than the combined wisdom of our own and every other age. And yet they are God's obedient servants. Their activity is held in check by His supreme will. They accomplish only such results as He in His wisdom sanctions. Every devil is, therefore, a consummate wizard; and every devil was acquainted with the hidden possibilities of electricity and the wonders of the X-ray long before Edison or Roentgen was born. The business of the fallen angels is to drag souls to hell; and, to further this purpose, they use all the resources of their wisdom. I can conceive that God Himself, after having put at man's disposal the authority of His sacred word and the guidance of His true Church, allows these spirits of darkness to test man's faith by the performance of wonders in the persons of iniquitous tools. Armed with this permission, the devil can communicate some of his skill to an unprincipled man. This agent, sacrificing everything to love of fame and greed of money, can turn his advantage to good profit; and weak-minded men and women, who hang on his words, will by degrees fall victims to the mistake of thinking they see God's finger, where men of faith and sound sense plainly discern the devil's tail. The next step in their downward progress is to banish the supernatural altogether from the horizon of their lives, and drift into unbelief, the paganism of modern times.

Their ruin is wrought by performances like the following. Their little idol, they say, reads in a dark room, with his eyes tightly bandaged. He sees with the soles of his feet. He readily and without previous study understands and talks a foreign tongue. He describes some distant capital, some celebrated park, never in the course of his life visited. He detects through the flesh the progress of a disease, and prescribes efficient remedies. He sees the soul through the walls of the body, reads its thoughts, its desires, its passions, and crimes. Now, these are marvels certainly; so striking withal, that I suspect the veracity of pretended witnesses to their reality. The utterances of these witnesses assuredly are not articles of faith; and, when my faith is silent in matters opposed to all the Physics and Philosophy I know, I beg leave to be incredulous. However, if brought face to face with these vaunted facts, I should still suspect a trick somewhere; and, if driven from even this corner, I should as a last resource fall back on the intervention of evil spirits, working with Heaven's sanction. From the science of Physics, I know that the eye, not the foot, is the organ of sight; that light is the natural medium of vision; and that, to be seen, an object must needs be present. From experience and the very nature of language, I know that hard study and continued practice are the only means appointed to acquire facility in a foreign tongue. From philosophy and theology, I know that the heart's secrets are a man's own and God's; and that, unless willingly betrayed by some outward emotion depicted in the face or movements, they remain sealed mysteries to outsiders. When, then, some wizard of no great reputation for piety or zeal pretends to upset by his unaided self all these well authenticated laws, my faith issues no command to believe; and I claim the privilege to doubt, and to doubt most uncompromisingly.

D. Ethics of Hypnotism. Enough, then, of the shallow pretensions of hypnotism in this last phase. A word, now, about hypnotism's danger in the case of the subject; and I am done. It has been unwisely compared in this matter of danger to the use of anæsthetics. The comparison is faulty in many respects. A person under the influence of anæsthetics is indeed no longer master of his body; but his soul is his own. A person under the influence of hypnotism is deprived of even that possession.

His mind and his will are at the mercy of the operator. Hence, though many a future of wrecked hopes dates its beginning from the imprudent use of anæsthetics, the use of anæsthetics is nowise forbidden, when proper precautions are taken. The strong right arm of a friend seated near can easily preclude every possibility of harm. But the strong right arm of a friend is powerless to shield the victim of hypnotization. Everything depends on the integrity of the operator. The victim's mind is active, his will is active; and yet over the one and the other the victim has as little control as persons asleep have over their own. He is absolutely at the mercy of the hypnotist for good or evil. He is not free to accept or reject the suggestions prompted. His mind can be filled, in spite of himself, with pictures that will torment his soul, and drag it down to hell, even when awake. Threats can drive him to the perpetration of filthy and horrid crimes. A martyr could, of course, resist these threats; but martyrs always die in full possession of their senses, and hemmed round about with the abundant grace of God. Even if no harm came of the experiment, when you reflect that, in surrendering yourself to the influence of hypnotism, you are simply putting yourself into the hands of another man, to be by him lifted up to Heaven or buried in the mire of sin, you cannot but consider the proceeding extremely dangerous and foully wrong. Every novice in the study of morality understands that the victim of hypnotism is not directly responsible for his actions during the precise period of the spell; but in hypnotism, as well as in drunkenness, we recognize two kinds of responsibility. When bereft of the untrammeled use of his free will, a man is capable of only indirect responsibility. But that same man, who, with his eyes wide open to the danger, submits to the process of hypnotization or drinks to excess, is directly responsible during the last moments of consciousness for whatever violence he does the laws of morality while intoxicated or hypnotized. In that last moment he makes deliberate choice of all the crimes and sins he afterwards commits, and must before God stand the consequences of his choice.

E. Church and Hypnotism. In this paper, which is by no means exhaustive of the subject, I have studiously avoided all reference to documents of the Church on the question in hand, issued at various intervals in her history. Suffice it to say that she is loud in her denunciation of everything savoring of hypnotism, of everything with even a remote semblance to that devil-worship, which is the crying evil of our times. The question has been already submitted to the Holy See for decision. Our Church, with all that caution characteristic of her proceedings, has declared against hypnotism only when it involves superstition, applies physical means otherwise forbidden, or seeks unlawful ends or objects. In medicine, when employed by a man of skill and integrity, with all due precautions against danger to the patient, its use, in view of the Church's decision, can hardly be condemned. Its employment for purposes of idle curiosity I should not hesitate to brand a crime. When it pretends to phenomena, that transcend the forces of nature, it is little short of idolatry or devil-worship. To even assist at hypnotic seances, may easily constitute a sin; to submit to the process of hypnotism, outside of real need in the field of medicine, rarely or never escapes the imputation of sin. We have no more right to enter the hypnotic state from motives of curiosity, then we have to get drunk for the purpose of knowing how it feels to be intoxicated. And, therefore, we Catholics must leave hypnotism severely alone. The less we have to do with these modern fads and cults, the better. We should be frightened from all participation in affairs of the sort by the reflection, that hypnotism and kindred practices are curses of modern civilization, and effective tools in the hands of the enemy for the destruction of faith and the damnation of souls.

PART II — NATURAL THEOLOGY

INTRODUCTION

We are now come to the crown and consummation of our work. Philosophy is our topic; and, if philosophy is knowledge of things in their last causes, this present department of the study, because it deals with God, the absolutely last cause of everything, more deserves the name than any preceding chapter. Natural Theology is more philosophy than Logic, Psychology or Ethics, and claims as such our deepest attention and utmost reverence. Theodicy is another name for Natural Theology, and was first introduced by Leibnitz. It means the justification of God, and was framed by its inventor with a particular view to what he considers the hardest problem in the whole study, the reconciliation of God's attributes with the evil in the universe. Theology itself means discourse or reasoning about God. Plato and Aristotle use the word. St. Thomas makes Aristotle call Orpheus, Hesiod and Homer the poets of Theology. Max Muller derives the Greek "Theos" from the Sanscrit, Deva, meaning light, splendor, the Brilliant. St. Paul describes God as dwelling in inaccessible light. St. Gregory calls the vision of God, incircumscriptum lumen, light without limit, a sky with no horizon. The epithet, natural, is prefixed, to separate this branch of the science from its near neighbor, supernatural or dogmatic theology. Wide differences keep the two apart. In Natural Theology we rely altogether on unaided reason, or our conclusions are quite independent of any special help from Heaven. We base no argument on Scripture or tradition, though as devout Catholics we are keen to the need of formulating no doctrine opposed to revelation as interpreted by the Church, the pillar and ground of truth. Dogmatic theology reserves to itself all such extraneous assistance; and, whereas we philosophers advance only such principles as approve themselves to the veriest pagan, and most consummate stranger to the written and spoken word of God, theologians properly so called have first recourse for argument to revelation, embodied in Scripture, the Fathers and the Councils, and make reason a species of appendage to faith. On this account *Natural Theology is best described in full as knowledge of God compassed in the light of reason. Dogmatic, on the contrary, is knowledge of God compassed in the light of revelation.*

Reason naturally enough precedes revelation, and in this respect Natural Theology makes the mind ready for supernatural. It puts on a solid footing what we call the praeambula fidei, the preliminaries to faith, and secures reason's voucher for truths that lie worlds beyond the sphere of reason's limited grasp and comprehension. In this sense philosophy is handmaid to theology, and the open book of creation is key to the sealed page of revelation. As compared with the knowledge of God we get from our catechism, the notions of God we derive from Natural Theology are dim, unfinished and pitifully indistinct. The most we can hope to do is establish the existence of God, vindicate to Him and explain His most characteristic attributes, and set in a clear light His influence, His intervention, His interference in the world's constitution and history. We therefore divide our treatise into three main parts, the existence of God, His attributes, and His influence or activity in created nature. In the first we contend that the one sound argument able to put the truth of God's existence on a solid basis, is essentially an a posteriori argument, derived from the contingent nature of created things, from the physical order apparent in the universe, from the moral order everywhere acknowledged, and from the common consent of mankind. In rejecting other arguments as insufficient and misleading we run counter to a host of opponents. We have to do with Ontologism as preached by Malebranche, 1715, Gioberti, 1852, Rosmini, 1855, and Ubaghs, 1856; with the ontological or a priori argument of St. Anselm, 1109, Descartes, 1650, Leibnitz, 1716; and with the treacherous attempt of Kant, 1781, to undermine all certainty about God's existence, by proclaiming it an impossible problem for the speculative reason, abandoning the belief to what he styles practical reason, an internal voice, categorically commanding the performance of good and avoidance of evil, a voice man cannot disregard without harm to his dignity, a voice without meaning in the event of refusal to acknowledge a supreme lawgiver. Jacobi, 1819, imitates Kant, when he reduces our certainty about God to a kind of irresistible spiritual feeling. Bonald, 1840, applies traditionalism to the same truth and restricts certainty to primitive revelation on the subject. Lamennais, 1854, was moved by the same line of reasoning to refer everything to the common consent of mankind, making it the universal criterion of truth. Hamilton and Mansel ascribe our certainty in the matter to harmony between the belief and our moral instincts. Herbert Spencer borrows his best arguments in favor of agnosticism from principles advocated by Mansel. All these several philosophers, from Kant down, are enemies in the camp, they are mere pretenders, and by setting truth on a crumbling foundation, easily overturned by truth's adversaries, they are doing the cause of righteousness and religion a world of wrong. Catholics among them, like Jacobi, Bonald and Lamennais, may have been sincere in their convictions; but they were stubbornly proud, and their sincerity is small recompense for the harm their theories have already done and still continue to do.

Our argument dates back to the days of Plato, 348, B. C., and Aristotle, B. C. 322. It was maintained by St. Augustine, 430, St. Thomas Aquinas, 1274, and all the Schoolmen; by Bacon, 1626, and Locke, 1704. St. Anselm, Descartes and Leibnitz acknowledged its cogency, and were far from resting their case on the ontological argument. In their writings all three draw on finite things to establish the truth of God's existence. Scientific minds of the first rank take sides with us, men like Kepler, Newton, Faye, Sir John Herschel, Sir William Thomson, and others too numerous to mention. We therefore have no reason to be ashamed of the position we take. The scientific world and the world of right philosophy are with us, and it would be the height of folly to bow down before the authority of crooked reasoners like Kant and Spinoza and Ingersoll, or giants of a later growth, like that Bowne of Boston University, who unblushingly says that theism, the fundamental postulate of our total life, cannot be demonstrated without assumption, and that it is strictly proved by nothing.

THESIS I

From created things of earth, from the order apparent in the physical universe, from the moral order naturally known to us, finally from the common consent of mankind, we prove a posteriori that there is a God.

Boedder, pp. 1–85; 149–233; 325–344. *Jouin,* pp. 219–228.

QUESTION

Agnostics are our chief opponents, and this term agnostic is but a Greek twist for our Latin ignoramus or Anglo-Saxon dunce. They make open boast of the title agnostic, and the term translated means the man who never knows. What in common language is an ignoramus, becomes in the smoother diction of polished refinement an agnostic. Herbert Spencer, Ingersoll and men of their ilk, who, for reasons best known to themselves, take sides against the universe of thought and champion the cause of wretches weak-minded and vicious enough to sacrifice principle to pleasure, and slink away from the most palpable responsibility catalogued in the duties of life, are by their own confession agnostics, and as such deserve small or no consideration at our hands. They are not honest with themselves, and the first step in the way to religious knowledge is sincerity. Their blind followers are more appealing objects of pity, and we pause to remind them that their leaders are by their own acknowledgment agnostics. Words are but words, and, whether the symbol used to express the condition be of Greek or Latin or Anglo-Saxon parentage, it is a dismal business to borrow knowledge from the man who never knows. The process is wonderfully like borrowing money from a pauper, feeding on the air, or reading by the light of night's inky darkness. Happily enough for Spencer and Ingersoll themselves, their ignorance is but partial; and though agnostics, when God or religion is in question, they are reputed oracles of wisdom in matters scientific and legal. The two are besides well equipped with the gift of fluency, ease and richness of expression. They have led thousands astray, and the philosophy of Kant, no doubt, proved their own undoing. Vigorous measures must be taken with them and their followers, no single concession must be made their empty vaporings, and we must guard against the mistake of that good easy man, Dean Mansel, who in the dual capacity of Protestant divine and lecturer at Oxford threw down his arms in the fight, declaring that faith in revelation alone, or the transmitted word of God, could be sufficient guarantee for certainty about God's existence. Champions thus faint-hearted and unskilled are a hurt to the cause they uphold, and unwittingly, perhaps, treat the devil to a victory, when they set up manikins easily overturned by a breath of wind.

There was a school of philosophers, named Traditionalists, who, though perhaps adverse to receiving into their ranks so radical an expounder of their tenets as this Oxford preacher, partook in no small degree of his notions, and were perhaps in some measure responsible for his wanderings. Tradition, they contended, handed down from father to son, as the depositary of a truth once communicated by God to mankind, is the groundwork of our belief in God's existence. Few were unthinking enough to maintain further that all other demonstrations establishing God's existence were idle and proved nothing. We ourselves make use of the very argument they advance, but assign it only its own modicum of importance, and are better pleased with the expression, common consent of mankind, than with tradition, a word always more or less suspected by merely natural philosophers. We venture to think it imperatively necessary and marvelously easy to convince an ordinary understanding of God's existence, without any recourse whatever to such extrinsic motives as the testimony of the race or the traditions of Christianity.

The Ontologists, under the leadership of Malebranche, whose acquaintance we made in Major Logic when discussing the criterion of truth, applying a test there shown to be inadequate, think that God's existence is made sure to our reason by that immediate knowledge of God, and by that familiar intercourse, which they fancy He has vouchsafed us. Apart from the two last theories, common to even a few Catholics, there are in the

Church two classes of philosophers, who, though a unit about the possibility and necessity of proving God's existence, separate when the species of argument allowable and conclusive enters into the question.

St. Anselm, supported by a smaller number of adherents, holds out for the validity of what we call an a priori proof. St. Thomas, and his followers are far more numerous, finds fault with such proof, and contends that man's reason can never in this matter attain to anything beyond an a posteriori proof. To the better understanding of these differences of opinion, it will much help to make clear the distinction between an a priori and an a posteriori demonstration. Priority in the ontological order is said with reference to the truth contained in the conclusion on the one hand, and on the other to the truths contained in the premisses. Of course, in the logical order, or in the order of existence in the mind, the premisses always precede the conclusion, no matter to what species the demonstration belongs; but in the ontological order, or in the order of existences outside the thinking subject, the reverse may be the case, and is the case in all a posteriori demonstrations. In an a priori demonstration, therefore, the truth bound up in the conclusion depends, in the order not of thought but of being, on the truths contained in the premisses. In an a posteriori the truth involved in the premisses depends, in the same order of being, on the truth contained in the conclusion. This priority or dependence may be twofold, physical and metaphysical. It is physical, when that peculiar to cause with reference to its effects; metaphysical, when that peculiar to essence with reference to attributes derived from essence. When, therefore, we come to decide on the question at issue between St. Anselm and St. Thomas, we have merely to ask and answer the question, Are the truths of the premisses, used in any conclusive demonstration of God's existence, dependent on or independent of the truth contained in this assertion, God exists? In our opinion the truths contained in the premisses are dependent on the truth expressed in the conclusion, and the only legitimate demonstration is, therefore, a posteriori. Thus, because God exists, created nature exists; because God exists, physical order exists, and so of our other arguments. God does not exist in the real order, the order outside of our mind, because created nature exists, or physical order, and so of the rest. Our knowledge of His existence is certainly brought about or caused by the existence of created nature, physical order and such. But such existence of God is existence in the order of thought, or logical; in which order, we said, the conclusion is always dependent on the premisses. St. Anselm's syllogism, if a demonstration at all, can with justice enough be denominated a priori. But a glance at its make-up must convince the mind that one of two faults is inseparable from it. It is either a begging of the question, or an unpardonable passage from the logical to the real order of being, from beings as they exist in the mind to beings as they exist outside the mind.

It runs as follows: God is the most perfect being, the being whose superior cannot be even conceived. But such a being cannot possibly be considered non-existent. Ergo God actually and really exists. Here is another form of the same argument: God is the most perfect being. But actual and real existence cannot be wanting to such a being. Ergo God really and actually exists. God in the first premiss can have two meanings, God within the mind eliciting the judgment or the notion of God, and God outside of that mind, or the objective reality of God. If the first meaning be chosen, it must undergo no change in the conclusion. Filled out, the conclusion will then read: God in the mind, or the notion of God, is the notion of a being endowed with real and actual existence. But this conclusion is not to the point. We do not wish to prove that our notion of God is such and such, but we wish to prove that God Himself is such and such. If the second meaning be chosen, the conclusion is indeed what we would have, but the question was begged in the Major. For in asserting there that God outside of the mind, or the objective reality of God, is the most perfect being, we at once clothe Him with real and actual existence, whereas the whole argument was instituted to discover whether God actually and really exists or not. Therefore, St. Anselm's argument must suppose from the very start that God exists. Based on this supposition, it is an admirable and conclusive proof that God, if there is actually such a being, can never have existed in mere possibility, but must have always existed really and actually. Briefly, it fixes with certainty the necessary mode of God's existence, not the fact of

His existence. The fact of God's existence must be derived from some other source. With St. Thomas we hold that the only legitimate source at our disposal is the world about us, the product of God's might; and that therefore passing from effect to cause, we argue a posteriori ad prius, or from what comes second to what comes first. Here is an instance of a proper a priori argument. The soul is a substance, simple and spiritual. But all substances, simple and spiritual, are immortal. Ergo the soul is immortal.

TERMS

From the created things of earth:

Creation was discussed at some length in Cosmology, and acquaintance with many of the remarks there made can with profit be renewed. We there proved that this world is the creation of some omnipotent cause. We proved the world produced from nothing, and production from nothing demands omnipotence. This conclusion was forced upon us by a consideration of the world's changes and modifications. They are plainly apparent to every observer, and to the reasoning mind they as plainly make manifest the world's contingency, and therefore its production by another. Contingency and actual existence are more potent signs of production by another than blaze and smoke are of fire. This other, or producing being, whose august prerogative it is to exist from eternity without ever being produced, and to create from the beginning of time everything in the universe but Himself, is God. Our notion then of God, from this first or fundamental view, is representative of a being unproduced Himself, and therefore without a cause; the Maker of everything else, and therefore the cause to which all else must be referred as effect. Unlike St. Anselm, we do not argue from this notion or logical being to the reality it represents. We begin with things sensibly present to us, and from the real order of existences about and around us we pass to the central existence of all, invisible indeed to our eyes of flesh, but none the less real on that account. Hence too our argument is a posteriori in that God's existence, the truth in the conclusion, is the cause not the effect of the world's existence, the truth in the premisses. *An actual existence, unproduced, necessary, non-*

contingent, is that which so exists from eternity that it is equally impossible for it to have never existed, to cease existing, or to experience a change in its mode of existence. An actual, produced, hypothetical, contingent being is that which at some period of time did not actually exist, which can in itself at any moment cease existing, and is capable of constantly undergoing changes in its mode of existence. Such are the created things of earth.

From the order apparent in the universe:

Order is the becoming arrangement or disposition of several things, based on fixed relations, and designed for the attainment of certain ends. Order is the work of reason, and rational agents work towards an end with knowledge and choice. This is a very general definition, admitting of applications innumerable, and too abstruse for any single individual, no matter how highly gifted, to follow to the end and describe. An astronomer can acquaint you with some of the wonders of intellect apparent in the heavens. If honest, he will tell you that life is all too short to pursue with anything like complete satisfaction one branch of his work. The botanist can find in the most neglected flower traces of an intelligence infinitely more capable than the skill, which enables the most consummate artist to trace even on canvas the despised flower's outlines, and attempt to fill in with tints that can be dreamed of, but never conveyed. The student of Natural History can, after years of painful research, communicate to admiring listeners a few of the baffling secrets hidden away in the anatomy and habits of animals. But with all their progress, all their devotion, no astronomer has yet produced a system of planets and stars comparing favorably with ours, no botanist or artist has yet produced a single violet, no Cuvier has yet constructed a diminutive house-fly.

Cicero, the poet of eloquence, thunderstruck at the various sights let in on his eyes, rapturously exclaims: "We scorn calling that thing a man, which, while gazing at the steady motions in the sky above, at the unvarying march of the stars, can be blind to the presence of an intellect in the work, can with stupid effrontery maintain that all is the result of chance, though no mind has yet measured the wisdom obtruding itself everywhere. Look at this earth of ours hanging in the middle of the universe, held together by the swing of its rapid revolution, clothed with flowers, fields of green, trees and fruits, so nicely scattered over its surface, that this otherwise tedious and wearisome multiplicity is toned by a variety, that ministers to pleasure without ever disgusting with surfeit. See too the streams of soothing coolness which flow on forever, the mighty rivers running down to the sea, their bank-slopes bright with the freshest green, the recesses of hillside grots, the jutting crags, the lowering mountains, the stretches of level plain. What a collection of beasts, how graceful the airy sweeps, how soft the songs of the birds! Must I lead in on the scene fair nature's king and guardian, him who keeps jealous watch over her vast extent, who checks the ravages of destructive brutes that would turn her into a desert, the growths of luxuriant vegetation, that would make of her a wilderness? Behold the meadows, the islands, the seashores, that glisten with his toil, dotted with his homes and his cities. Were man's eyes once so touched by Heaven as to see as plainly as does the mind these wonders, could he for a moment doubt about God's existence?" Thus Cicero. Epicurus and his herd, because it was more convenient for them, and less a reproach to their gross lives, pretended to see only a blind chance at work in nature, and scouted the idea of final causes or ends. In Ontology we upset this ignoble view of nature; and, in opposition to the imaginings of Epicurus, advanced solid reasons in proof of our belief that every agent works unto an end, be that agent God, angel, man or creature inferior to man. It is hardly worth while to here repeat what was there said. It will be sufficient for us to again reflect upon it.

From the moral order naturally known to us:

We base our argument on no set system of revealed or natural religion. We discuss man's instincts in their nakedness, whether Catholicity has ennobled and elevated them, whether Protestantism has weakened and poisoned them with uncertainty, or whether Mohammedanism has degraded and almost submerged them in the sink of sensual vice. Our platform is as broad as the earth and takes in all shades of belief, all the variations of creeds revealed by God, or manufactured by men. We appeal to that whisper, which, perhaps more faint and indistinct in the bosom of the grosser pagan of savagery than in the refined Christian of virtuous civilization, nevertheless manages to make itself heard, when the tumult of passion is loudest, and when its voice is most unwelcome. We pretend only to show the necessary connection between the existence of God and that familiar monitor, which prompts man to sin in the dark, and drives the guilty soul to recesses, whence it would, if possible, shut out the light of an unseen eye. Man may have faith of no description whatever, he may be the veriest heathen or pagan alive, but he has a conscience. It is an awkward possession on occasions, a companion whose dogged persistence is at times extremely uncomfortable. But there it is, and there is no help for it. It is God's minister, and we can no more get rid of it, than we can get rid of ourselves. It is the executive of a moral force; and, extending to secrets over which policemen have no control, it exercises a wider and more effective influence. The moral force, whose interests it advances, is familiar to all as the Natural Law. *Law in general, for want of a fuller definition, we here describe as the prescription of a superior forbidding or commanding some certain action.* Its effect in the subject is an almost instinctive impulse to consider himself bound by the strictest kind of moral necessity to acquit himself of a duty, and stand away from the object under ban. *The Natural Law we can with sufficient correctness call that prescription which is founded on the very essences of things, independently of all merely human activity; and manifested to man by the pure light of reason, without any profound elucubrations in the philosophic lore of right and wrong.* It forbids actions intrinsically evil, prescribes actions, the non-performance of which would be intrinsically evil. *Conscience is reason, inasmuch as it advertises man of his duty in this matter, praising him, chiding him, accusing him, as circumstances require.* This argument extends to deeper details than the mere existence of God. It proves God a supreme being, a rewarder and avenger, infinitely holy and just, all powerful and knowing to a degree absolutely without bounds. The dictates of conscience are not simple figments of the mind, without any foundation in reality, owing their entire being to the work of the intellect. They are as stern facts as the mind itself. They rise up and declare themselves, whether the man wishes to entertain them or slight them. The mind never creates them, it simply perceives them. If remorse depended on ourselves alone, it would seldom annoy us.

Common consent of mankind:

It is safe to say that the tendencies of modern science are atheistic. Certainly nature is not to blame for this perversion of her lessons. She silently but eloquently puts forth the claims of God; and reason, untrammeled by any sordid passion, distinctly and gladly hears her whispers. But pride distorts the sermon, and hearkens to only its own uncertain conclusions. Passion cannot entirely blot out sentiments born with the man, but it can and does deaden these sentiments, and so obscure them that they virtually disappear. No wonder then that after long years of intimacy with erring self-conceit men find themselves with scarcely a vestige of truths implanted in their very nature, and originally ready to burst forth spontaneously. The devil went so utterly blind with pride that, though much closer to God's august presence than we, he one day lost consciousness of God's might, and challenged Omnipotence to battle. Who is going to be surprised then, if weak, ignorant men, with passions alert and strong, away off from God's absorbing countenance, wrap themselves up in themselves, and refuse to pay to a being infinitely their superior the homage of acknowledgment? For a species of atheism the devil was hurled from Heaven; for a species of atheism more ignoble still, no corner in hell can be found too warm. Angelic atheism had, to my mind, some redeeming features; but human atheism, which is never more than practical, unsupported by any theory with the least shadow of substance, is extremely abominable. There may be practical atheists, men degraded and dull enough to openly profess unbelief in God, to shape their lives much as they would, if there were no God; but no human heart has yet been so poorly moulded by God as to honestly believe that its Maker does not exist.

It is not my intention to enter into the literature and remains bequeathed to us by nations coeval with the birth of the world, to interpret hieroglyphic inscriptions traced on the tiles and sepulchres of Babylon and Egypt, nor even to lay before you the results of devoted research among their ruins. Volumes have been already written on the subject, and the almost unanimous verdict of students, worthy of credit, is that belief in God's existence is as old as the world itself; that, though very absurd notions have crept into religious systems such as those of Greece and Rome, the fundamental idea of the actuality of some superior existence has uniformly been cleaved to. Here at home the Puritan ministers Roger Williams and John Eliot, who were among the first white men in close contact with the Indians, persistently declare that they never once in the course of all their wanderings happened on a single red man, not persuaded of the existence of God. Darwin and his materialistic followers may theorize and theorize, may give out as their deeply rooted conviction that man began as a monkey, and, after successive stages of evolution, by a subtle and fatal use of Dialectics hit upon, among other erroneous principles, that of God's existence. "Descent of Man," vol. 1, page 204. Ingersoll may prate about ignorance, fear, prejudice, the cupidity of priests and what not. Facts nevertheless stubbornly refuse to give way to theories; and, though I spend a year endeavoring to prove a horse a tree, I reap for reward of my pains only obloquy, shame and the reputation of being a fool. Plato has somewhere in his voluminous works this pithy saying, "Greeks and all the peoples outside Greece profess belief in the existence of God." Cicero takes the one sensible view of variety of creeds, when he says, "Among men there is no race so completely uncivilized as not to know, though ignorant perhaps of His true nature, that a God must be acknowledged." Plutarch, the celebrated historian of ancient heroes, replying to a certain opponent of his, remarks, "If you travel much, you will no doubt visit cities without walls, without kings, without dwellings, without resources, without a currency, without a literature. Nobody has yet discovered a city without temples and gods, without rituals, oaths, shrines; without sacrifices instituted to call down blessings and avert evils."

Polytheism, or the worship of several gods, is an absurdity in itself; but it none the less clearly points out the tendency of the human mind, and establishes none the less solidly the fact for which we here contend. Besides, polytheism invariably recognized one divinity superior to the rest, and so, virtually if not explicitly, was a profession of monotheism or one-god-service. Jupiter was God with the Romans; Zeus, God with the Greeks; Juno, Apollo, Mars, Diana, Venus, were princes and princesses in Jove's kingdom, endowed with many high prerogatives, but denied that supremacy which could alone make them gods.

God:

It is not our business to prove that God is one in substance and triple in person, that He once descended to earth and assumed human nature. We are in the domain of natural theology. The mysteries of the Most Holy Trinity and the Incarnation belong to supernatural or revealed theology, and presuppose the gift of faith. The God, whose existence we establish in this present thesis, is the one ens a se in the world, the unproduced and necessary being; the first cause of everything, Himself without a cause; the all powerful, all wise, all holy, all just being, who presides over the interests and destiny of man. Later we prove Him the being whose superior cannot be even conceived, and from this prerogative all others flow. He is therefore infinitely perfect, infinitely simple and peculiarly one. He is an utter stranger to change, eternal and immeasurable.

PROOFS I, II, III, IV

I. a. There exist beings which were produced. But produced beings ultimately suppose as cause a being non-produced. Ergo, this non-produced being, or God exists.

With regard to the Major. There exist beings which undergo at least accidental changes. But such beings are produced beings. Ergo, produced beings exist.

With regard to this Minor. An actual non-produced being can undergo no change. Ergo, the beings in question are produced beings.

With regard to this Antecedent. An actual non-produced being is a necessary being. But a necessary being can undergo no change. (In what state would it be necessary? In none.) Ergo, an actual non-produced being can undergo no change.

With regard to the Minor. Multiply men beyond the number of the stars, and to the whole multitude no higher epithet can be applied than that of rational. Increase of number could never result in changing their dignity to that of the angelic or divine. Majus et minus non mutant speciem. Even so with produced beings. Though they include everything in the universe, one alone excepted, they must ever and always be styled produced beings, and must therefore have their actual existence from something outside of themselves. Outside of themselves, however, since they take in the whole round of produced beings, there can be only the non-produced being, whom we reverently call God. Production from another is an attribute essential to things subject to change; it is not an element that may be present or absent, and still have the same influence on their actual existence. Without production there is for them no such thing as actual existence.

N.B. Produced beings can come from produced beings as from proximate causes, not as from ultimate causes. All these proximate causes are produced beings, and no matter how much you multiply them, you will never get from the collection a non-produced being. All the plants in the world will not make a horse. Produced beings and non-produced being differ as widely as plant and horse, specifically; yea, even more widely. But this collection of produced beings is unintelligible without a cause. Otherwise you would have an effect without a cause. This cause must be outside the collection, which embraces all produced being, and must therefore be a non-produced being, God.

b. Everything actual is either produced or non-produced. But it is impossible for all to be produced. Ergo, there exists at least one non-produced, God.

With regard to the Minor. Everything produced is an effect. But there can be no effect without a cause. Ergo, it is impossible for all to be produced.

N.B. Beings at this moment existing and beings that have already existed form a series, closed at least as far as this end of the line is concerned. Since an actual indefinite series is impossible, it must be closed also at the other end of the line. Since, further, the last being at this end of the line is a produced being,— otherwise it would be a cause with no effect whatever,— the last being at the other end of the line, or the first being of the series, must be a producer only, as the producers must always be just as many as the beings produced. The first being in the series cannot produce the second, and then be itself in turn produced by the second. For through the instrumentality of the second it would produce itself, or exercise an activity, which by supposition it does not yet possess.

II. There exists in the surrounding universe an order of things undeniably wonderful. But such an order supposes as capable cause some being, in intellect far above the visible works of the universe, an all-wise being, God. Ergo, God exists.

With regard to the Major. Its vastness, variety, intricate simplicity, perfection, long continuance, make this world's order truly wonderful.

With regard to the Minor. This order arises not from the essences of its constituents, because they are things subject to change, and therefore wholly indifferent of themselves to this or that combination. It arises from neither hap-hazard nor accident. Otherwise, nothing at all, or at most a cause without intelligence would be on an equal footing with a cause full of intelligence. Wherefore it has its origin in some being wholly distinct from, and immeasurably superior to, the whole visible universe, the being we know as God. The establishment of an intelligence greater than any with which we are acquainted, would serve to confound atheists; but the intelligence here displayed is nothing short of infinite. It is the intelligence of the actual non-produced being already proved, and therefore infinite.

III. Everybody at times, even against his will, feels himself urged by the most exacting kind of moral necessity to perform some actions and omit others. But this natural impulse betokens the existence of some supreme Lawgiver, a rewarder and avenger, absolutely holy and just, all powerful and omniscient. Ergo, God exists.

With regard to the Major. The sting of conscience, remorse of conscience, are by-words, and represent a psychological experience that falls to the lot of saint and sinner alike.

With regard to the Minor. Our inability to escape from pleasant and irksome feelings, attendant on good and evil done, is an unerring sign that the being responsible for these emotions is extraneous to ourselves, superior to us, human nature's supreme Lawgiver. Reason is rather passive than active in this matter of conscience. It does not precisely shape these dictates itself, it merely perceives them, in much the same way as it perceives universality. If their presence or absence depended on our will, unpleasant pangs would be exceedingly rare. Neither is conscience still, when once its message of reproof or congratulation is conveyed. It further excites a dread of future punishment, a hope of future reward, and therefore proclaims the existence of an all-powerful avenger and rewarder. The deeds falling under the blame or praise of conscience are not necessarily outward and open to the gaze of the world. They are oftener, perhaps, thoughts and intentions, hidden from men's eyes, divulged to not even a father, mother, husband or wife, but so securely wrapped up in the saint's or culprit's bosom as to go out only with death and descend to the grave with him. Surely, then, if our fear and hope have any foundation at all, and to think otherwise is absurd, the being, who inspires the one and the other, must be possessed of a vision infinitely more piercing than any falling under human observation.

IV. It is a judgment ratified by the common consent of mankind, that there exists a divinity or God, to whom worship is due. But such a judgment cannot be false. Ergo, God exists.

With regard to the Major. This first premiss is largely a matter of history, and has been so often and so overwhelmingly verified, that any further details on the subject would hardly be an addition to the facts already gathered, and indisputably substantiated by men of established probity and learning. Suffice it to say that atheists themselves do not attack the universality of the belief. They rest content with a vain inquiry into the motives prompting the belief. Fear, they say, cupidity and fraud, prejudice and ignorance are at the bottom of this huge mistake, not nature. But their assertions are emptier than the air that gives them voice. Fear is the parent of atheism, not of belief in God. It is a fact of history that the most fearless and most courageous of nations have ever been loudest in their profession of God's existence, and sincerest in their reverent worship. A man never assumes the dread responsibilities entailed by belief in God out of fear. It is a characteristic of fear to shirk responsibility. On second thought I should hesitate to denominate fear the cause of either atheism or belief in God. Fear in the one case and the other is an effect of certainty about God's existence, and would be wholly meaningless and easily divested, could that certainty be once weakened. It is just as silly to deny the existence of God, as it is to deny that well grounded fear and respectful reverence, which it prompts. Cicero made of Epicurus, a fair counterpart of our Ingersoll in point of blasphemy, the following reproachful but honest remark, "I never yet in the course of a life-time met the man, who stood more in awe of what he professed to regard idle grounds for fear, death, namely, and the gods." It is impossible to believe that recalcitrant men were ever so short-sighted and servile as to allow overbearing and greedy rulers, spiritual or temporal, to thrust on them this to the rebellious most irksome belief. I rather fancy that fraud and cupidity have been obstacles to its growth and propagation. No human law, attended with so much and so persistent inconvenience, would be long tolerated by a single people, to say nothing of the whole world. Prejudice may exert a wide influence, when it countenances ease and remissness, or ministers to any passion. But its influence is limited indeed, when it stands in the way of self-gratification and self-indulgence. The circumstance that a father and mother followed such and such a line of belief, may be of great weight with the young and uneducated, when a religion is to be chosen. But men are wont to grow out of youth and diffident ignorance. They are not slow to put aside prejudices less important in their bearing on life than this. Besides, prejudice in the case of the child does not incline him to belief precisely in God, but to a particular kind of belief in God. Ignorance is perhaps the emptiest of all the causes alleged by atheists. Aristotle, St. Thomas, Cicero, Plato, Kepler, Newton and all learned men of note are living illustrations of that beautiful saying ascribed to Bacon, "Sips of philosophy may indeed lead up to atheism, but fuller draughts lead the soul on to God."

With regard to the Minor. A judgment ratified by the common consent of mankind cannot be false, because it takes its rise in rational nature as such; and reason as such, or reason per se is infallible, unless we want to make man a being designed for the truth and destined to never compass it; unless we want to make reason an instrument designed to defeat its own purpose. *Every such judgment has four qualities, separating it from whatsoever other judgments, no matter how universal. 1. It has a claim to universality, to long duration and unchangeableness as well among ruder as among more civilized peoples. 2. It has a claim to exact agreement with all the rules of right reason. 3. It has a claim to absolute freedom from any such cause as prejudice, ignorance and the like. Its universality is sufficient guarantee for this claim. 4. It has a claim to the exclusive inculcation of moral and social truths, not of scientific truths. Small harm comes of scientific mistakes, moral mistakes reach to eternity. Nature provides for morality, not for science.*

PRINCIPLES

A. From Boedder. Nat. Theol., pp. 15–24.

Ontologists contend for no intuitive vision, such as the elect enjoy in Heaven. They contend for direct consciousness of God's existence. Our ideas, they say, are occasioned by sensations, they are not caused by them or the mind, but by God immediately present, like a sun in the middle of a thinking world.

Answer. We must make an effort to feel sure of God's existence. It costs labor to dispel doubts.

Matter is direct object of mind, not spirit; like owl in midday, when confronted with spiritual. The idea of God's existence is implanted in us by God, inasmuch as He gave us a reason capable of at once grasping His existence.

If we saw God immediately, we should see His essence. We see everything in God as we see everything in the sun, in principle of knowledge, not in object known.

B. Objections raised by Ontologists:

1. Notion of infinite cannot be gotten from finite. We have notion of infinite. Ergo, immediate.

2. Harmony of order. God first. Ergo idea of God ought to be first idea and immediate.

3. God, man's last end, first object of will. Ergo, first object of intellect and immediate. God is first truth. Ergo, first known.

4. God alone intelligible by Himself, creation intelligible only in God. Ergo, God first and immediate.

5. Universals, based on direct intuition of God, because eternal, necessary, unchangeable. Ergo.

Answers. 1. Infinite can be gotten from finite analogically, by positivo-negative concepts.

2. This harmony is not needed except in perfect knowledge like God's. In human knowledge truth is possible without this order. We can know a book first, and then its author.

3. To be last end, God must be known and wished not first, but somewhere in life or after death. God is subsistent truth, not truth in the abstract and common to creatures. Skeptics can deny the second truth, not the first.

4. Creatures have existence distinct from God, though not independent. Existence is basis of intelligibility. Ergo, creatures have intelligibility distinct from God. God is cause of their intelligibility, as He is of their existence.

5. They are negatively eternal; logically, not physically. God is physically and really eternal, necessary and unchangeable. Otherwise universals would be gods.

C. Difference between St. Anselm, Descartes and Leibnitz:

St. Anselm argues from notion, God the greatest being that can be conceived. Descartes argues from notion, existence contained in clear and distinct idea of God. Leibnitz argues from notion, God possible, because no contradiction proved in concept of God.

Answer. All forms sin because unwarranted passage from ideal to real. Monk Gaunilo pointed it out in St. Anselm's time. He refuted argument with story of the Lost Island, greater than any conceivable, inscribing his work, Opusculum pro Insipienti, a reference to the Scripture, The fool hath said in his heart, There is no God. The Lost Island must be a reality, because the greatest conceivable island. Anselm answered by saying that his argument was good for only the infinite being, not for finites.

Answer. St. Anselm assumes that the idea of infinite being is not a contradiction, and this without warrant, unless he first appeals to an a posteriori proof. Suppose many self-existent beings, and no being would be infinite.

D. Agnostics especially deny an intelligent first cause. They admit some kind of first cause, like the forces of matter, nebular hypothesis, atoms and such.

Answer. Our unproduced cause must be intelligent because some of its effects, men, are intelligent; it is infinite because unproduced. Ergo, no begging of question. Opponents deny a finite intelligent first cause. Ergo, no need to prove God infinite. Later we prove God infinite from the notion of necessary or actual non-produced being.

E. Urraburu: Theod., D. 1, c. 2, a 1, vol. 7, pp. 89–95.

1. Contingency of things created not yet proved. Ergo.

2. Though individual creatures are contingent, collection may be necessary. The door is not the house, neither is the window; but all the parts together can be called the house. One horse may not be able to haul a load, equal to the strength of five. Not lawful to argue from distributive to collective. Ergo, all contingents.

3. In the supposition of an infinite series there would be no first cause. Ergo, all contingents.

4. A can produce B, and then disappear to be later produced by B. Ergo, all contingents.

5. World could be eternal, and therefore necessary. Ergo, no first cause, and all contingents.

6. A necessary being can be from another, or produced. Ergo, all contingents.

7. Conclusion follows weaker part. Contingent in premisses. Ergo, necessary out of place in conclusion. "Latius patet conclusio quam praemissae"; from contingent to necessary.

Answers. 1. Contingency proved in Cosmology. Change proves contingency.

2. Not lawful, when distributive is the collective inadequately taken, I grant; when the distributive is the collective in no sense whatever, I deny. Necessity belongs to contingents not even inadequately. In contingents there is not even a partial aptitude for necessity. Ergo, necessity cannot be said of collection. The door is the house inadequately taken, and so is the window. No contingent being is the necessary being inadequately taken.

3. Infinite series, an absurdity, because series denotes some first and infinite denotes no first; square circle. Whether absurd or not, the whole infinite series of contingents must have

an outside cause. In a crowd of one hundred, to have a hundred whipped men, either somebody outside the hundred must whip, or somebody in the hundred must whip himself, or be whipped by another, whom he has mediately or immediately whipped. The cause of the series is in or outside the series. If out, necessary being; if in, each has cause, and one will mediately or immediately be cause of itself.

4. A ought to have cause before it produced B, not after. Otherwise it could not perish after its production of B.

5. World could be eternal by its very essence, I deny; by favor of the first cause, I grant. Only a thing eternal by its very essence is necessary, a thing eternal by favor is contingent.

6. A necessary being can be ens ab alio, or from another, when it proceeds from a first cause working necessarily, not when it is necessary by its very essence.

7. This axiom is a rule regulating the formal truth of syllogisms, and the weakness in question is that of negative as compared with positive, particular as compared with universal. It has no bearing on the relative dignity of truths in premisses and conclusion. Necessary being occurs in premisses, and therefore has right to a place in the conclusion. Contingents presuppose necessary. Contingents exist. Ergo, necessary exists. We do not derive God from contingents, but from necessary connection between necessary being and contingents. A necessary being or God exists necessarily not contingently, because, though contingent beings in the premisses are contingent in themselves, when once placed in existence, they necessarily exist; and God in the conclusion exists the same way, necessarily. The inquiry cannot be pursued to infinity.

F. From Urraburu: l. c, pp. 97–102.

1. Creature-causes are enough to explain effects. Ergo, no first cause.

2. Spencer. World cannot be ens a se. Ergo, no ens a se possible.

3. Mill. Neither experience nor reason proves first cause. Experience teaches only second causes. Reason is no voucher for principle of causality. Experience alone vouches for sufficiency of cause; and experience teaches that effect can surpass cause. More perfect beings are evolved from less perfect; world from nebulous mass.

4. Present things have beginning. Not so primal elements, which are eternal.

Answers. 1. Enough, immediately and proximately, I grant; remotely and mediately, I deny.

N.B. A first cause must always be supposed.

2. A stone cannot understand. Ergo, nothing can understand.

3. Experience is silent about first cause, does not deny. Principle of causality is not due to experience, it is analytic. Life in less perfect explains evolution to more perfect. Supposing the nebular hypothesis true, God gave the nebulous mass power to become world. Certainly the nebulous mass cannot be without cause. Ergo, first cause.

4. Primal elements are contingent, and could never begin without cause, even if eternal.

G. From Urraburu: l. c, pp. 104–107; pp. 111–124.

1. Numbers are greater and greater without greatest conceivable number. Same of bodies. Ergo, contingent beings, a pari, without necessary, ens ab alio without ens a se.

2. According to argument, a most perfect man ought to be the cause of all other men. Absurd.

3. God ought to be primus motor immobilis. He is not, because of intellect and will. Faculties are eternal, thoughts and wishes are in time. God passes from potency to act. Ergo.

4. Vital faculty moves itself. Ergo, vital faculty is God.

5. An eternal world would not be in potency, but would be actus purissimus. Ergo.

6. Primal elements of world get motion from their essence. Ergo.

Answers. 1. No parity, greater and greater numbers are always in same class. Same of bodies. Ens a se and ens ab alio are in different classes. Numbers will not give bodies.

2. Essence is the same in all men. No man is more perfect than another in essence. Essence of ens a se is different from essence of ens ab alio.

3. God moves Himself without dependence on another. The axiom, Omne motum ab alio movetur, is said of physical motion, not of metaphysical, like thought and wish. Created intellects and wills pass from potency to act, not God's. He is actus purissimus. His intellect and will are from eternity, like-

wise His thoughts and wishes. Effects ad extra are in time. Terms are in time. Aristotle, when he calls God primus motor immobilis, means that there is in God no physical motion, motion peculiar to inert bodies, which is always from and by another. Plato says that God moves others by moving Himself, and he is talking of uncreated metaphysical motion, thought and wish. Thought and wish in creatures are self-motion, work of intellect and will, though they must always be started by another. Intellect and will move themselves, but under motion from another. The will wishes under, not from and by, motion from the intellect; the intellect thinks under motion from the species. Thought and wish in God are self-motion without dependence on anything distinct from intellect and will. God's intellect is God's will, and both are God Himself.

4. Adequately and without dependence on God, as first cause, I deny; inadequately and with dependence, I grant. Vital faculty moves itself under motion from another. God moves Himself without such dependence.

5. It would be in potency after its creation, and therefore in itself in potency before creation.

6. Primal elements get not existence from their essence. Even in this hypothesis God is needed.

H. From Urraburu. Order in world. l. c, pp. 130–142.

1. Kant: a. From analogy between nature and art. Ergo, not certain.

b. Argument proves need of architect, not need of creator of matter.

c. Finite effect calls for no infinite cause.

2. God not omnipotent, because as such He ought to be able to use means out of proportion with effects. Finite causes can do as much as God.

3. God would have to sanction everything done in the world, like capture of fly by spider.

4. Atoms could combine to form order in the world. Organism and wonders it can perform. Type in an urn after a sufficient number of pourings would assume the form of Virgil's Æneid.

5. No order in the world:

a. No finality; some creatures have no purpose, rudimentary organs, parasites, bacilli, pain.

b. We ought to know whole world to be able to decide finality.

c. World a machine. We ought to know end of whole world, and how each part conspires to that end.

d. Like shooting a million guns to kill a hare; seeds lost; a few saved by chance to perpetuate species; geniuses lost by poverty, carelessness of parents, laziness and such.

Everything from chance, no finality.

Answers. a. Argument not from analogy, but from metaphysical principle, order is the work of intelligence. Order in nature calls for mind as well as order in art. Analogy used to illustrate, insisted upon, because it serves to disprove atheism. Relative notion of God's intelligence enough; absolute, not needed. The world is not so perfect, but that it could be more perfect. But everything in the world has some point of perfection. Imperfections are relative, and in harmony with perfection as a whole.

b. This architect, being ens a se, must likewise be the creator of matter. Besides, we use the argument to prove God a reality, not to prove Him the creator of matter.

c. Finite effect cannot always be produced by finite cause. Examples are creation of world, knowledge of future free contingents. Enough, immediately and proximately, I grant; remotely and mediately, I deny. A second finite cause could produce the world, but dependent on a first infinite cause. This finite effect ultimately calls for an unproduced, and therefore infinite cause.

2. Omnipotence can use means out of proportion, means intrinsically repugnant, I deny; intrinsically possible and out of proportion, I again distinguish, with ordinary power, I deny; with absolute power, I grant. God always employs His ordinary power. Absolute power means omnipotence without regard to other attributes; ordinary power means omnipotence viewed in connection with other attributes like wisdom, justice and the rest.

3. God would have to sanction, with His approval, I deny; with His permission, I grant.

4. Atoms could form order under direction of first cause; not otherwise. Organisms get their power from first cause. The forces of matter directed by an intelligence can accomplish wonders; not otherwise. We are not ignorant of what the forces

of matter can do when left to themselves, and when guided by God or man. The example of Virgil's Æneid and type is little worth.

a. The type are made by intelligent beings.

b. They are placed in an urn, poured through a hole, and set on proper ends; intelligence.

c. They occupy a finite space, stand in forms; not verified in atoms.

The order apparent in brute work comes from God. The laws supposed by Evolutionists to guide matter in its operations are meaningless, unless there exists a Legislator.

5. a. Some creatures have no purpose known to us, I grant; known to God, I deny. Many ends are assignable to rudimentary organs, bacilli, parasites, pain.

b, c. It is not necessary to know all the order in the world. We know enough to establish God.

d. Not like hunter and hare in case. God shoots where hare is, the million guns shoot a million hares. Not every seed is meant by God to grow to a plant. Some are meant to supply food to the birds, and these in turn preserve such seed as become plants. Geniuses are to be evolved with dependence on men's free will. Not all are intended by God to fully develop.

I. From Urraburu. Common consent. l. c, pp. 158–164.

1. Atheists numerous.

2. Other universal opinions proved false. Examples are, motion of sun, no antipodes.

3. Different opinions about God rob consent of universality.

4. Polytheism can be proved from common consent. Ergo.

Answers. 1. Practical atheists are numerous, I grant; theoretical, I deny. Atheists with the Greeks were men who denied the gods of the state; and they were better theists than their neighbors, e. g. Socrates. The Hebrews are called atheists by Pliny. The atheists of to-day rest on fool reasons. They deny a personal God, not a first cause. There never was a nation of pantheists or atheists.

Barbarians are poor examples to cite in favor of any system, passion kills moral instincts. Buddhist philosophers are atheists, not the common people. 500 millions of people, few philosophers.

2. Scientific, not ethical. See page 215.

3. Different opinions, about God's existence, I deny; about God's qualities, I grant.

4. Polytheism never universal, Hebrews always monotheists; philosophers wise to absurdity. Jupiter alone God; not lasting, because dead; against reason.

J. From Urraburu. Moral order, conscience. l. c, pp. 166–171.

1. Remorse disappears with crime. Ergo, no criterion.

2. Believers are sinners as well as atheists.

3. Other motives able to keep men virtuous, honor, esteem, self-respect.

Answers. 1. Remorse disappears, I deny; weakens, I grant.

2. Believers are sinners, because they are free. Motives for sin fewer and weaker in believers.

3. Other motives, universal and sufficient, I deny; particular and indifferent, I grant.

K. From Urraburu. General. l. c, pp. 173–181.

1. Infinite good ought to exclude evil.

Answer. From Himself, I grant; from others, I again distinguish; if necessary agent, I grant; if free agent, I deny.

2. The good are afflicted, the wicked prosper.

Answer. Affliction meant for higher good, I grant; affliction not meant for higher good, I deny. Uses of adversity.

3. Energy in world, enough to explain things.

Answer. Placed in it by first cause, I grant; had of itself, I deny.

4. Qualities of God not proved.

Answer. Existence not proved, I deny; qualities, I grant. An sit and quid sit.

5. Spencer:

a. Infinite duration inconceivable.

b. God is not finite beings. Ergo, not all being, not infinite.

c. Absolute has relations, mind, will, creation.

d. Has consciousness, if free; and that says relations.

e. God can do all things and can do no evil. He punishes and pardons. He can foresee and prevent evil, and yet permits it.

Answers. a. Simple infinite duration can be conceived somehow, not in itself; successive cannot. Eternity means no beginning, no end, no succession.

b. God contains all finites virtually and eminently. To be finites formally would be an imperfection.

c. No real relation in God, only logical, which adds nothing real to God, mere external denomination.

d. No real relation.

e. One act, different terms; moral evil as such needs no cause, it is nothing positive. He permits and does physical evil for good reasons. He permits moral evil without doing it; men are free.

Other seemingly contradictory qualities urged by Agnostics: He is everywhere and nowhere; immovable and works ad extra. He is good without quality; large without quantity; whole, without parts; free and unchangeable.

6. Kant.

We prove necessary being infinite, and then infinite being necessary, or necessarily existing. Ergo, our argument is a priori.

Answer. We prove a posteriori existence of necessary being, and then in turn this being is infinite because necessary. And all the while God is real, not notional, as with St. Anselm. Our argument is not from an idea, but from the real existence of things in the universe. Once God's existence is proved real, His other attributes can be demonstrated from ideas. Our argument would be a priori, if it ran this way: The necessary exists. Ergo, the contingent exists.

7. God is imaginary, no real being.

Answer. We know God by analogical concepts, belonging to Him alone, as to a most real being. God is pictured as a man only because of our weakness and limitations. Our concept of God is objective, inasmuch as it follows our concept of physical realities. It is not logical like St. Anselm's. All the analogy is between God's attributes and man's, not between the existence of a necessary being and that of contingents. Relation of dependence between God and creatures is real on the part of creatures; and in this thesis we want to prove the existence of God, not His perfections. There is a distinction of reason, on our part, between God's essence and His existence, and therefore we can reach one without reaching the other.

L. From Boedder, pp. 149–233. *Traditionalism:*

1. Faith and science have different objects. Existence of God, a dogma of faith. Ergo, above reason.

Answer. Motive makes difference, science based on reason; faith, on the authority of God's word. Some dogmas above reason, others not. God's existence, object of science as well as of faith. God reveals truths within reach of reason, to lessen difficulty. Men incapable and lazy. Knowledge would come late in life. There would be more room for error.

2. Impossible to pass from finite to infinite. Ergo, tradition needed.

Answer. Impossible at one bound, not by successive steps.

M. First Cause — Kant, Spencer, Mill. Boedder, Nat. Theol., pp. 152–165.

Kant: 1. Ontological proof unsound.

Answer. We agree.

2. Uncertain about principle of causality.

Answer. That is scepticism.

3. Must fall back on ontological.

Answer. We argue a posteriori; from contingent to necessary, and then to infinite.

4. Argument from design fails. Architect needed, not creator, unless recourse is had to ontological proof.

Answer. We prove creator a posteriori.

5. Mere intelligent mind enough.

Answer. Not enough; must be outside of order and creatures.

Spencer: 1. Self existent is inconceivable. Ergo, atheism, pantheism and theism are wrong; agnosticism right. Self existent, without beginning, impossible to conceive, because of infinite past time.

Answer. Impossible to materialists, who recognize only organic or sensible knowledge. God's duration is not time, but eternity; and in eternity there is no succession; everything is at once.

Mill: 1. Our argument, because world is changeable, it needs a cause. Add, and this cause is without a cause, and you have the truth. Elements of world are essentially unchangeable. Ergo, no need of cause.

Answer. Essentially unchangeable elements would be incapable of changed combinations, and these combinations would have to be effected by another.

2. Causes within our experience had their cause. Ergo, no such thing as cause without a cause.

Answer. They have their causes, because they are creatures and contingent. It is not of the essence of causation to have a cause, but an accident or circumstance due to contingency.

3. Conscious production requires a mind, not unconscious production, and world's production may be of latter kind. Besides, effect can be superior to cause, as in tree and seed.

Answer. Unconscious production would not explain conscious creatures. Effect cannot surpass cause; life and organism explain seeming departure from rule. Tree not superior to its complete cause.

N. Physical order or design. Mill, Lange, Mallock. Boedder, pp. 165–182.

Mill: 1. Mechanism of eye explained by survival of fittest, by chance, exclusive of finality.

Answer. This is only pushing the difficulty back. Self-constructing machine calls for even higher intelligence. Same as old theory, fortuitous concourse of atoms, and this calls for intelligence.

2. Paley's watch gets motion from without. Organisms are different, and get motion from within.

Answer. Same as the old theory, anima mundi, and this calls for an outside cause, self-existent. Monism and pantheism are wrong. Dualism is right, God and the world.

3. Omnipotence needs no design. It can use any means.

Answer. It cannot use intrinsically impossible means. By absolute power it can use any means, not by ordinary power, and it can freely use either.

Lange: 1. Clumsy providence, great waste of organisms.

Answer. Bread and eggs no waste when meal for the philosophers, and yet seeds are destroyed in their making. A best world is impossible, except in relative sense. God's absolutely last purpose is His own extrinsic glory. His relatively last purpose is the happiness of mankind. He chooses and uses best means for this twofold purpose.

Mallock: 1. God misses bull's-eye oftener than He hits it.

Answer. It all depends on what the bull's-eye is. If it is the maturity of all seeds, yes; if it is His glory, no.

O. In general, Darwin. Boedder, pp. 182–200.

According to his son Francis, Darwin never denied the existence of God. He first lost faith in the gospels, then faith in God. He was a non-aggressive agnostic. He has three objections to argument from design:

1. There is no more design in organisms than in course the wind blows. All adaptation in nature cannot be referred to creative design. Instances, rocks from precipice to form house, change of rock-pigeons into fantails, innocent man struck by lightning, swallow devouring gnat.

Answer. Every effect in creation was foreseen by one act of the mind, and at the same time ordained.

2. Rudimentary organs serve no purpose.

Answer. Man need not know purpose; angels perhaps know. Clown visiting artist's workshop and amazed at utensils. St. Augustine has fine passage on this subject. A surprised fly on the top of Liberty Statue. Many assignable purposes, balance of organism, excretions removing material from blood.

3. Suffering in sentient beings, without purpose. Men and animals. Bacilli in human organism, cat teasing mouse.

Answer. Not for suffering's sake; God is not cruel or wanton. Some higher purpose, patience, precautions for health. Natural Selection regulates things for Darwin, but Natural Selection calls for intelligence in Creator.

4. Different opinions about God.

Answer. About qualities, I grant; about existence, I deny.

5. Origin of things an insoluble mystery. Ergo agnostic.

Answer. He grants premisses and connection, but refuses conclusion. That is skepticism.

6. Mind sprung from amoeba cannot solve problem.

Answer. This is false humility. The mind is spiritual, the work of creation, and sprung from no amoeba. Darwin finishes thus: "I have had no practice in abstract reasoning, and I may be all astray."

P. Pantheism — Spinoza, Fichte, Hegel. Boedder, pp. 200–209.

1. Spinoza. Whole system based on definition of substance.

"That which is in itself, and is conceived by itself alone, that is to say, that of which the concept can be formed without involving any other concept."

Answer. Definition is ambiguous. It can mean a complete individual physical being, as distinguished from its properties and accidents, and this is correct; or self-existent being, independent of every other being as subject of inhesion or producing cause, and this is pantheistic and wrong. Taken the second way, there is only one substance, God; taken the first way, there are many substances.

2. Fichte: The Ego is all reality or God. Knowledge of existences separated from the Ego impossible. This feature of theory was suggested by Kant's doctrine about the speculative reason's inability to have certainty regarding the objectivity of things. The most expeditious way to solve the difficulty was to remove the object altogether, and make the world one infinite subject, God. God, therefore, is all, and we are but modes and accidents of God. The most expeditious way to cure pain, is to kill the patient. Fichte could find no bridge to carry him from real subject to real object. If he sat down and thought hard of the reality of his opponents, the process might prove a help.

3. Hegel took the other alternative and did away with the subject. With him God and Idea are one. This is to say that Being and Idea are one. The statement is true of God alone, not of men. In God, because of His simple essence, being and idea are one. Everything in God is one, His divine essence. With Hegel the universal alone is real, the singular is unreal; and this theory dates back to Plato. He confounds things as they are in themselves with things as they exist in our minds. Of course the concept of being in general embraces all, God and creatures. But no concrete reality corresponds to such concept. It is a logical being, with mere foundation in fact. In Hegel's theory all men would be one man, and a single death would be the race's destruction.

N.B. Monists are atheists, because their god is no God at all.

Q. Aristotle and necessity of eternal motion, or an eternal world. Boedder, pp. 209–214.

Aristotle admitted God, but had no idea of creation or production from nothing. Hence his mistake. He has three arguments to prove the world eternal:

1. A thing to be changed must exist, and a thing to exist must be changed. Ergo, eternal change.

Answer. World comes of creation, production from nothing, and this entails no real change.

2. Time means motion, and time had no beginning. Ergo, motion is eternal.

Answer. Aristotle mixes time with duration. There are two kinds of duration, time and eternity. Time means succession and has beginning. Eternity means no succession, and has no beginning. Aristotle urges and says, before the first moment of time there was no time. But the word before means time before the first moment. Ergo, the very expression means that time had no beginning.

Answer. The word before is said of imaginary time, it is a help to language; or it may refer to eternal duration preceding time. Kant uses same argument to prove the world eternal. Empty time is impossible; and, unless the world exists from eternity, there would be empty time preceding its creation.

Answer. Empty time is impossible, it is no time. Real time began with the created world. Eternity alone existed before that.

3. Motion is from God. God is unchangeable. Ergo motion is eternal.

Answer. God is free. His creative act is eternal, its effect appeared in course of time. Like king's decrees. They are made to-day, go into effect next year. Cousin urges a similar difficulty; God had to create from eternity or not at all. Ergo, world eternal.

Answer. He chose freely to create from eternity and have effects appear in time. God is essentially a cause, only inasmuch as He can cause, not inasmuch as He actually causes. He is a cause by extrinsic denomination when His effects appear. King and law, above.

R. Dean Mansel — Limits of Religious Thought. Eight lectures at Oxford. Boedder, pp. 214–232.

His conclusion, difficulties are insuperable, but only subjective, not objective. Faith in Christ is enough. Spencer calls this eternal war between our mental faculties and moral obligations, the radical vice of religion. Here are Mansel's insuperable difficulties:

1. The absolute and infinite being must contain all finite perfections and imperfections, all evil possible and actual.

Answer. Created perfections are in God not formally, but eminently, stripped of their imperfection. Privation, like evil, is not in God at all. Beauty is not lessened by its representation in wood, metal, stone; God is not lessened by creatures, imperfect representations of Him.

2. The absolute being cannot be a cause, which says relation to an effect. It cannot be infinite because of the added perfection accruing from new relation.

Answer. A free cause like God says no real relation. Effects work no change in God. All the change is extrinsic to God. He is cause from eternity, His effects are in time. God is His thought, not merely the cause of His thought. There are no accidents in God, nothing but substance.

3. Consciousness destroys the absolute. It is relative, saying subject and object.

Answer. That is hardly true of our own consciousness, much less of God's. In God's knowledge subject and object are not distinct. Even in our own case, consciousness can have self for object. Subject and object are necessarily distinct only in sensible knowledge, not in intellectual knowledge.

4. God's attributes are opposed to His simplicity.

Answer. His essence, in virtue of its self-existence, contains without division and composition, equivalently and supereminently all conceivable perfections.

5. He is omnipotent, and yet unable to do evil.

Answer. Evil as such is a privation, and no reality. God cannot start to do something and do nothing. He is the cause per accidens of evil, inasmuch as He is the cause per se of whatever physical reality attaches to moral evil.

6. God's wisdom and freedom are irreconcilable.

Answer. His decrees are from eternity, and as free as they are eternal. There is a difference between necessarily or infallibly knowing and knowing with necessity.

7. God cannot be a personal being, because personality is a limitation and a relation.

Answer. Personality is subsistence of an intelligent nature.

Subsistence means the existence of a natural whole, as distinguished from the existence of the component parts of a natural whole. Arm and the body are examples of non-subsistent beings. The soul enjoys incomplete subsistence. The whole man is a subsistence. Our notion of personality involves no idea of relation or limitation. Personality is not consciousness, though it implies consciousness. Besides, consciousness does not necessarily imply difference between subject and object. In psychological reflection subject and object are same.

S. Ingersoll, the American Agnostic.

Agnosticism in this country had an able defender in the person of Col. Robert G. Ingersoll, who two or three decades ago traveled from city to city, delivering lectures with the avowed purpose of shaking belief in the existence of God. He acquainted the world with no new information, serving up only the age-old difficulties answered time and time again. But he was a speaker of remarkable skill, able to garnish his lies with all the graces of eloquence; and religious error, never without its charms for the wicked, borrowed new attractiveness from its advocate's smooth diction, splendid imagery and rhetorical cunning. At the height of his success he ventured an article in the *North American Review* of December, 1889. It was entitled, "Why Am I an Agnostic?" and can be considered a fair specimen of his methods. We purpose a running commentary on the article, quoting him verbatim, and answering as circumstances require.

"The cruelties of a supposed Deity"— Can we account for the cruelty of the judge, who condemns the murderer to death by hanging; for the cruelty of the king, who throws into prison the wretch presumptuous enough to slap him in the face; the cruelty of the mother, who makes the flesh of her boy tingle for some misdeed or other; the cruelty of the farmer, who lines the road to his orchard with watchdogs; the cruelty of the husband, who looks on and sees his wife die; the cruelty of the railroad director, who sits in his office and reads of lives cut down by his locomotive; the cruelty of the surgeon, who lances the wound to effect a cure, who lops off an arm to keep the heart going? We can; and it is no harder to account for the cruelties of a supposed Deity.

"Why? why?? why???" Because He knew that sufferings

patiently endured in this life for His sweet sake, are pledges of eternal felicity, and that Heaven is the reward of only heroic sacrifices; and because He knew that timely chastening is most salutary medicine, and that briars scattered over some paths have led the travelers to pastures, from which roses would have diverted them; and because He knows that eternity will furnish ample time for the adjustment of differences, and the renewal of the quality of justice between destroyers of souls and of bodies and their victims; because of innumerable other reasons, which will occur in myriads to the mind of him, who sits down and consults his own heart and his own unbiassed judgment.

"The man who knows the limitations of the human mind," is no Agnostic, unless the word has changed its meaning. In sooth he is more gnostic or knowing than ordinary men, for whom the terms, Creator, Preserver, Providence, have not lost all meaning. The man who fails of ascertaining first or final causes, of comprehending the supernatural, or of conceiving of an infinite personality, so far from knowing the limitations of the human mind, is ignorant of its most elementary capabilities. The Agnostic can give no value to human testimony, as he can, if logical, give no value to the testimony of intrinsic evidence itself. As soon as he gives any value whatever to one or the other, no matter how insignificant, he ceases to be an Agnostic.

The conclusions to which a mind comes do not make or change the objective realities, which form the basis of the conclusion. The judgment a man forms can be tainted with prejudices and ignorance; but such judgments, as well as those free from all taint, in nowise create or modify the realities in themselves, which exist before and after all human judgments with precisely the same characteristics. God's existence does not depend on the fact that mankind universally recognizes it, but this recognition depends on the fact that God exists. God's existence is the foundation, its recognition is the house. This universal recognition would in other words be impossible, unless God in reality existed. However, under given conditions, such for instance as had place before the creation of man, God could have existed and been entirely independent of all outside recognition. Even now, though it is impossible for Him to exist without a definite relation to man's recognition, this relation is not that of dependence; it is not the relation between man's knowledge of God's existence and that existence itself.

It does occur to man that it is necessary to account for the existence of an infinite personality. In the opinion that there can be a designer, who was not designed, there is no absurdity whatever, if absurdity means a contradiction in terms. Man does not take it for granted that matter was created and that its Creator was not. He does not assume that a Creator existed from eternity without cause, and created what is called matter out of nothing. Man, or at least man as a thinking animal, assumes nothing, takes nothing for granted in this matter, but what Ingersoll himself and men with a grain of common sense assume and take for granted. In our thesis on Creation we proved to the satisfaction of the thoughtful that matter was created, and that its Creator was not. We proved too, and later on will more explicitly prove, that this Creator existed from eternity without cause, and that He created what is called matter out of nothing.

"How could such a being be intelligent?" He Himself, or His unfathomable essence contained subjects enough, and more than enough for thought. He could know Himself.

"How could such a being be powerful?" Suppose that a giant never struck a blow, never lifted a pin from the ground, never once exerted the mighty force within him on outside objects, would he therefore cease to be powerful? His essence was from the beginning, to suggest an idea and a multitude of ideas. What would be the consequence, if relations did not exist in the sense in which Ingersoll understands them? Ingersoll's mind is so that it can conceive aright of very little in matters of a higher order, and nature has its Maker to thank that in the present state of things matters depend very little on Ingersoll's understanding or misunderstanding them; and the sooner he wakes up to the full force of this little truth, the better.

After all the works written on the subject, only ignorant stupidity can confound creation with production without an efficient cause. Nobody can conceive of production destitute of both material and efficient cause; but production without a material cause only, is easy enough of conception. We postulate nothing in this matter. We have already proved the existence of God, and He can well be efficient cause of creation.

"We cannot conceive of the destruction of substance." His reason for this assertion is threadbare and worthless, upset time and time again. His persistence in clinging to all such worn out and long exploded notions, is only another proof that Ingersoll is either very ignorant as far as acquaintance with books is concerned, or very insincere. We cannot conceive of the destruction of substance, forsooth, because we never saw it destroyed, nor otherwise experienced a sensation tallying with its destruction. We could not, for precisely this same reason, conceive of substance as it exists. We see and touch only accidents. Yet Ingersoll must feel sure that he has come to the knowledge of or conceived substance, as it exists. He cannot, however, he complains, conceive of substance destroyed or annihilated. The indestructible certainly cannot be created; but outside of God everything is destructible, and therefore admits of creation.

"These questions should be answered by every one,"— not according to the structure of his mind, but according to the truth, according to the facts before him and visible to him.

"In the realm of thought majorities do not determine" for the wise; but they generally have the truth on their side. The flagman at a street-crossing does not determine the certain approach of the train; but it is highly dangerous to cross the tracks, when he signals you back. A gathering of clouds in the sky does not necessarily determine a downfall of rain; but when the clouds huddle together, it is imprudent to fare forth attended by a high silk hat, without a rainstick or some such protection.

"Each brain is a kingdom, each mind is a sovereign," but some brains are kingdoms blessed with anarchy, some minds are dethroned and puling sovereigns. The universality of a belief tends always to prove its truth. In certain circumstances, as in this question of God's existence, it absolutely proves its truth. Belief in God and belief in the devil were produced by neither ignorance, nor fear, nor selfishness. It is a fact of history that the most ignorant nations have been the least religious, and that the most fearless and most magnanimous peoples have been most steadfast and consistent in holding to the notion of a divinity. Old Greece and old Rome are certainly far from being open to the reproach of ignorance, cowardice and selfishness. But old Greece and old Rome were in the days of their primal vigor devout servants of the beings, unworthily of course regarded as gods, and their splendor faded away only when this piety lost its hold on the races, and they strove to forget God. Agnosticism is the fatal fruit of supine ignorance, of unmanly fear, and narrow selfishness.

The savage would not have invariably fallen prostrate, and called on the Unknown, unless the Unknown were made familiar to him by the promptings of nature, an unerring guide on occasions. This saving lesson of nature could not be lost, but through the long night of savagery it grew brighter and stronger, till to-day there is no conviction more widespread, more firmly rooted. The undimmed lustre and unflagging strength of this lesson are sufficiently accounted for by the fact that, though dispositions, and customs, and prejudices, and fears, and ignorance can all undergo changes, man's nature and its fundamental teachings are immutable, and undergo none of the vicissitudes of time. The savage's heart told him, more plainly than did his eyes reveal colors, that by his actions he could offend and displease this Unseen, but well understood Being. He took every care to propitiate God, and call down God's blessings. To-day our patriotic fellow-citizens rear enduring shafts to Lee, Grant, and hosts of others, who deserved well of their countrymen. Even so the savage, untutored save by nature, hewed out of stone or wood what he conceived to be an image of this unseen being, and set it up in some conspicuous place, where it would minister unto holy thoughts. If some minds among them were gross enough to confound the deity himself with these images, they belonged to idolaters, and fell victims to an ignorance almost as excusable as that which prompts the reiterated nonsense of misguided Protestants, touching Catholicity's reverence for images, relics and other objects of devotion.

Integrity of life, the savage felt, was a bond of union between Heaven and earth, and the virtuous or the priests had characteristics that endeared them to God, and served as claims for more intimate and friendly intercourse with the Sovereign Lord of all. Nowadays impulse teaches the most cultured and the most unsophisticated alike, that a favor is most readily obtained from the great through the intercession of a friend. The god represented rudely in stone did not answer prayers and protect his worshippers of old, precisely as our God to-day seems not to answer prayers, seems not to protect His worshipers. The prudent mother descends not to the silliness of complying with her hopeful's every request. No miracles were ever wrought by idols of stone, but miracles of the Christian era are plentiful part and parcel of the world's history. Some eyes are so that, let their owners try as they will, they can never see blue otherwise than as green; some heads are so that an abundant crop of hair nevermore will grace them. Asses, they say, can be made enjoy a meal of shavings by adjusting spectacles of the proper hue. Even so, Ingersoll's mind is so that it is forced to the conclusion that substance is eternal, that the universe was without beginning and will be without end, that the substance of things is from eternity to eternity. Constellations will of a surety fade, but not from the infinite spaces. The mind capable of grasping infinite spaces, should find little difficulty, it seems, conceiving an infinite being, or God. Yes, the questions of origin and destiny seem to be beyond the powers of the human mind, often alas! only because the owner of the mind is too lazy and too dishonest to tax the mind's powers to their fullest. I have fallen in with many a dull boy, far beyond the powers of whose mind the open mysteries of algebra seemed to be placed.

Love of parents and reverence for ancestors are motives not to be spurned in choice of an opinion or dogma. But they are not the real groundwork of a philosopher's certainty about the existence of God. The fact that they persuade or urge to the belief should not certainly be taken for proof conclusive that the belief itself is to be departed from. In fact the weight of authority is on its side, and the mother's creed should not be departed from until satisfactorily proved false. But Agnostics and Free-thinkers are assuming a large contract, when they undertake so to illumine mankind as to make evident the falseness and hollowness, they fancy existing in our certainty about the reality of God. I do not believe in the existence of God, because my mother and father believed in it before me; but because my own individual reason teaches me that such belief alone is proper and justified by events about and around me. There can be in religion many sorts of progress; but in point of dogma there can be no progress. The one religion in Adam's time and the time of the apostles, was dogmatically as perfect and as true as it is to-day, and as it will be at the end of all time. The one true religion can be more and more widely spread, and can claim, as the years roll on, more and more subjects; our knowledge of its dogmas can grow, can pass from implicit to explicit; but it was at the very origin of the race as pure and as perfect and as true as it will ever be. There may be progress in science, there may be progress in astronomy, geology, philosophy; but in religions progress as such is impossible.

The Christian is sure that Mahomet was an impostor, not simply because the people of Mecca declared him no prophet, but from signs also that to any student of history are far more unerring and unmistakable. Besides, the confession of the people of Mecca with regard to their leader and prophet, would have more weight in any court of justice than the denial of Christ's Messiahship by Israel, whose sceptre and sway Christ came to abolish.

The seven articles taught a man are not rolled up and crammed down his throat; but they are proposed to his consideration, and, unless reason has deserted him, he accepts them; and, without a sigh of hesitancy, though they entail upon him severe sacrifices and trials, he makes them the pole-star of his pilgrimage.

If the average man seems to Ingersoll to merely feel, it is because the truth of God's existence is so patent and so imbedded in our very nature, that reason accomplishes its work with all the ease and facility commonly observed in operations of the feelings.

There are unmistakable signs, by which the average man can settle for himself whether his God is the true God or not; whether the will of the true God is contained in his version of the Holy Scriptures or not; whether the only true Church is the one to which he belongs or not. There is no reason whatever why the average man should spend a single day in uncertainty on these several points. Notice what a falling away from his first position is evident in the stand here taken by the Agnostic. He started out hymning the impossibility we are under of ever arriving at certainty about God's existence. The question is now not about God's existence, which no longer seems to be disputed, but about the existence and choice of the true religion.

Multiplicity and variety of religion are no argument against the existence of God. On the contrary, they are a weighty element in the group of proofs adduced by the Theist against the Atheist. If the average Christian had been born in Turkey, he would not have been a Mohammedan, unless he willfully closed his eyes to the light, and locked his mind to the entrance of all thoughts in unison with reason. To escape the gross error of Mohammedanism, he would not have had to read controversial works, or peruse tracts spread broadcast. He would have had simply to sit down and seriously think the matter over. God has not left His creatures entirely to their veriest whims and vagaries in choice of religion. He has endowed reason with a sort of instinct, which, unless unduly tampered with, weakened or annihilated, is unexceptionably sure to lead man to the proper knowledge of his Creator, and of the service most pleasing to Him. If the average man believes implicitly in the religion of his country, because he knows nothing of any other, and has no desire to know, the fact is no necessity imposed upon him by nature; but is due to either his intellectual inactivity or incapability. The true religion courts examination, and her deepest and firmest believers are those who have investigated other creeds, and come away with an utter disgust for their hollowness and wretchedness.

It is unparliamentary and unkind to accuse anybody, no matter how misguided he may be, of deliberately telling a lie. But misunderstanding hardly does justice to the wide departure from the truth, evident in this assertion of Ingersoll, "Then these same Christians say to the inhabitants of a Christian country. You must not examine, you must not investigate; but, whether you examine or not, you must believe, or you will be eternally damned." Christians say, If the result of your examination is refusal to believe, and you live up to it, for the small pains taken to arrive at the truth, and for rejection of nature's most salutary and most unequivocal advice, you will be eternally damned. The right to examine involves the necessity to accept and reject, not to accept or reject. It involves the necessity to accept one and reject every other, if the examination is to bear any fruit at all. It by no means involves the necessity of rejecting all. Else it would be a futile endeavor and mere waste of time and pains. Christians have examined, and their search has not been without result; and they have freely given to the world the conclusions attained to. If Christians read the Koran or the religious writings of India and China, the opinions transmitted to them by their ancestors, if properly transmitted, would undergo no change whatever, except perhaps in intensity of disgust for the absurd systems there woven together. They have read Ingersoll without harm, and, as between Ingersoll and the Koran, the Koran has fewer points of danger.

Christians are more rational than to think only that the true religion, which succeeds in staying volcanoes, earthquakes, conflagrations. God has designs on the world, with which He cannot, as it were, Himself interfere, and the will of vicious man is a power against which no force can hold its own. The real God looks on and smiles complacently at the calamities that befall His servants, as they befell Job, because He knows what a weight of glory the sufferings of this present time lay up in Heaven, and because He knows full well that the pains of this life are as nothing, compared with the joys of the life to come. God does not necessarily favor His servants here below, because eternity is the more proper period to devote to such return of thanks. This is rather a place of probation, in which the patience, and love, and sacrifice of His friends are tested. For my part, I never feel easy when the current of life runs smooth. There is about quiet and absence of trouble an atmosphere of self-distrust, of dread that everything is not right, and that God has perhaps stricken my name from the roll of candidates for honor and conspicuous service. I almost fancy that God is engaged in advancing the wages of past efforts, and making payment in full now for what I would rather have accumulate interest here, and be handed over in bulk only in Heaven. The prosperity and ill-luck of nations alike depend upon the providence of God; but neither the one nor the other is an infallible sign of His pleasure or displeasure.

Infidels and Agnostics and heretics alone have neither praise nor blame for any man, no matter what his creed. In this point at least they are true to themselves, and to the tenets they adopt. But the Catholic who has truth, and who is conscious that he alone has truth, is and ever will be at war with the disseminators of false and pernicious doctrines. One error can live at peace with another error, it can crave for peace, when truth is nigh. But truth can never lie down with falsehood. Truth is essentially pugnacious, and cannot, without being recreant to itself, throw down its arms, till everything is drawn unto it, till its reign is absolutely universal. This fact will account for the intolerance of Catholicity and the dilly-dallyism of Protestantism. This fact is a sufficient reason for Rome's battle cry of, No Compromise, and the Pope's refusal to hear of half-measures towards reconciliation. Truth cannot be reconciled with falsehood. Sooner will the earth and the sky meet, sooner will the wolf make truce with the lamb. A creed can be good, no matter what manner of man professes it; but no thoroughly good man can long slave to an essentially bad creed. "The brain of man has been the trysting-place of contradictions," but truth is sure to always win before the day is over. "Next to finding truth, the greatest honor must be won in honest search"; but search without any result but falsehood is lamentable indeed, and deserving of honor hardly even when truth is impossible as a result; when such result is impossible, and known beforehand to be impossible, search is pitiable in the extreme, as waste of time and of otherwise profitable labor.

Ingersoll examined the religions of many countries and the creeds of many sects, in much the same way as the boy who once attempted to read without having mastered the alphabet. There are fundamental ideas, which must first be pondered and appreciated, before an examination can be productive of proper conclusions. One of these fundamental ideas, to which he is apparently an utter stranger, is the historical fact that this earth of ours is accursed of God, and that suffering and sorrow patiently borne are the coin, with which the Son of God Himself purchased His glorious Resurrection, with which, therefore, we His brothers by adoption are to purchase Heaven. Ingersoll's preference for Shakespeare is of about as much value with men of sober thought, when judgment is to be passed on the inspired writers, as the seven-year-old's preference for Mother Goose's Melodies, when judgment is to be passed on the masterpieces of Homer, Sophocles, Demosthenes, Virgil, Horace, and Cicero. In one case and the other ignorance accounts for the perverseness of taste. Humboldt, Darwin, Laplace, Huxley and Tyndall, though guilty of many gross inaccuracies, and eaten up with a false estimate of their abilities, knew more about science than any knowledge the writer of Genesis betrays. But Moses talked and wrote to be understood by the men of his time, he made no pretensions to scientific knowledge of a later date, and, in communicating his rude notions about geology and astronomy, is nowise worthy of blame. His business was to narrate the conduct of God with His people, and, in knowledge bearing immediately on his subject, he was incalculably far in advance of the modern thinkers, who out of inane levity laugh at him. What Moses intended to say was true. In matters of science he intended to say what appeared to the senses, and not what was scientifically accurate. We ourselves say that the sun rises and sets.

"We believe in the accumulation of intellectual wealth," not in the stowing away of intellectual garbage and trash. We believe in the intellectual wealth, which has the true ring of genuine gold, which has truth stamped all over it, which frees men from fear, and makes its owners light and buoyant with the spirit of the liberty of the children of God, and with that exuberance of feeling possible to only a deep, and solid, and eternal love of God. Let us by all means acknowledge our ignorance, when the subject is beyond our ken or the sphere of our activity; let us reverently leave to God's time the depths of mysteries, which elude our weak and limited reason. But let us be men enough, when knowledge entails pain and sacrifice, that can be shirked by a profession of ignorance; let us then, I say, be men enough to rise up and say, We do know.

THESIS II

God is infinite, altogether simple, and essentially one.
Boedder, pp. 85–109; *Jouin*, pp. 228–238.

QUESTION

In our first thesis we proved the existence of God. Unlike St. Anselm, we kept always in the order of objective reality. We did not pass from an abstract notion to the concrete existence of a being represented by that notion. On the contrary, we began with the concrete realities about and around us, contingent beings in the universe, and deduced from these concrete contingents the concrete existence of a concrete cause, producing them, Himself not produced. God is, therefore, as real, live and physical a being as His effects. He is no mere notional or logical reality, or abstraction existent in the mind alone, with no claim to a place in the objective order of things. He is the First Cause, set at the head of the series, terminating at this end in an effect. The notion effect touches Him not. He is a producer merely, the cause of everything, with nobody and nothing outside for His own cause. He is His own full explanation, deriving neither His being nor His attributes from aught else. He is the one being a se in the universe. Everything else is a being ab alio. *These expressions a se and ab alio, interpreted, mean that, whereas God is the absolutely necessary being, everything else is contingent. As the absolutely necessary being, actual existence attaches to His person in much the same way as roundness to the circle, rationality to the man. Actual existence is, therefore, of His very essence, it is as impossible to think God non-existent as it is to think a square circle. It is quite possible to think everything else non-existent, because actual existence is a favor conferred on everything else by the single necessary being, God.*

We come now to the attributes of God. And here we must remember that we are talking after the manner of men. Attributes are accidents, and in strict language God is without accidents. Accidents connote imperfection, and are wholly incompatible with necessary being. And yet the imperfect nature of our knowledge constrains us to hold speech of God's attributes, much as we talk of His eyes, hands and ears. God has no eyes, hands or ears; but He possesses within Himself whatever perfection these several organs secure to their owners, without the limitations attendant on sense-perception. In the same way, God has no attributes, and yet we ascribe to Him whatever perfection attaches to simplicity, unity, immutability, eternity, immensity, wisdom, justice, pity and other qualities. The necessary being is His attributes. Hence in exact language God is wisdom, is justice, and mercy, and pity. His essence is His all, and everything in God is one. Attributes overlap each other in God. Justice and mercy are one and the same thing in God, His undivided and indivisible essence, though we conceive and think them as distinct and separate realities. One single cause can be the root-principle of many different effects, and God's essence can display itself now as wisdom, now as justice, now as mercy, without undergoing any intrinsic change whatever. Among these so-called attributes of God we reckon some fundamental, others accessory. Their respective importance is wholly responsible for this division. The fundamentals in our eyes serve as basis for the others, and the three established in our present thesis are accounted such. To prove whatever other attributes of God, we regularly appeal to His infinity, simplicity and oneness; and these in turn are rooted in His aseity or self-origination.

TERMS

God, the supreme being established in our first thesis; the being a se, with self for single origin; first cause of everything; creator of Heaven and earth; infinitely wise and holy, and just; the artificer of creation; the rewarder of the just, and avenger of the wicked; man's last end; the universally acknowledged Lord and Master of created and contingent being. Infinite wisdom, holiness and justice flow as corollaries from our first thesis. Here we intend to prove God infinite in every respect, and we take for granted only what we already proved.

Infinite — This word can prove misleading, because of the double meaning it involves in Latin, if not in English. In Latin it can mean unfinished, incomplete, a thing still in potency to some finish or perfection; and this is what we call infinite in privative sense. It denotes a being not yet in possession of some due or needed perfection. It must be plain that infinite is not asserted of God in this first sense. Infinity of the kind is imperfection, and imperfection has no part in God. Infinite can likewise mean a thing that has no end or limit; a thing, from which no perfection is absent; a thing so perfect that nothing greater can be conceived or thought; and this is what we call infinite in a negative sense, or in positivo-negative sense. God is infinite after this second manner. His perfections are without bound and limit. He is so great that nothing greater can be conceived or thought.

All-perfect and infinite are very much alike. *All-perfect,* when restricted to actually existent perfections, falls short of the infinite; when made to embrace as well all possible perfections, it coincides with the infinite. *Infinite* is the better term, because it explicitly removes all limits, and this the term, all-perfect, fails to do. Infinite is *part negative, part positive.* It is the explicit denial of all limits, all imperfections, and the implicit affirmation of all actual and possible, or real and thinkable perfections. The perfections within our acquaintance are of many different kinds. Of these some are *simple* in the sense of unmixed, and embody in their concept no suspicion of imperfection; others are *mixed,* and involve in their very essence a touch of imperfection. Fair examples of the two are wisdom and science, or knowledge gotten by intuition and knowledge gotten by the roundabout and laborious process of reasoning. In common with all perfections these two exist in God. Science is as much His possession as wisdom. And yet science is an imperfect perfection; and, to do God no offense, we must maintain that science exists in Him quite otherwise than as wisdom exists in Him. Other examples of mixed perfections are quantity and courage. Quantity is essentially finite and connotes parts; courage postulates an element of danger for its owner.

Simple perfections are predicated of God one way; mixed perfections, another. We distinguish three possible ways, formally, eminently, virtually. A perfection is *formally* resident in a being, if it belongs to the being in the full and complete sense of its definition or essence. Whiteness is thus a perfection of a white wall. A perfection is *eminently* resident in a being, when present, not in the complete and full sense of its definition or essence, but by way of inclusion in some equivalent perfection of a higher order. Sense is thus contained in intellect; and angelic knowledge is not formally, but eminently sense-knowledge. To contain a mixed perfection eminently, is more in God than to contain it formally, because it is to contain the mixed perfection in an infinite, not a finite way. God cannot formally contain a mixed perfection, He cannot eminently contain a simple perfection. A perfection is *virtually* resident in a being, when present causally, inasmuch as the being is equal to the task of producing the perfection in question. All the perfections of an apple are thus contained in the parent tree, and every created perfection is thus contained in God. Mixed perfections have no formal existence in God, but only eminent or virtual. Created simple perfections exist formally in God as simple perfections, eminently and virtually as created; formally, because they exist in Him in the full and complete sense of their definition or essence, which by supposition involves no imperfection; virtually, because He produces them; eminently, because the same or an equivalent perfection in God embraces them in a surpassing way. Thus, wisdom in God, considered as His essence, or the resultant of His different perfections, is equivalent to perfections specifically infinite, and to an infinite number of perfections in each species; and this is the same as saying that wisdom in God is in reality every other conceivable perfection, infinite in point of number and in point of intensity. This is not true of created wisdom, or wisdom in man.

In the ontological order, the objective order, the order of things as they are, all perfections are in God first, principally, properly, and in an infinite manner; and they descend from Him to creatures by the method of participation, secondarily, metaphorically, by grace of a figure of speech. In the logical order, the subjective order, the order of thought, or of things as we think them, all this is reversed; and perfections as they exist in creatures come first to our knowledge, principally, properly, and in a finite way; and from them, as from effects, we rise to God their cause by affirmation and negation, ascribing to God what is perfect in them, removing from God what is imperfect in them, always with due regard to the excess or eminence the divine nature demands. These analogical or metaphorical notions help us to only an inadequate or incomplete knowledge of God's essence; and therefore our knowledge of God at its best is essence-knowledge in only a wider sense, inasmuch as we become aware of many attributes altogether absolute, intrinsic and essential to God.

In spite of its imperfection our knowledge of God is still true, even though our mode of knowing the infinite is different from the infinite's mode of being; because, while attributing these perfections to God, we strip them of the manner of existence peculiar to them in creatures. Thus, in a confused and obscure way we arrive at their mode of existence in God. On this account we know in a measure, and in a measure we know not what God is. We know not with adequate, complete and literal or proper knowledge; we know inadequately, incompletely, figuratively and by analogy. Life in man, because created, is metaphorical life when compared with life in God. Face, for instance, is said univocally of a human being, analogically of a portrait. What a beautiful face! is an exclamation applicable to persons and pictures. The face of the man is even less superior to the face in his portrait than whatever perfection in God is to the same perfection in His creatures. In the objective order things on earth are the analogues of God in Heaven; in the logical order God is the analogue of things on earth.

Hence we are far from classifying God with creatures, when we attribute to Him perfections of the same name as perfections His creatures enjoy. To classify two or more beings under the same species, the beings in question must be exactly alike under at least one aspect. Thus, we are justified in classifying men under one species, human, because individuals of the race, no matter how marked and numerous their differences, are exactly alike in their possession of reason. But God and creatures are exactly alike under no single aspect. Even in point of being, the most general notion within our acquaintance, they are different. God is being a se; creatures are beings ab alio. And this difference is brought out in the expression, God is wisdom, while man merely has wisdom. God is whatever is, man has things that are.

Locke thinks that our notion of infinite is gotten from the addition of finite to finite, but he is sadly mistaken. No such addition results in more than the finite. For this very reason an infinite number and an infinite space are equally absurd. Number is a collection of units, and no such collection is so great that the addition of another unit is inconceivable. If it ever became infinite, the removal of one unit would make it finite, and its infinity would be made up of the remaining finite number and the removed finite unit. Space is made by the dimensions between the surfaces of a body or bodies. These dimensions can never become so large as not to allow of a larger. If space were infinite, a part, say a cubic inch, would be contained in it an infinite number of times, and infinite number is absurd. No less so is infinite space. Number and space can readily be conceived as indefinite, so great that every assignable number and every assignable space are as nothing in comparison with them; but the indefinite, while unlimited in potency, is always limited or finite in fact.

Spinoza in his pantheistic way writes, God is not infinite. He is nothing but the energy of nature scattered in creatures. Hobbes teaches that the infinite means nothing more than our own want of power, as who should say, we know not whether God is without limit, and wherein His limitations consist. Some Traditionalists and Scholastics maintain that reason cannot prove God infinite; but in the main the position they take admits of explanation.

Altogether Simple — physically and metaphysically. Simplicity is the denial of composition. A compound being has parts, a simple being has none. These parts may be physical or metaphysical. *Physical parts* are realities quite independent of the mind, one different from the other, uniting to form a complete being called the whole. Instances are, body and soul in man; head, arms, trunk, limbs in body; mind and its thoughts in soul; hydrogen and oxygen in water; matter and form in body and water.

Metaphysical parts are concepts, dependent on the mind for their reality, with foundation in fact, one different from the other, uniting to form a complete being called the whole. Instances are, animality and rationality in man; essence and existence in soul.

Logical parts are concepts dependent on the mind for their reality, with no foundation in fact, different aspects of one and the same thing, uniting to form a complete being called the whole. Instances are, memory, mind and will in the soul; man and brute in animal. The soul is really distinct from its faculties with an inadequate distinction. This is far from making the faculties physical or metaphysical parts of the soul. They are different views of one and the same soul. The soul is each of its faculties and more besides. Wholes are physical, metaphysical or logical, according as the parts constituting them are physical, metaphysical or logical. A thing physically simple can be considered a metaphysical or logical compound. The soul is an example. A physically simple substance can be considered a physical compound in combination with its accidents. The soul admits of this composition, and it is far from affecting the soul's substantial simplicity. It has no existence, when the soul is considered apart from its accidents. Logical composition is compatible with physical and metaphysical simplicity. The thing in question is simple and without parts, logical composition results from viewing this simple being under different aspects. Man and brute are no physical or metaphysical parts of animal, because man is animal, and brute is animal. Animality and rationality are metaphysical parts of man, because man is neither animality nor rationality, but a combination of the two. They are not physical parts of man, because they are mere concepts, and never exist as such outside the mind. Memory, mind and will are neither physical nor metaphysical parts of the soul, because memory is the soul exercising a certain function, mind is the soul exercising another function, and will is the soul exercising a third function. Logical composition is altogether on the part of the thinker, and leaves the being's simplicity untouched. It can therefore be without harm recognized in God. Metaphysical composition offends against perfect simplicity, and must be excluded from God. It is a quality native to everything less than God, be it an angel or a soul. Everything less than God, every contingent being, is certainly made up of the metaphysical parts, essence and existence, one of which is not the other, the two uniting to constitute the being in question, whether angel or soul. Existence is of the essence of a necessary being, one is the other, and there can be no union or composition between one and the same thing. Physical composition is grosser than metaphysical, and with all the more reason has no place in God. *And now to resume. Physical composition goes into these classes, matter and form, integral parts, substance and accident, accident and accident, substance and substance. Metaphysical composition goes into essence and existence, genus and difference. Logical composition goes into faculties of soul, genus and species.*

Simplicity means more than unity. One means undivided, simple means indivisible. Unity excludes division, while it is compatible with composition. Man is an example. Simplicity excludes composition as well as division. The soul is an example. Viewed substantially the soul is physically simple. Viewed with its accidents it is a physical compound; but, as before remarked, this physical composition affects not the soul itself, but the soul in connection with its accidents, which may be present or absent without at all touching the soul's substance. There is no substantial composition in God, because a physical substantial whole is made up of, and dependent on, parts different from itself, and God can be dependent on nothing different from Himself. There is no accidental composition in God, because an accidental physical whole results in part from an accident, an accident is an added perfection or modification, and to God no perfection or modification can be added. There is no metaphysical composition in God, because its foundation is contingency, as is evident in essence and existence; and there is no contingency in God, the one necessary being. The metaphysical composition of genus and difference is absent from God, because He can be classed under no genus. He is perfectly similar to creatures in no respect, and genus is constituted by mutual and perfect similarity in some one respect. His justice, on account of its independence, is not perfectly similar to any created justice; and so of His very being and the rest. Animal in man is perfectly similar to animal in brute. Each divine attribute coincides with the divine substance; and each implies the rest, though it fails to express them. His attributes are absolutely inseparable in their application to objective reality. They are not metaphysically compounded, though metaphysically distinct. Compounded things must be distinct, but distinct things need not be compounded. The Three Divine Persons are really distinct, but they are not compounded into one Godhead, because they are really identical with the Godhead. The Three Persons are virtually distinct from the Godhead, but they are not virtually compounded into the Godhead, because the concept of each Divine Person involves the concept of the Godhead. Therefore, the mystery of the Trinity is not opposed to the physical or metaphysical simplicity of God.

Essentially one. Unity is the denial of division, and pertains to whatever being is in itself undivided. Units or ones are of as many different kinds as there are degrees of unity. The whole world in spite of its divisions can be called one in virtue of *logical unity, a figment of the mind with no foundation in fact.* The world is no more a real one than two separate loads of sand are one load. The connecting bond between its parts is wanting. Other units are real ones, in virtue of a *real unity, nowise dependent on the mind for its reality,* and this because they are actually undivided or indivisible or, though divided and divisible, held tight together by a connecting bond. An inch, a foot, a yard is called a *mathematical one or unit,* inasmuch as it is a basis or foundation for number or measure. Whatever can be called a being is *a transcendental one,* and this again goes into *individual and formal ones.* Peter is an *individual one,* inasmuch as he is not only undivided in himself, but also separated from everything else; and whatever exists in the world of realities is affected by this individual unity. *Formal unity belongs to essences,* making them ones, though they are compounded of different notes. Man in spite of rationality and animality is one after this fashion. *Simple beings vindicate to themselves the highest kind of created unity, called that of indivisibility. They are one in such a way that they are not only undivided but indivisible in themselves.* Physically considered, the soul rejoices in this supreme degree of unity. Metaphysically considered, it lacks the quality; for God alone is both metaphysically and physically simple. *Unity of composition* belongs to beings resulting from union of two or more principles intended by nature to form them. It renders a thing actually undivided without removing the possibility of division or separation; and man, as composed of body and soul, is such a unit. *The unity of art* belongs to works of skill or mechanism, which, having no very close physical connection between their parts, preserve throughout a sort of order and relation. A house, a coat, a chair are ones of this sort. *Unity of aggregation* is in force where things have among themselves no other connection than that of nearness of position, as may be seen in a heap of stones, a pile of sand, a mound of earth. After all, these different varieties of unity, because proper to creatures, have little or nothing to do with our thesis. We here affirm of God a oneness peculiar to Himself, and altogether outside the range of created nature. *Essential unity* can be predicated of no creature; *transcendental unity* in some or other degree is the highest of which it is capable. *Essential unity makes God one in such a manner that He is not only undivided and indivisible in Himself, but He is the only God, the only one of a kind, and a class by Himself.* God is no genus like animal. He is no species like man. There are many men, there is only one God. Again, the Latins had two words for our one: unus and unicus. God is more than unus or one; He is unicus, and we have no English equivalent, excepting perhaps unique. God the Father, God the Son, and God the Holy Ghost, are not like man A, man B, and man C. The Three Divine Persons have one and numerically the same individual essence; each of the three men has his own individual essence, and that of A belongs not to B or C. As St. Thomas puts it, the oneness and commonness of human nature are not an objective reality, but a subjective consideration; while the actuality signified by the divine essence is one and common as an objective reality. In separate human natures we have not real identity, but only similarity; and in the Three Divine Persons we have real identity of nature. We are not concerned with the Trinity, that question belongs to dogmatic theology. We have but to prove God one in essence.

It is hard to comprehend how men could make a mistake in this matter of God's oneness; but the fact stands, whatever its explanation; and while God in modern times is made one too few, in ancient times He was made several too many. Polytheism is opposed to Monotheism, and is of many different kinds. Some contend that it was the primitive form of religion, and that by successive stages of evolution it grew, as civilization advanced, to Monotheism. But these men have small or no regard for the Bible. Genesis is clear evidence that Adam and all his posterity down to the time of Abraham worshiped one God. Idolatry saw the beginning of polytheism, and the Chaldeans would seem to have been its first promoters. The stars and planets were divinities in their eyes. From them the mistake passed to the Egyptians and Phœnicians, the Greeks and the Romans. Men and the devil were responsible for idolatry. Men got themselves ready for the abomination in a threefold way: They allowed their esteem for relatives and heroes to usurp the place of God in their thoughts. They allowed their admiration for works of art to exceed due bounds. They dulled their minds by grosser crimes, and fell away from right knowledge of God, to fasten their hearts on creatures of surpassing beauty or power. The devil finished the work by making the idols his oracles and instruments in the performance of various prodigies. The sin assumed many different phases, astrolatry, demonolatry, anthropolatry and fetish-worship. With the Greeks no mountain, hill, river or spring, no tree or plant was without its divinity. Varro counts up 300 Jupiters and 6,000 lesser gods. The Hindoos had 33 million gods; some say 300 millions. The Japanese maintain pagodas where as many as 33,333 deities are worshiped, each with its own statue. The ancient Mexicans honored at least 2,000 gods. The Egyptians were famous for the queer beings they selected as objects of worship, onions, garlic, crocodiles, snakes, dogs, cats, hawks, crows, goats, scorpions, bats, mice, cows.

Lamennais, on this subject of idolatry, makes a statement not borne out by history, and Protestants employ it against Catholicity's veneration of images. He maintains that pagans gave their idols only relative worship, of the same nature as that accorded images by Catholics. But pagans themselves bear opposite witness, and they ought to know their own minds better than Lamennais. They testify that they regarded their idols gods, no mere representations, and paid them absolute worship. In cases where pagan worship was merely relative, the gods their idols represented were false gods, and all such worship was decidedly wrong. The old Greeks and Romans were examples. We Catholics render absolute worship to God alone in person, relative worship to His images. The homage we pay the Blessed Virgin Mary and the saints, as well personally as in their statues, is purely relative. In person they are mere creatures like ourselves, though closer friends to God; and their statues are possessed of no divinity, but persevere without change the material of which they are made. A piece of marble shaped to represent Washington gets more honor at the hands of Americans than the same piece of marble ready for work in the sculptor's studio; and Americans are no idolaters.

DIVISION

Three Parts, I, II, III
I, Infinite; II, Simple; III, One

PROOFS

I. God is infinite.

1°. The absolutely necessary being, God, cannot be finite. Ergo, God is infinite.

With regard to the Antecedent:

It would be absolutely necessary inasmuch as it is infinite, or inasmuch as it is finite in such or such a degree. But neither holds true. Not the first, because in that case all finites would be absolutely necessary, or incapable of change; and our experience is other. Not the second, because in that case, since no finite is so great that greater and greater cannot be conceived, there would be an endless multitude of absolutely necessary beings, whereas there can be but one absolutely necessary being. If there were two absolutely necessary beings, they would have different essences. If one had actual existence for essence, the other could have only possible existence for essence, and would be contingent. It would therefore be at the same time necessary and contingent, a square circle, a contradiction in terms.

N.B. When we say that a thing is whiteness itself, that a wicked deed is baseness itself, that an orator is eloquence itself, we are captive to the notion of infinite our argument contains. We merely contend that God is infinite, because He is being itself, ipsum esse. As whiteness, baseness and eloquence are forms conceived in the mind as bases of certain specific qualities or perfections, so being is the form conceived as basis of every quality or perfection conceivable. Being is basis of whatever perfection, because unless it is, it is nothing. Therefore, in ascribing being to God as His essence, we are ascribing to God every conceivable perfection in every conceivable degree, which is infinity.

2°. An actual being is infinite, when it suggests no sufficient reason for limit. But God, as unproduced, is such a being. Ergo, God is infinite.

With regard to the Minor:

In case of a produced being its efficient cause suggests limit. It is due to this particular cause and no other. The unproduced being is without efficient cause, and limit can accrue to it only in virtue of its essence. Its essence, however, can exclude no simple perfection and no mixed perfection, when rid of its imperfections. Essence excludes only what conflicts with essence, only what in combination with essence would provoke contradiction. But contradiction is out of the question, where, as in this case, everything is affirmation. On the one hand God is being itself, ipsum esse; on the other, simple perfection and mixed perfection, when rid of imperfections, are pure affirmations without a trace of negation. Contradiction is impossible without a negation or denial. A square circle is a square-not-square.

3°. God is the actual or possible maker of all else, actual and possible. But the maker of all else is infinite. Ergo, God is infinite.

With regard to the Minor:

The maker of a thing gives the thing its perfections. Nobody gives but what he first has. Ergo as maker of all else, actual and possible, God has all perfections, actual and possible, which is infinity.

4°. All conceivable perfections are either unproduced and necessary, or produced and contingent. But the absolutely necessary being ought to possess both kinds, and therefore be infinite. Necessary perfections partake of the necessary being's nature, and cannot exist apart from it. Contingent perfections exist only by favor of the necessary being's efficiency; and, since nobody gives but what he first has, this necessary being possesses all the actual and possible perfections resident in His effects, actual and possible. Possible perfections are producible, and get their producibility from God.

5°. Actual creative power is infinite. God is creator. Ergo, God is infinite.

With regard to the Major:

Actual creative power is infinite, because it produces something from nothing, and is independent of every outside agency.

PRINCIPLES

A: Infinity is perfection, perfection means finish, and is of two kinds, relative and absolute. Perfection makes a thing perfect, and a thing can be perfect in two ways, simply perfect and perfect after a manner, or perfect privatively and perfect negatively. *That is perfect after a manner, which has everything its nature demands for wholeness and completeness; and creatures as well as God are perfect in this sense. That is simply perfect, which has every perfection, every conceivable degree of being and reality, and every perfection is its due in such sense that no perfection at all can be absent from it either privatively or negatively.* When some perfection is absent from a thing, that thing is called imperfect. A perfection is privatively absent from a thing, when the thing's nature demands its presence or possession. A perfection is negatively absent from a thing, when the thing's nature makes no such demand, when the thing's nature is complete and whole without the absent perfection. Sight is privatively absent in a blind man; negatively absent in a stone. A blind man is privatively imperfect, a blind stone is negatively imperfect, and a negatively imperfect thing can be a privatively perfect thing. In the case of God, because all being or reality is His due, as the ens a se, the absolute, the necessary, to be negatively imperfect would amount to being privatively imperfect too. Sight can be absent from the stone without rendering it truly and really imperfect, nothing can be absent from God without rendering Him truly and really imperfect; and this presence of everything in God constitutes His infinity.

B: God is the greatest conceivable being. No greater, no better being than God can be conceived or thought, because His essence is being, He is being itself. In other words, He contains within Himself the plenitude or completeness of all being and the reality of every perfection.

C: God is first principle. But first principles are imperfect, because they unite to form something complete and perfect. Ergo, God is imperfect.

Answer: God is first principle in the sense of efficient cause, I grant; in the sense of formal or material cause, I deny.

D: That is perfect which is finished, completed, totally made. But the term "made" has no place in God. Ergo.

Answer: Taken radically or in root, perfect means made, I grant; taken in its true and universally received sense, I deny.

St. Gregory explains. As best we can, we proclaim in a stammering way the lofty attributes of God. Certainly, what is not made cannot in strict language be called completely or totally made, or perfect. But, because a thing in process of making passes from potency to act, we denominate perfect whatever actually exists, whether its mode of existence is perfect or imperfect.

E: Infinity involves a multitude of perfections, and therefore destroys simplicity. Ergo.

Answer: These perfections are many a parte rei, as a matter of fact, separate realities outside of the mind, I deny; many a parte mentis, as a matter of thought or notional, constituting one physically simple reality in God, I grant. St. Thomas explains. A king's power in much the same way contains all the scattered particles of authority resident in his officials.

F: God is all being, and this sounds like Pantheism.

Answer: God is all being in the sense that He is the formal being of everything else, in the sense that nothing has being but God, I deny; in the sense that no grade of perfection, no degree of being can possibly or actually exist without in some way belonging to God, I grant. This illustration may serve to elucidate things. The fact that some man is a substance, with a body, life, sense and intellect, is far from eliminating or annihilating other substances, bodies, life, senses, and intellects. In the same way the fact that God is all being, or possesses within Himself the plenitude of being, is far from denying the existence of other beings and other realities besides God and distinct from God. If God is creator, there must be other beings proceeding from His hands, and dependent on His might for existence.

G: To be is God's essence. But naked being says nothing of life, or knowledge, or freedom. Ergo, God is imperfect.

Answer: God's essence is being of itself subsistent, I grant; abstract being, which bases the actuality of whatever exists, I deny. The being we affirm of God is, like His wisdom, a concrete and subsistent reality. The being we affirm of creatures is an abstraction of the mind, with no concrete substantial reality in fact. Hence being embraces in God every possible and actual perfection. Our way of thinking makes these perfections different formalities from God's being, but in reality they are one and the same with His being.

H: The infinite cannot be a person, because a person is distinct from others, and distinction means limit. So the German Transcendentalists argue.

Answer: God is infinite and undetermined negatively, not privatively — Privatively means without actuality, unfinished, lacking some further perfection. Negatively means with actuality, and without limit; lacking no perfection, but distinct from everything else.

PROOFS

II. God is absolutely simple, (a) no physical composition in God; (b) no metaphysical composition in God.

(a) The physical parts in God would be beings a se or beings ab alio. Were they beings a se, each part would be infinite and God, without the others. Were they beings ab alio, a collection of contingent beings would constitute a necessary being, and this is absurd.

(b) Every metaphysical compound can be conceived as different from what it in reality is. But this is impossible in God, the necessary being. Ergo, God is metaphysically simple.

With regard to the Major:

Peter is a metaphysical compound inasmuch as he is made up of possible and actual existence. He can be stripped of actual existence, and conceived as a mere possible. Animality and rationality in the man admit of the same mental separation, and one can be conceived without the other.

With regard to the Minor:

Because God's essence is actual being, He can be conceived or thought only as He actually is, and to think Him actually non-existent, or to think Him in some different state or condition, involves intrinsic contradiction.

PRINCIPLES

A: One simple cause produces one simple effect. Ergo, God is not simple.

Answer: When the cause is a necessary agent, I grant; when it is free, I again distinguish, if it is one and simple in fact and in power, I grant; if it is one and simple in fact, manifold in power, I deny.

B: Compounds are better than simples. Ergo, God not simple.

Answer: In the world of bodies, I grant; in the world of spirits, I deny. Composition perfects bodies; simplicity perfects spirits, and God is a spirit.

C: If simple, God could be completely and entirely known, or comprehended. Ergo.

Answer: He could be known whole and wholly, I deny; He could be known whole, but not wholly, I grant. Because He cannot be known wholly, He cannot be comprehended. St. Thomas explains. The measure in which God can be known is infinite, man's mind is finite. Ergo, man cannot wholly know God. There are no parts in God. Ergo man must know Him whole, or not know Him at all. Comprehension is perfect knowledge, and knows its object in every conceivable detail.

D: Every compound can be reduced to its simples; and, to avoid infinite series, we must come at last to some absolutely simple thing. Ergo, God is not the only absolute simple.

Answer: Nothing outside of God escapes metaphysical composition.

E: God has many perfections. Ergo, God is not simple.

Answer: Many in themselves, I deny; many in our mind, I grant. God's essence is one, and equivalent to many.

F: In God there is something common and something proper, nature and personality. Ergo.

Answer: The common and proper are in fact one and the same thing, I grant; not one and the same thing, I deny.

G: To be one in one is more simple than to be one in several. God is one in several. Ergo.

Answer: If that one is itself in the several, and the several are constituted by personalities and relations, I deny; if that one is a distinct thing in the several, I grant. God is one and three; but the three are one in essence.

H: The Three Persons in God are three things, according to St. Augustine. But three things give composition. Ergo, God is not simple.

Answer: Three things have composition, when united among themselves, I grant; when not united, I deny. St. Thomas explains. The Three Persons involve no composition. The Three Persons, compared with God's essence, are one and the same with it; and therefore there is no composition, which demands union.

I: Equality and inequality are in God, as in Trinity and towards creatures. Likeness is in God, man being made to His image and likeness. But quantity is basis of equality and inequality, quality is basis of likeness. Ergo, accidents are in God. Ergo, God is not simple.

Answer: Accidents are in God as they are in creatures, I deny; virtually in God, God's substantial perfection is equivalent to the perfection contained in quantity, quality and other accidents, I grant.

J: Wisdom, justice and the like are accidents in man. Ergo, in God, and He is compound.

Answer: Accidents in man are not accidents in God, because nothing is predicated univocally of God and creatures.

K: God can be thought without goodness, wisdom and the like. Ergo, they are accidents.

Answer: God can be thought incompletely without them, I grant; completely, I deny.

L: God can be a species under substance, when substance is taken to mean a being in itself, without reference to the mode of its origin. One species would be a being in itself, whose essence is existence, God; the other species would be a being in itself, whose essence is not existence, creatures.

Answer: Taking substance in this precise sense, being in itself, whose essence is existence, could not be ranged under it as under a genus, just as an animal, that would be by its essence a rational animal, could not be ranged under animal, prescinding from rationality and irrationality. God is transcendental substance, not predicamental. He is substance and everything in transcendental sense, as creatures are beings. Everything is being, not everything is substance.

PROOFS

III. God is essentially one.

God is a being of such sort that no greater or more perfect can be conceived or thought.

But in the event of several gods, none would be such. Ergo, God is essentially one.

With regard to the Minor:

Each of these several gods would be equal. But he who has no equal is greater than he who has. Ergo, a greater can be conceived. If one of the several could hinder the others, the others would not be omnipotent. If one could not hinder the others, he would not be omnipotent.

PRINCIPLES

A: There are two kinds of unity, transcendental and mathematical. The first is constituted by absence of division; and God is more than undivided, He is because of His simplicity absolutely indivisible. Ergo, His transcendental unity is of the highest. He is besides mathematically one. He is the only one of a kind, possible as well as actual. And this is what we mean when we say that God is essentially one.

B: These several gods could agree to always do and wish the same thing. Ergo, no conflict.

Answer: If this agreement were necessary, they would not be free, and that would be an imperfection. If the agreement were free, their condition would be mutual dependence, differences and displeasure would be possible, and that would be imperfection.

C: The Three Persons are not three gods, because they have numerically one and the same nature. Though really distinct among themselves, each is identical with the one divine nature, each is infinite, each is in the others, each formally possesses all the perfections of the others, because God's essence is God's perfections, and each Person is identical with the one divine essence.

D: God, as the most perfect being, ought to be able to produce a being like Himself. Ergo, several gods.

Answer: The axiom is true of beings, whose nature can be multiplied in different individuals, I grant; of the being whose nature cannot be so multiplied, I deny.

E: God would not be omnipotent or supremely good. Ergo.

Answer: An essentially infinite being cannot be the effect of omnipotence, because a produced being of the kind is an intrinsic contradiction. Omnipotence need only be able to produce greater and greater effects, without ever exhausting its efficiency.

F: Solitude, or the state of being alone, is an evil. Ergo, several gods.

Answer: In a being sufficient unto itself, I deny; in a being not sufficient unto itself, I grant.

G: A nature, that exists in several really distinct persons, cannot be one. Ergo, God is not one.

Answer: In question of created beings, I grant; in question of God, I deny. Faith teaches the mystery.

H: The common consent of mankind favors polytheism as much as monotheism. Ergo.

Answer: Regarding Polytheism, the consent of mankind was never universal, enduring, reasonable or a matter of genuine tradition. It was not universal, because the Hebrews always worshiped one God, and wise men among the pagans, like poets and philosophers, acknowledged one supreme ruler, usually Jupiter. It was not enduring, because from creation to the deluge monotheism was universally recognized, and long after the deluge the same system prevailed. Since the dawn of the gospel, the better, if not the greater, part of mankind professed monotheism. It is unreasonable, because several gods are an open contradiction, and the gods of antiquity were characters of the lowest type, animals of the most repulsive nature, plants and even lifeless objects. The demons perpetrated seeming miracles and forged sham prophecies, to propagate polytheism.

I: A form can without contradiction be multiplied, when it is not its own individuation. But God's form, His essence, is His own individuation. St. Thomas explains. That in virtue of which a thing is this particular thing, cannot be communicated to others. That in virtue of which Socrates is a man, can be communicated to others; but that in virtue of which Socrates is this particular man, cannot be found outside of Socrates himself. If therefore in virtue of one and the same thing Socrates were a man and this particular man, several men would be just as impossible as several Socrates. And this is what happens in the case of God. God is His nature; Socrates is not his nature. In virtue of one and the same thing, His essence, God is God and this particular God. God therefore is one. S.T. 1.q.11 a 3.

J: Every created thing is one by its essence; but, since it always consists of potency and act, it involves at least metaphysical composition.

K: Oneness in created things involves denial of only physical, not metaphysical division; oneness in God implies denial of metaphysical division as well.

L: Finite perfection under the same genus can be manifold, not infinite perfection.

M: In question of finite natures, plurality removes no perfection; in question of an infinite nature plurality introduces imperfection.

THESIS III

God is unchangeable, as well physically as morally; He is besides eternal and immense.

Jouin, pp. 228–238; *Boedder*, pp. 233–256.

DIVISION

THREE PARTS, I, II, III

I, UNCHANGEABLE; II, ETERNAL; III, IMMENSE

TERMS

Unchangeable. Change is passage from one state or condition to another. Physical change affects the being's nature; moral change, its will. Intrinsic changes have place inside the changed being, and are absent from God; *extrinsic changes* affect outside beings, and are compatible with divinity.

PROOFS

I. (a), Physically; (b), Morally.

(a). *1°.* God is the being determined by sheer force of essence to actual existence; His existence is His essence. Everything in God is one. But determination to actual existence involves determination to an actual mode of existence. Ergo, God is determined to an actual mode of existence.

With regard to the Major. This actual mode is as much part of His essence as actual existence itself, and existence in this actual mode, because it belongs to God's essence, admits of neither removal nor change. Ergo, God is physically unchangeable.

With regard to the Minor. An actual existence cannot be without its own fixed mode, any more than actual motion can be without its own fixed direction and velocity.

2°. Physical change in God would be to worse, or better, or an equivalent. Change to worse, because an imperfection, is out of question in the infinite. Change to better is no less absurd in the infinite. Change to an equivalent presupposes the possibility of two infinites.

(b). Moral change is change of will. It means modification of plan, already conceived, or a halt in will-process, implying that now at last God begins to wish or not wish a thing.

1°. Such a change would arise from some physical change in the mind of God, or from want of knowledge, or from instability of purpose. But God is incapable of physical change; and, because infinite, He is a stranger to ignorance and inconstancy.

2°. Because His intellect and will are infinite, God as a matter of fact can by a single act of His will arrange the universe and its every minutest detail. Ergo, He must be supposed to have once for all made such disposal of everything by a single eternal wish.

With regard to the Consequent:

Apart from the reproach of inconstancy, no reason can be assigned for delay on God's part with regard to any single decree of His providence. He had to make no experiment, to become aware of His freedom. That would derogate from His knowledge; and prudence would preclude useless trial. Nor had God reason to fear that the result of an eternal decree, like a sick man's cure to be realized in the course of time, would fail His expectations. The omnipotence of His will centres in the circumstance that the external effect of His wish begins to exist, not at the precise moment when He wishes, but at whatever remote moment of time He chooses and decrees.

PRINCIPLES

A. When He works, God moves Himself with a species of motion improperly so called. He works without passing from potency to act. He is always in action, never in potency.

B. It is one thing to change one's mind, and quite another to wish a change in things. By one and the same act of the will a person can wish one thing and another to happen at different times.

C. Freedom implies in God as well as in creatures indifference with regard to the object; but this kind of indifference is extrinsic to the agent. Freedom in creatures further implies indifference to the act of choice itself, and this indeed is intrinsic to the agent, and involves real change. But the latter species of indifference is absent from God, because the act of His will is always from eternity.

D. To wish, viewed actively, touches the term or object of the wish; viewed passively, it touches the wish itself, inasmuch as it is an immanent act. To pass from one wish to another, viewing the wish actively, is no change; but to pass from one wish to another, viewing the wish passively, involves change. God is always in act, and a stranger to wishing, viewed passively.

E. God can wish and not wish with the one act, because all the difference is in the outside term, not in the act itself.

F. The use of freedom in itself implies no change; considered in its term or effect, it implies change in created agents on account of wishing viewed passively; and this view of wishing is not verified in God.

G. Love and hate in God are one and the same act in point of principle, different acts in point of term or object.

H. God passes from the condition of non-creator to that of creator by an act eternal in point of principle, temporal in point of term or object, not by an act temporal in point of principle.

I. In God there is in reality no time before, no time after, but only according to our way of thinking.

J. It is quite correct to say that God with a single act of the will wishes this, later wishes that to happen.

K. Freedom means power to change one's mind.

Answer. In creatures, I grant; in God, I deny. Freedom in creatures is weighted with imperfection, in God it is free from same.

L. Prayer changes God's mind.

Answer. Prayer leaves God's mind as it was from eternity. In the event that prayer was to be neglected, God's mind would have been other from eternity.

M. To pass from hate to love is change.

Answer. In beings capable of potency, I grant; incapable, I again distinguish: change on the part of God, intrinsic, I deny; change on the part of the term or object, extrinsic, I grant.

N. God assumes new denominations and these betoken change.

Answer. New relative denominations, I grant; absolute, I deny. A white wall, without any change on its part, becomes like another wall treated to a coat of white paint.

O. Incarnation involves change in God.

Answer. Change in humanity assumed, I grant; in God assuming humanity, I deny.

II. God is eternal.

TERMS

Eternal. Eternity formally taken is duration essentially without beginning, without end, and without succession. Duration is a thing's continuance in being, or the period a thing lasts. Time, the duration proper to creatures, has three opposite characteristics: it embraces a beginning, an end and succession. Causally, eternity tallies with the definition of Boethius, "Interminabilis vitae tota simul et perfecta possessio." The perfect possession of life without limit and all at once. No beginning, no end; no past, no future; indivisible now or present; one single fixed point, admitting of no division, vested with all the perfection of successive duration. Eternity is duration like time in every respect save succession and limit. When we talk of the past and future in God, we are consulting our own weak and imperfect power of thought and speech. Eternity must not be conceived as time infinite from front and back. That indivisible point, described as eternity, coexists with all real happenings in the course of time, and therefore admits of extrinsic division. Eternity is intrinsic to God, and therefore a necessary attribute; coexistence with things created is extrinsic to God, and necessary only in the hypothesis of creation, properly speaking no divine attribute.

PROOF

He is eternal, who goes on existing without beginning, without end, and without succession.

But God goes on existing without beginning, without end,

and without succession, because He is the absolutely necessary and infinite being, and because He is unchangeable.

Ergo, God is eternal.

PRINCIPLES

A. The eternity essences and possibles have is a gift they enjoy at God's hands, God's eternity is His own by favor of His essence. They are eternal by participation; He, without participation.

B. Inasmuch as eternity coexists with this precise moment, it does not coexist with any set moment of the past or a future year.

C. Eternity becomes no larger with time, just as the soul becomes no larger with the growing body. Neither soul nor eternity has large or small, because both are simple, indivisible and without quantity. A point on the bank of a stream with the water flowing past.

D. God created eternity in the wide sense, not in the strict sense; of others, not His own. God is eternity.

E. Boethius. Nunc stans makes eternity, not in reality, but after our way of thinking. God is eternity.

F. God is before and after eternity, in aeternum et ultra, Exod. 15.18, in wide sense, not in strict.

III. God is immense.

TERMS

Immense. Formally taken, immensity is infinite filling existence, or infinite spiritual occupancy, or infinite capacity to be spiritually present. Considered in cause or principle, it is the power of infinite presence. With regard to body space, it is an intrinsic and essential attribute of the divine nature, in virtue of which God is intimately and substantially present to every conceivable place and thing, possible as well as actual.

We distinguish three kinds of existence: *circumscriptive,* proper to bodies; *definitive,* proper to the soul and angels; and *filling or all pervading,* peculiar and proper to God. Their differences admit of easy understanding. Immensity is not precisely omnipresence. The whole difference between the two lies in the reality or absence of creatures. Immensity is the root of omnipresence, and independent of creatures; omnipresence presupposes their existence, and is therefore hypothetical, extrinsic to God, and an attribute only when confounded with God's immensity. To say nothing of the hypostatic union in Christ and the union of grace in the souls of the just, God is in creatures after a threefold manner:

He is in things by His essence or substance, inasmuch as He substantially exists wherever a creature exists or can exist, that is everywhere, even in imaginary space. This is the presence of which our thesis speaks, and it accrues to God from the fact that He is the actual or possible cause of all things actual and possible, and the impossibility of action from a distance renders it necessary. A body is after this manner in the space it fills, and the soul's presence in the body is of the same nature.

God is in things by His power, inasmuch as everything in nature is subject to His rule and authority, inasmuch as He keeps all in being and coöperates with all. In much the same way the king is in all his kingdom. *He is in all things by His presence,* inasmuch as all things come under His notice and knowledge. After this fashion a man can be said to be in a whole room, though he occupies only a definite portion of the same. By His essence-presence God pervades all things; by His power-presence He preserves all things; by His presential presence He comprehends all things. Every actual being, whether a spirit or a body, has two locations or wheres, one intrinsic the other extrinsic. A thing's intrinsic location is constituted by its substance, it is an absolute quality, and quite independent of surrounding objects. Extrinsic location is the spatial relation a thing bears with some neighboring object, affecting it, when a body, with contact of mass or quantity; and, when a spirit, with contact of influence. A body's extrinsic location is determined by the outer surface of some enclosing medium; its intrinsic location is determined by its own outer surface. The enclosing medium can be changed, removed, or destroyed without at all influencing the thing's intrinsic location. Adsence would be the right term for intrinsic location, as presence is for extrinsic. God's intrinsic location is His immensity. It is without bound or limit, permeating and pervading everything, as much an actuality in imaginary as in real space.

PROOFS

1°. Immensity is a simple perfection, infinite in the case of God, and actual. But no perfection of the kind can be absent from God. Ergo, God is immense.

With regard to the Major. It is simple because it involves no imperfection. Immensity is infinite definitive existence; and, in virtue of definitive existence, the soul after its own measure surpasses whatever material atom or body. Definitive existence, proper to the soul, is a closer approach to immensity than circumscriptive, the badge of bodies. It is infinite in the case of God, because infinite essence calls for infinity in every particular, even in the matter of coexistence with outside objects. God's coexistence is infinite in itself; finite by accident, because outside objects are finite. It is actual, because God is pure act, with no suspicion of potency, and whatever belongs to His intrinsic constitution is always from eternity to eternity.

2°. As a matter of fact, our world actually exists in, and is enclosed by, imaginary space. God ought to enjoy the same perfection. Imaginary space is not altogether nothing. It is emptiness stretching in every direction, without a body in sight, but fit always to be filled with bodies. There is nothing to prevent God from creating an angel, or a man, or anything else, in imaginary space; and, in the event of such a creation, to save Him from change, we must consider Him a reality in imaginary space, prior to the production of the angel or man. Real space is the world's intrinsic locus, imaginary space is its extrinsic locus. Both are equally God's intrinsic locus.

PRINCIPLES

A. Heaven is said to be God's special and proper abode only after a manner, and inasmuch as He there manifests Himself by way of reward to the elect.

B. God exists in foul places, without at all contracting harm. God is distinct from the places He occupies, and no physical union intervenes. The sun can serve for illustration.

C. God approaches us and withdraws from us only in a metaphorical and figurative sense.

D. In imaginary space nothing but God exists, with imaginary space for intrinsic locus; and nothing but God, far from being pure and simple nothing, is a mighty large something.

E. The terms here and where are applicable to not only actual but also possible bodies.

F. Chrysostom and Augustine say that God is nowhere, because He cannot exist in place. That kind of existence is characteristic of bodies.

Answer. They deny circumscriptive and definitive presence of God, not filling or pervading presence. In much the same way they contend that God does not exist in time, meaning that His existence is a stranger to succession, without at all questioning His coexistence with time.

G. God is indivisible, and cannot be in two places or times.

Answer. There are two kinds of indivisibles, one of quantity, the other outside of quantity. A point and a moment are instances of the first kind. The soul, an angel and God are instances of the second kind. A point or a moment cannot exist in two places or times; but by their influence, not by their mass or quantity,— they have none — the soul, an angel and God can be in many places and many times.

H. What exists whole and entire anywhere cannot exist outside of that place. Ergo.

Answer. What exists whole and entire by wholeness of quantity, I grant; by wholeness of essence, I deny. Whiteness in whole wall, and in part of the wall, can serve for illustration.

I. The stronger the agent, the more able to work from a distance. Ergo, God need not be present to His effects.

Answer. Always with a medium, I grant; otherwise, I deny. Actio in distans, is a contradiction.

THESIS IV

God knows all past, present, future, possible and futurible things.

Jouin, pp. 238–242. *Boedder*, pp. 255–290.

TERMS

God's knowledge. God, because infinite, is a spirit enjoying the most perfect conceivable kind of life. Only simple perfections are formally in God, mixed perfections exist in Him virtually and eminently. Intellectual life, manifest in thought and wish, is the one kind of life free from every admixture of imperfection, the one brand of life deserving the title simple perfection. All created life, intellectual as well as sensitive and vegetative, is a mixed perfection and has no formal being in God. Life in God is pure act, with no suspicion or trace of mere potency; it is substance, and no accident; it is identical with God's own essence; infinite and wholly devoid of parts. And what is true of God's life is true of His knowledge. God's knowledge is God's life, God's substance, God's essence. His knowledge is one single act, not made up like ours of many different acts. In God's knowledge all the multiplicity is in its terms or objects; in our knowledge every new term or object calls for a new act, and acts in our case are as numerous or multiplied as the terms or objects of our knowledge. There is no past or future with God, everything is present. God with one single act of His mind reaches whatever is capable of being known, in all the wide range of its knowability. And the reason is plain. Otherwise a higher and better intelligence could be conceived or thought, and God's knowledge would fall short of being infinite. He knows all things, and knows them exhaustively or comprehensively.

The determining principle of God's knowledge, the agency substituting in God for the imprinted intelligible image in our knowledge, the actual and sufficient reason of His knowledge, is His divine essence. His essence is term-object as well as motive-object of His knowledge. On this account God's essence is the one primary object of His knowledge. Everything outside of God is a mere term-object, a secondary object of His knowledge. All this, to preclude difficulties, and free God from suspicion of dependence for His knowledge on things outside of Himself. In addition to our essence we have need of the imprinted intelligible image to understand, because of our indifference and potency to actual knowledge, ignorant now and knowing a moment later. God has no such need. His essence is enough to explain all, as He is pure act, and a stranger to mere potency. God's essence is primary object of His knowledge, because it is what He first knows, and that by which He knows everything else. It would be wrong to say that God has many ideas in the same sense as ourselves. He has but one idea, and this single idea is representative of whatever is knowable. His idea is one, its terms are without number. If God knew one thing after another, like ourselves, He would know an infinite number. But, as a matter of fact, He knows infinite things all at once and by the same single act. No absurdity attaches to infinite multitude, but to infinite number, which is multitude measured with some unit for standard. God's essence is different from aught else, and yet it is the means God employs to know aught else, because it eminently and virtually contains everything else.

Past, present, future, possible and futurible things. God's knowledge is threefold: 1, *knowledge of vision,* 2, *knowledge of simple intelligence,* 3, *intermediate knowledge; with actuals, possibles, and futuribles for respective objects.* In Scholastic language God's knowledge is: *scientia visionis, scientia simplicis intelligentiae, and scientia media.* We repeat that there is no past or future with God, everything is present. Knowledge in God comprises no many different acts, God's knowledge is one act, and God's knowledge is His substance. The names we employ are derived from the process human knowledge follows. We see only actually present objects, we understand essences whether present or absent, and we discourse of things that are not, but would be in the event of a certain condition's fulfillment. *Therefore God's knowledge of vision has for object things vested with actual existence, whether in the past, the present, or the future.*

His knowledge of simple intelligence has for object pure possibles or essences never vested with actual existence. His intermediate knowledge has for object futuribiles, or free conditioned futures, or futures dependent on a double condition, the exercise of free will along with some different and distinct condition. Conditional futures are not the same as futuribles. Conditional futures are reducible to absolute futures; and, as such, form part of God's knowledge of vision. Futuribles are not reducible to absolute futures or mere possibles, and so constitute a third object of God's knowledge, distinct from objects embraced by God's vision and simple intelligence. The knowledge in God concerned with futuribles is called intermediate, because it partakes of the nature of both vision and simple intelligence, without being identical with either. Their possibility in the abstract is matter for simple intelligence, and their impossibility in the concrete is matter for vision; and the divine knowledge embracing the two we denominate media or intermediate. Simple intelligence is necessary knowledge in God, and precedes every free decree, not in the order of time or of nature, but of power or origin. Vision is contingent knowledge and follows a free decree, not in time but in nature. Intermediate agrees with simple intelligence, inasmuch as it precedes every free decree; it differs from same, inasmuch as it is contingent knowledge. Intermediate agrees with vision, inasmuch as it is contingent knowledge; it differs from same, inasmuch as it precedes every free decree. A futurible is more than a possible viewed precisely as such, and therefore it is outside the range of simple intelligence. It is a possible with a bearing on actuality, destined in default of a condition to never materialize, and therefore it is outside the range of vision.

For obvious reasons God's essence is called the necessary object of His knowledge. Things outside of God, like past, present, future and futurible things, are for equally obvious reasons called the contingent or hypothetical objects of God's knowledge. The past is what once was and is no more; the present is what now is; and the future is what is going to be, though nothing now. A necessary future depends on created causes that follow necessary law, like the next eclipse. A free future depends on free will, whether mediately or immediately. An instance would be, John will eat to-morrow at nine. A future, whether necessary or free, is said to be absolute, when its originating cause is effective and prerequisite conditions are verified. It is said to be conditioned, when its cause and conditions never materialize. This last sort of future is known as a futurible, and is what would happen in event of certain conditions, but never will happen because the conditions will not be verified. An instance would be, Were John invited to the game, and he never will be invited, he would excuse himself on the plea of business. Were miracles worked in Corozain, and they never will be worked, its people would be converted.

About God's knowledge of past and present there can be no difficulty. Such knowledge is within man's reach, and it would be blasphemy to reckon God inferior to man. About futures and futuribles the question is not so easy, and calls for proof as well as explanation. Past and future say a relation to the present. They are respectively a long or short distance behind or in front of the present. God antedates everything, and God always exists. When events are taken as terms of God's decrees, God antedates them in time; when they are taken as these decrees themselves, God is simultaneous with them in time, prior to them in nature. In our case the future often becomes a reality only after we cease to exist, many events in the past were actual realities before we began to be; but in the case of God nothing of the kind can possibly happen. He is present to whatever future, He is present to whatever past; and all this in virtue of the double fact that past, present and future are bound up in His decrees from eternity, and that He always was, always is, and always shall be. Time works no change in God, it works changes in things outside of God. We know the present because it is an actual reality. We know the past because it was once an actual reality. We can guess at the future without precisely knowing it, because it never was and is not now an actual reality. But with God, in virtue of His eternal decrees, the future is as much an actual reality as the past and the present. All things are futures with reference to God, because His existence precedes them; all are presents, because actual from eternity in His divine decrees; all are pasts, because He outlives them all.

Whatever has a determined being has a determined truth, and determined truth is the one requisite for knowledge on the part of the mind's object. Whatever is, is knowable; and everything knowable is necessarily known to the infinite mind. That past, present, future, possible, and futurible things are, is plain from their several definitions. The past is that which was; the present is that which is; the future is that which will be; the possible is that which can be, but never will be; the futurible is that which can be and never will be, but would be under certain conditions not to be verified. To resume, there can be no difficulty about God's knowledge of past and present things and of necessary futures. Free futures are of two kinds, absolute and contingent. In absolute free futures the consent of the will is the one requisite condition for their knowledge. In contingent free futures, or futuribles some added condition attaches to consent of the will. To the mind of God necessary futures are as much facts as the past or the present. Absolute free futures are as much facts as necessary futures, in the event that God knows beforehand how the will is going to choose. This foreknowledge must in no way interfere with human freedom; and in this particular we clash with such Thomists as advocate physical predetermination. Contingent free futures or futuribles are as much facts as necessary futures, in the event that God knows beforehand how the will would choose, were certain conditions verified. In futuribles God must know two things, the will's choice and the conditions to be verified.

About absolute free futures St. Augustine says: "As your memory of past events never forced them into being, so God's foreknowledge of future events never forced them into being." Dante beautifully explains the thing, when he compares the bearing of God's foreknowledge on a free agent's future acts with the bearing of a spectator's knowledge on the direction a ship takes under influence of wind and tide. The will in course of time never chooses this or that because God foresaw the choice, but God foresees the choice because the will is going to so choose. God's foreknowledge is not the cause of our choice; our choice, on the contrary, is the cause of God's foreknowledge; not indeed the determining cause, which is His essence alone, but the terminating cause, or conditio sine qua non. What God foreknows, necessarily happens; but we recognize a twofold necessity, antecedent and consequent. Antecedent necessity has play in necessary causes, and has play prior to the act; consequent has place in free causes, and is subsequent to the act. Antecedent destroys freedom; consequent is compatible with freedom. Even a free act must be, when it is once placed or put. God's knowledge of free futures, like man's freedom of choice, acknowledges consequent necessity, it repudiates antecedent necessity. God's knowledge, like all knowledge, presupposes its object; but this precedence of object is precedence of termination, not of determination. God's knowledge in point of determination precedes its object in the order of time as well as of nature, when there is question of men's free acts taken as realities. In much the same way God's knowledge depends on our freedom terminatively, not determinatively; and terminative dependence is no intrinsic imperfection in God. The reality of a futurible is not absolute, but only hypothetical; and one as well as the other can base knowledge.

DIVISION

Three Parts — I, II, III

I. Past, present, and possible things. II. Necessary futures and absolute free futures. III. Contingent free futures, or futuribles.

PROOFS

I. 1°. Knowledge of past, present and possible things is a simple perfection. Ergo, it exists in God.

2°. Man enjoys this knowledge. Ergo, God a fortiori enjoys the same.

II. 1°. God knows whatever is vested with determined or set truth, and is therefore knowable. But necessary futures and absolute free futures are vested with determined truth. Ergo.

With regard to the Minor. Whatever event as a matter of fact has place in the future is nothing vague or undetermined, even before its occurrence. Before its occurrence it is a something as set and fixed as it is after its occurrence, of course in the logical not in the real order.

2°. In the matter of actuality the future is no worse off than the past; and yet nobody hesitates to ascribe knowledge of the past to man himself.

3°. It is unworthy God to suppose that He learns by degrees, or to think that to know the future He must wait till it happens in the real order of things.

4°. Without this knowledge of necessary futures and absolute free futures God would be no effective ruler of the universe. Such knowledge is a requisite for providence.

III. 1°. Every statement regarding futuribles contains set or fixed truth, and therefore futuribles are knowable objects. But God knows everything knowable. Ergo, God knows futuribles.

With regard to the Major. The thing is plain in absolute free futures. Regarding Peter in fixed conditions one of two contradictories must necessarily be true. Either he will sin, or he will not sin. He cannot do the two things, sin and at the same time not sin. The thing ought to be equally plain in contingent free futures or futuribles. Regarding Peter in different conditions one of two contradictories must necessarily be true. Either he would sin, or he would not sin. He could never do the two things, sin and at the same time not sin.

2°. Without this knowledge of futuribles God, desirous of some effect, would have to make trial of several different means. But every such need is derogatory to God's dignity. Ergo, God knows futuribles.

3°. Knowledge of futuribles is a very desirable perfection. Ergo, it belongs to God.

4°. Knowledge of futuribles is a requisite for providence. Ergo, it belongs to God.

5°. All men ascribe this knowledge to God. Ergo.

Scholion I. About Absolute Free Futures.

The fact that God knows absolute free futures and futuribles is easy enough of comprehension, but the process by which He knows them is somewhat obscure. And first with regard to absolute free futures. Some Thomists maintain that God knows them in predetermining decrees. These decrees are wishes on the part of God, ordaining the future act prior to all foreknowledge of the agent's behavior. Therefore the last reason why God knows absolute free futures is because He formulates a decree, establishing the future event prior to all foreknowledge of the future event itself. To bring about such events God therefore employs physical predetermination, He energizes the will by antecedent pressure. *This predetermination, according to Goudin, a good Thomist, is a quality transient in nature, communicated to the will, and binding the will, without a chance of escape, to a fixed act.* These decrees unduly exalt God's power, to insult and destroy man's feedom. *We maintain, therefore, that they are superfluous and hurtful to human freedom. They are superfluous for four main reasons.* Physical predetermination is not needed to explain God's quality of

a, first cause,
b, His supreme dominion,
c, His foreknowledge, or
d, the will's indifference.

a. These four facts are enough to constitute God first cause of man's free acts:

1. He makes the will and its energies.
2. He predetermines it to good in general, the summum bonum.
3. With the help of the other faculties He sets the will in motion by proposing some particular and finite good.
4. He contributes to the act by simultaneous coöperation with the will.

b. Dominion is twofold, moral and physical. God's total dominion is manifest in His bestowal or refusal of coöperation, and in His arrangement of circumstances with a view to this or that foreseen act of the will.

c. God's foreknowledge is abundantly explained by His intermediate knowledge, in conjunction with His decree to coöperate with the will.

d. The will's indifference is active as well as passive, and must not be tampered with by any stress brought to bear on its inner nature. Mere passive indifference leaves freedom incomplete, active gives it completion and finish. This active indifference can be said to be objectively lifted by the good in question, not effectively. It is formally lifted by the will itself engaged in actual choice.

Physical predetermination is hurtful to human freedom, because it is a prerequisite for every act of the will; and, when once present, the will is no longer able to omit the act or put its contrary. But freedom is on all sides admitted to be that capacity of the will, in virtue of which, with every prerequisite for activity present and verified, the will is still able to omit the act or put its contrary. All Thomists consider physical predetermination a simple prerequisite. Billuart tries to get round the difficulty with the help of a time-honored distinction, sensu composito and sensu diviso, compound sense and divided sense. And he alleges this example. A man seated cannot walk. True in compound sense, untrue in divided sense. In much the same way, the will with physical predetermination cannot choose in compound sense, though it can still choose in divided sense. No parity. Physical predetermination is a prerequisite for willing; sitting is no prerequisite for walking. You can separate sitting from walking, you cannot separate physical predetermination from willing. Nobody can walk while he remains seated, and nobody can choose when compelled by physical predetermination. A man seated can change his position, a man willing cannot get away from physical predetermination. Were sitting a prerequisite for walking, no man could ever walk; and, because physical predetermination is a prerequisite for willing, no man can ever choose. This potency to choose in divided sense is no potency at all; because the one prerequisite for the contrary act, namely physical predetermination, is forever wanting. Every such potency is metaphysically irreducible to act, and therefore vain and empty, a mere figment of the mind, and of no practical use whatever. Freedom of the sort would be lame and halt, altogether incomplete, because forever without its essential prerequisite, corresponding physical predetermination. It would be freedom to put one set act, and that is no freedom at all. To omit the act, to put its contrary, would be altogether out of the question, because physical predetermination to one thing or the other would never be verified.

Billuart thinks he sees a resemblance between his physical predetermination and the foreknowledge of a man's free act we vindicate to God. They are both prerequisites, but there the resemblance ceases. Predetermination imposes antecedent necessity on the will; foreknowledge imposes only consequent necessity, because it presupposes man's actual exercise of his freedom. Billuart then appeals to mystery, saying that God in some strange and hidden way moves the will in a manner befitting its nature. But mysteries are matter of revelation, and God is their author, not Billuart or the Thomists. Besides, mysteries involve no contradiction, and free will physically predetermined is a square circle. We admit the maxim, omne movens motum, motion on the part of a mover precedes movement in the thing moved. But God is mover enough without physical predetermination. He moves the will by implanting in it a natural desire for happiness, a leaning towards good in general, the summum bonum; by the proposal of particular goods, and by simultaneous coöperation with the will in all its acts. To the objection that God in our system would be unable to get from man whatever act He wants, we answer that God is still supreme Lord of animals, plants and stones, though He cannot squeeze a thought from them. Besides, grace, coupled with consent and foreknown as such, can enable God to get from man whatever act He wants.

P.S. God and the will together choose, or determine the man's act; but God must not on this account be called its determining cause. God and the eye see together, vision is a body-act, accomplished with the help of organs; and yet God must not be said to see corporeally or employ organs. All this about absolute free futures and physical predetermination, according to Thomists their single explanation. Therefore, with Thomists God knows absolute free futures in these physically predetermining decrees. We reject all such decrees in the matter of absolute free futures; and must otherwise explain God's manner of knowing them. God of course knows all things, past, present, future and futurible in His essence as in formal object. When we say He knows things in anything else, we mean to introduce no new formal object, but merely assign the root-reason why His essence represents absolute free futures and futuribles to His intellect. We maintain that God knows absolute free futures in themselves and in a mutual combination of His intermediate knowledge and a resultant decree. He knows absolute free futures in themselves, because they are in His essence only eminently, and He must know them formally; because they must influence His intellect at least intentionally, as the sound of the bell when one has vowed to say a Hail Mary when the bell rings; because they are the root-basis of the divine knowledge touching them. He knows absolute free futures in a mutual combination of His intermediate knowledge and a resultant decree, because this is the process. If I gave Peter grace A, Peter would consent. I will give Peter grace A. Ergo, Peter will consent. The Major is a matter of intermediate knowledge; the Minor is a resultant decree.

PRINCIPLES

A. Opponents object and say, God knows things inasmuch as He is their cause. We distinguish: By vision for actuals, by intelligence for possibles, by intermediate for futuribles. Necessary futures belong to vision; absolute free futures and contingent free futures or futuribles, to intermediate. For explanation see page 272. The medium God employs, when He knows absolute free futures in themselves, is infallible, because His knowledge is posterior, not prior to act's futurity. Things would stir God to knowledge in sense of objective conditions, not in sense of physically determining motives. At most, things would be intentionally determining motives, and no imperfection or dependence attaches to that kind of motive. In no sense of the word must God be said to know absolute free futures in physically predetermining decrees, because man's freedom must be kept intact.

B. Regarding God's way of knowing futuribles, the Thomists introduce as mediums what they call subjectively absolute, objectively conditional decrees, decrees actually had but suspended in effect till a condition is verified. We deny every such decree in God, while ready to recognize subjectively conditional decrees, not what is, but what would be. God knows futuribles not in these decrees of the Thomists, but in themselves, inasmuch as the actual existence they would have in the event of a certain condition is the ultimate reason and basis of God's knowledge touching them. Scripture is witness to God's knowledge of futuribles in St. Matthew 11–21. "Woe to thee, Corozain, woe to thee, Bethsaida; for, if in Tyre and Sidon had been wrought the miracles that have been wrought in you, they had long ago done penance in sackcloth and ashes." Besides, were God without this knowledge, He would be held to the unworthy expedient of making trial or experiment. In Matthew Corozain and Bethsaida stand for the Jews; Tyre and Sidon, for the Gentiles. Miracles were worked for the Jews, not for the Gentiles. The Jews in spite of miracles failed of conversion; the Gentiles would have been converted in the event of the same miracles. And Christ reproaches the Jews as guilty of a heavier condemnation than the Gentiles. Hence we argue. Had God foreknown the conversion of the Gentiles in these decrees of the Thomists, the Jews could have objected and said that the Gentiles would have done only what they could not help doing, and would have deserved no credit for their conversion. Physical predetermination would have converted the Gentiles in the event of miracles. The reproach made the Jews would be unreasonable, because through no will of their own they were without physical predetermination, a necessary prerequisite for conversion, and the Gentiles would be possessed of the same. Nor will it do to say that the Jews were denied physical predetermination because of their sins. Successive sins would then result from successive privations of physical predetermination, and progress would be made towards an infinite series.

Billuart has two reasons for thinking this complaint of the Jews without foundation:

1. They had sufficient grace; they had the power, though that power was of no avail without physical predetermination. And he appeals to these examples. Fire is able to burn, bread to nourish, mind to understand; though the fire must be applied, the bread must be eaten, and the mind must have species or images. To this we answer that sufficient grace of this kind confers only a tied up power, nowise reducible to act. It is like handing a man a sword, binding him with ropes, and then telling him to defend himself. The predetermination is a prerequisite.

2. The hardness of heart and ingratitude displayed by the Jews account for their privation of physical predetermination. But this is only to move the difficulty back. Predetermination is refused now, because it was refused on a former occasion.

C. This passage in St. Paul would seem to favor Thomism: "He hath mercy on whom He will, and whom He will He hardeneth." Rom. 9.18. But the apostle is talking of a call to the faith, not of predestination. Men called to the faith have not merited the favor, men not called to the faith miss the favor because of their sins. Besides, predestination is in everybody's power; physical determination was not in the power of the Gentiles. Intermediate knowledge in God explains the problem of free will, it fails to explain why God confers merely sufficient grace on one man, efficacious grace on another; and this is the burden of St. Paul's lesson. God's will is the explanation.

Scholion II. About Futuribles.

And now the question arises, how does God know futuribles. We just proved that God knows absolute free futures in themselves, and in that combination of intermediate knowledge and decree already explained. Here we maintain that God knows futuribles in themselves, inasmuch as the actual existence they would have in the event of a certain condition bases as root-reason God's knowledge of them. God is said to know things in themselves and in Himself; and the two sayings must be kept apart. There can be no difficulty about God's knowledge of all things, actual, possible and futurible in Himself, or in His essence. His essence is His primary object. His essence is all things. His essence is cause of all, it is to God what species or image is to us. He knows His essence, and in it all things else. To know a cause comprehensively, is to know all its effects; and all things are in God's essence as effects are in their causes. Ergo, God knows all things in Himself. The contingent reality of futuribles is in God's essence as well as the actual reality of pasts, presents and necessary futures.

All the difficulty turns on God's knowledge of things actual, possible and futurible in themselves. Actuals, whether past, present or future, and possibles can readily be known in themselves, because they have a reality of their own, actual or possible as the case may be. Futuribles are different. They would seem to have no reality of their own, being neither actuals simply nor possibles simply. Futures are of two kinds, necessary and contingent. Necessary futures are reducible to actuals, and therefore belong to knowledge of vision. Contingent futures are of two kinds, absolute free futures dependent on choice as single condition, and contingent free futures or futuribles, dependent on a double condition, choice for instance and miracles. Matters of vision and intelligence are known in predetermining decrees; absolute free futures and futuribles are known prior to any predetermining decree. Hence the need of intermediate knowledge in God. Futuribles are like possibles, inasmuch as they will never be reduced to act; they are unlike possibles, inasmuch as they would be reduced to act in the event of a certain condition. They are like actuals, inasmuch as they would be reduced to act, having contingent actuality; they differ from actuals, inasmuch as they never will be reduced to act. The same is in a measure true of absolute free futures; and they belong to neither vision nor intelligence, but to intermediate knowledge. Their reality in God's mind precedes every predetermining decree, unlike actuals, possibles, and necessary futures.

Therefore, absolute free futures are known in themselves and in the combination of intermediate knowledge with resulting decree, which is by no means predetermining. In themselves, because God must know their formal being, not merely their eminent being, which alone exists in His essence; because they must themselves as formal object intentionally stir God's knowledge; and because they are root and basic condition for God's knowledge of them. In the combination of intermediate knowledge with resulting decree, to save man's freedom from harm or diminution.

Futuribles are known in themselves, and in a kindred combination of intermediate knowledge with resulting decree, by no means predetermining. In themselves, because what is true of the absolute reality of absolute free futures is true of the contingent reality of futuribles. In the combination of intermediates knowledge with resulting decree, by no means predetermining, to save man's free will from harm or loss. The decree in this latter case denies for instance miracles, and posits the consequent non-occurrence of conversion. The decree is subjectively absolute with regard to miracles, subjectively conditional with regard to conversion. Thomists teach the contrary. When we say that futuribles are not known in decrees, we mean Thomistic decrees, subjectively absolute. Bellarmine and Molina talk about supercomprehension of the will, and they mean our combination of intermediate knowledge and resulting decree. Futuribles have a reality all their own, not physical of course and absolute, but moral and contingent; and that suffices to base their truth and save the axiom, omne verum est ens. Their reality is not a physical reality they have, but a moral reality they have in virtue of the physical reality they would have in event of a certain condition.

PRINCIPLES

A. Three kinds of knowledge in God, necessary, free, and intermediate. Necessary antedates every decree, cannot be absent. Free follows a decree, can be absent; intermediate antedates every decree, can be absent.

B. When the Fathers say that men are lost and saved because God wills it, they are using "because" in illative, not causative sense, e. g. Antichrist will seduce many because Christ foretold it.

C. Salvation in first act is from God; in second act, from God and man. Ergo, in full and complete sense from the two together.

D. Grace given to Peter, and grace given to Judas, the same intrinsically and physically, not extrinsically and morally. Grace given to Peter extrinsically different, because foreseen by intermediate knowledge in conjunction with consent.

E. Man saves himself not as cause, but as putting the indispensable condition, coöperation with grace. God gives the grace that saves, man only puts the condition. Ergo, God saves rather than the man.

F. Intermediate knowledge is not the reason why grace is given. It is merely directive of God, and God can allow this. The Pelagians made the mistake of thinking that intermediate knowledge is the reason why God gives grace.

G. To reconcile God's foreknowledge with man's freedom. God's foreknowledge is eternal, and in point of time antedates our free acts. Intentionally, objectively, and terminatively our acts antedate God's foreknowledge, and they shape it. Our acts are necessary only with consequent necessity. Hence it is true to say, God foresees that Peter will consent, and Peter can refuse to consent.

H. God's knowledge of vision is neither the directive nor effective cause of our free acts. God's wisdom is in some sense the cause of things. Ps. 103.24, "Thou hast made all things in wisdom." Directive cause is intelligence and intermediate. Effective is will in a decree, no knowledge. Proof: Acts would not be free, because God's knowledge of vision is based on a predetermining decree. St. Augustine says, God's knowledge is no more the cause of free acts than our memory is the cause of past events. Damascene says, God's knowledge of our free acts is no more their cause than the doctor's knowledge of a coming disease is its cause. Our conduct precedes God's knowledge with priority of causation improperly so called, it is determinative of God's knowledge as object and mentally, not physically.

THESIS V

God has a will, necessary with regard to Himself, free with regard to creatures.

Jouin, pp. 242–245. *Boedder,* pp. 290–325.

TERMS

Will. That God has a will hardly needs proof after proving that He has an intellect. Scripture is plain and removes all doubt from the minds of believers. "Whatsoever the Lord pleased, He hath done." Ps. 134.6. "He loves justice, and hates iniquity." Ps. 44.8; and these acts call for a will. To will is a simple perfection, and as such cannot be absent from God. Besides, there is no knowledge without desire, and God has most perfect knowledge. Even dead things like stones, and live things without knowledge like plants, have tendencies. Only live beings with knowledge have elicited appetite. Appetite has good for object, and good can be sensible or intellectual, material or spiritual. The will tends towards good and away from evil. Tendency towards is love, tendency away from is hate. Whatever emotion of the soul is free from imperfection can be attributed in strict sense to God, others only by way of figure. Desire with respect to extrinsic things and delight are species of love that involve no imperfection. Aversion is a kindred species of hate. Hope, fear, sadness, remorse, despair, anger, are absent from God, and are ascribed to Him only figuratively, by comparison with man. Hope and despair imply a superior; fear, and sadness, and anger imply harm proper to self; remorse means change of heart. Hatred in God involves none of the disturbances it involves in man.

In reality and formally speaking, God's will is God's essence; and His infinite simplicity is the reason. And yet we keep them apart in our mind. God's will is entitatively one act, terminatively many acts; by nature simple, virtually compound. His one wish equals every possible wish, and touches all possible objects. God is at the same time the principle of His wishes and their object, though with our minds we distinguish between the principle of God's wishes and their objects. The distinction rests in the fact, that, because God is infinite, His one wish equals many, and because the act of wishing one thing is not, at least terminatively, the act of wishing another. Creation is proof that God's will can turn on things outside Himself. Differences in object are responsible for our division of God's will into will of good pleasure and will in symbol, antecedent will and consequent, conditional and absolute, with effect and without effect.

A word about each:

Will of good pleasure turns on what God really and truly wants. *Will in symbol* resembles the written legal instrument among men. God's will is seen in some external act. At times in Scripture God makes plain by the turn events take what He wants, the opposite of what He might be supposed to want. Examples are the sacrifice of Isaac by Abraham, and the silence imposed by Christ on the cured leper. St. Matt. 8.4.

Antecedent will in God means what He wishes in the most absolute manner, without regard to particular circumstances. *Consequent will* means what He wishes with an eye to particular circumstances. With antecedent will He wishes the salvation of all, saint and sinner alike. With consequent will He wishes saints saved and sinners lost. Hence it is plain that God can wish with consequent will what He previously fought against with antecedent will. Their theory of physical predetermination drives the Thomists to limit the particular circumstance in question of consequent will to the beauty of the universe and a display of justice. These motives had all to do with the wickedness of Judas and the holiness of Peter. The man's use of his free will is the circumstance on which we insist. God's antecedent will prescinds from man's use of his free will, His consequent will takes this circumstance into account. Conditional will in God means a wish subject to a condition, and the condition hangs on man, not on God. Absolute will carries no condition, and is always fulfilled. Will with effect and will without effect explain themselves. No absolute will of God is without effect, conditional will is often without effect. With the same antecedent will God wishes all to be saved and wishes to bestow on all the means of salvation. In one case His antecedent will is conditional, in the other absolute. Every consequent will of God is absolute and with effect. Sometimes will with effect is not consequent, though it is absolute on the part of God.

Free. The formal object of God's will is His own goodness. It is what first and of itself moves His will; and, being alone infinite, is alone in proportion with His faculty of wishing. The primary material object of God's will is God Himself; the secondary material object is every being outside of God, because all share in the goodness of God. When God Himself is object, God's will is not free; when creatures are object, God is free. Freedom is immunity from necessity or from restriction to one line of conduct.

There are two kinds of freedom, because there are two kinds of necessity, physical and moral. We are talking about physical freedom, not moral. Two kinds of physical freedom, because there are two kinds of physical necessity, extrinsic and intrinsic. Immunity from extrinsic necessity is called freedom of spontaneity or freedom from violence. Immunity from intrinsic necessity is called freedom of choice, or of indifference, and is of three kinds, contradiction, contrariety and specification.

With regard to moral evil or sin, God enjoys no freedom of contrariety. He simply must hate sin, He simply must love virtue. With regard to metaphysical and physical evil He enjoys freedom of contrariety. We leave God's decrees out of the question, because they are eternal and banish suspension of will from God. Freedom in our thesis means that whatever creatures God wishes to come into being, He wishes them in such a way that He could have not wished them. No imperfection must attach to God's freedom. Therefore it must be conceived, not as indifference on the part of a potency to be reduced to act, but as indifference on the part of an act, put from eternity, to touch this or that object, as indifference to whatsoever term outside of God.

Division — Two Parts, I, II. I, Necessary; II, Free.

PROOFS

I. **1°.** Infinite will cannot be indifferent to infinite good perfectly known. Ergo, God necessarily loves Himself.

2°. A well ordered and holy will cannot but love a being infinitely deserving of love. Ergo God necessarily loves Himself.

II. 1°. God's will is free with regard to what things He knows to be contingent. But God knows creatures to be contingent. Ergo, God's will is free with regard to creatures.

2°. Creatures are particular goods, and no adequate object for even a finite will. We ourselves can embrace particular goods, we need not embrace them. They are no adequate good, and not necessarily connected with God's existence.

3°. Prayer proves free will in God. It supposes God able to grant or refuse the favor.

4°. Liberality implies same. A favor is a gift that can be withheld without wrong, and liberality means the bestowal of a favor.

PRINCIPLES

A. 1°. God has no end or good distinct from Himself. He is good and end for Himself and for all besides.

2°. A perfectible will is a moved mover, not a divine will.

3°. Will of God, viewed in principle, is God's being; not when viewed in term, unless His essence is object.

4°. God's will is not stirred by creatures. His essence stirs Him to wish creatures, always as secondary object.

5°. God's purpose, when He seeks outside objects, is not to perfect Himself, but to communicate His goodness to others.

6°. God's wish is one formally, many virtually.

B. 1°. God's wish is eternal, viewed in principle; temporal, viewed in term; its necessity is consequent, not antecedent.

2°. God's wish regarding outside things is identical with His essence after the manner of a transient, not an immanent act.

3°. God's wish would be contingent, if He could not wish after wishing; not, however, if He can not wish before wishing.

The first implies change, and therefore contingency; the second implies no change.

C. 1°. The necessity, with which God knows things outside, is consequent on His decree to create, and consequent on the free acts of men.

2°. God knows only the possibility of things with antecedent necessity, not their future reality or futuribility. He knows the latter with consequent necessity, dependent on free will and the realization of conditions.

D. Freedom in creatures, because it involves potency, is a mixed perfection; not in God, because it is act, and no potency.

E. We conceive God's will as able to determine itself; in itself, and as a matter of fact, it is determined from eternity; in such a way, however, that it could have otherwise determined itself.

F. The act by which God loves Himself and creatures is entitatively the same, not terminatively. It is necessary entitatively, not terminatively, unless His essence is object.

G. 1°. Freedom of contrariety regarding moral good and evil is no perfection, and is absent from God.

2°. God can draw good from evil; and with God, to permit evil is good and no harm.

Scholion. To reconcile God's freedom with His immutability.

God's freedom must not prejudice His immutability. New volitions must not be new realities in God. They are new relations, but non-mutual. All the change is in the outside term they affect, not in God their author. The relation is logical on the part of God. God is really the same before and after the world exists. On the part of creatures it is real. Creatures are different before and after God's wish. The thing in God that makes Him free, that makes Him now wish and then not wish creatures, is God's substantial volition, His very essence. There are no accidents in God. Wishes in us are accidents, in God they are a substance, they are Himself, His essence.

In God freedom stands with immutability, because it rests on the surpassing and infinite actuality of His substantial volition. On account of its infinite actuality volition in God can without change, increase, diminution, lean or not lean towards creatures in a way beyond our mental grasp. When He leans towards creatures, He wishes them, and they are terms of His act. When He leans away from them, they are no terms of His act, and He wishes them not. The mystery of God's freedom lies in this, that His volition, enduring the same substance without change, views outside things in different lights, wishes some, not wishing others. The act of volition in God is necessary and eternal, its termination is free and in time. Hence term or object is the important factor in God's freedom. No free act entitatively taken can be absent from God, a free act terminatively taken can be absent from God. The act by which God loves Himself is necessary, the act by which He loves creatures is free. No contradiction, because the act is necessary and free under different respects, entitatively and terminatively.

The act constituting God free is God Himself, and this act is not considered in itself, but inasmuch as it connotes terms or objects. The infinite nature of God alone explains the wondrous efficacy of this act. Finite acts, like our own wishes, are quite other. As soon as my free act exists, it becomes necessary. It is called free, because it proceeds from an indifferent potency; and, at the very instant of its doing, it is done in such a way that, prior by nature to its doing, it could have been left undone. Of course, when once done, it is necessary, and no longer free, it is shackled to its formal object. An act in God is free, not because it proceeds from an indifferent potency. There is no potency in God, He is all act. Act in God is God Himself, and therefore of no act in God can it be said that, prior by nature to its doing, it could have been left undone. An act in God is free, because in virtue of its infinite and substantial actuality it looks effectively, or leans with life-giving efficacy towards one or other of two outside objects. In this way an act, necessary and immutable in itself or entitatively, by virtue of this look or tendency induces change in an outside object, connotes the outside object, and is free in its causative capacity.

Another explanation. In every act of wishing, a created will undergoes an intrinsic change, because it passes from potency to act. It undergoes no additional intrinsic change because it chooses, or wishes with freedom. God in the act of wishing undergoes no such intrinsic change, because passage from potency to act has no place in God. He is act, and act alone. And therefore no intrinsic change attaches to God's will when it chooses, or wishes with freedom. Hence God can be said to wish or not wish from eternity, because no intrinsic change, no passage from potency to act, is incurred in the double process. Creatures cannot be said to at any fixed moment wish and not wish, because the double process in their case involves intrinsic change, passage from potency to act.

THESIS VI

I. Creatures, to continue in being, need positive and direct conservation on the part of God.

II. Creatures, to act, need physical and immediate coöperation on the part of God.

Jouin, pp. 250–253. *Boedder*, pp. 344–370.

Division — Two Parts, I, II. I, Conservation; II, Coöperation.

QUESTION

I. There is nothing in the nature of a contingent being to make its continued existence necessary, and all creatures are contingent. Only the necessary being enjoys this property, and independence in the matter of continued existence means independence in the matter of origin. Continuance is only a mode of existence, modes follow substance; and contingents are as helpless regarding continuance in being as they are regarding original existence. As nothing in their nature demands first origin, and creation alone accounts for their first appearance in the universe of existences or realities; so nothing in their nature demands continuance in being, and conservatism alone accounts for their perseverance in the universe of realities. The quality of contingence in creatures makes conservation as much a need as creation; and, as all contingents are necessarily created, all contingents are necessarily conserved.

TERMS

I. Conservation means divine activity responsible for a creature's continuance in being. It can be negative or positive; direct or indirect. *Negative conservation* is simple non-destruction, policy of hands off, e. g. when we refrain from killing a neighbor. *Positive conservatism* implies actual influence on the thing conserved, e. g. food sustains life. In negative, the preserver does nothing; in positive, he does something. *Direct conservation* exerts immediate influence on object, and it is a species of continuous production, e. g. the shape of a vessel sustains the shape of the liquid it contains. *Indirect conservation* wards off destructive agencies, e. g. salt sprinkled on meat kills germs.

Sense of thesis. God positively and directly keeps in existence every contingent being, and without this divine activity no contingent being could continue in existence. Deists are of opinion that God after creation left the world to itself, to its own native forces, physical and chemical, and to unchanging laws.

PROOFS

I. 1°. Unless creatures need positive and direct conservation, God cannot annihilate them. But God can annihilate creatures. Ergo, they need conservation.

With regard to the Major. The term of annihilation is nothing. A positive act cannot have nothing for term. Ergo, annihilation can be accomplished only by withdrawal of positive and direct conservation.

With regard to the Minor. God's supreme and absolute dominion demands it. Creatures can exist only as long as God wants them to exist, and no longer. Even man can destroy the work of his hands.

N.B. Immortality of the soul is no limitation of God's power, because God's own attributes forbid soul's destruction, and God's attributes are God Himself.

2°. St. Thomas.

What depends on another for its being, as opposed to its making or production, depends on that other for its continuance in being. But all creatures depend on God's immediate work for their being. Ergo, they need conservation for continuance in being.

With regard to the Major. Dependence in making lasts while making continues, and then ceases. A pari, dependence in being ought to last while being continues.

With regard to the Minor. Effects depend on cause for their being, when they can be produced by no other cause; for their making only, when they can be produced by another cause.

Every effect of a creature can be made by another cause, e. g. son, house. Nothing can be made without God's coöperation. Primal matter, angel, soul depend on God for both being and making. They must be created.

3°. Without this dependence, God's dominion would be less perfect than it is. Ergo.

PRINCIPLES

A. What cannot but be, needs no conservation. But actual creatures cannot but be. Ergo, they need no conservation.

Answer. Actual creatures cannot but be in hypothetical sense, not in absolute sense. God alone cannot but be in absolute sense. The hypothesis is plain. Actual beings cannot but be as long as they remain actual. They can not be, when they cease to be actual.

B. Nothing, whether a house or a wall or anything else, depends on man for its being. Things depend on God for their being (esse); on man for their making (fieri). For this reason a house can endure without further activity on the part of its second cause or man, not without activity on the part of its first cause or God.

C. Things tend towards nothing negatively, not positively; and this tendency is no argument against immortality. The soul has no need of indirect conservation. It needs direct.

D. The soul's immortality is indeed natural, but not absolute; and its self-conservation is indirect, not direct. Its spirituality and simplicity are salt preserving it from the destructive and corruptive germs of materiality and composition. God directly conserves the soul.

E. Conservation is a continuance of the act of creation, not a renewal of the act. Everything in God is one. Conservation and creation are one and the same act, the terms of the act are different. Creation therefore is not sufficient to explain creatures, conservation is besides needed.

F. A substance is a being that stands in itself, exists of itself, without need of inherence in another as subject. This circumstance is no argument against conservation. Substances depend on God for their existence, they are independent of creatures. Accidents on the contrary depend on creatures for their existence, they cannot naturally exist without some substance for subject of inhesion.

G. The reason why a house can continue to exist without its builder, hot water without fire, is because they do not depend for their being, but for their making on builder and fire. They depend on God for being and cannot continue without Him.

H. A creature able to continue without conservation would reflect more credit on God's omnipotence.

Answer. Square circle. Necessary and contingent. God could not annihilate.

I. Indirect and accidental conservation of bodies is within the province of creatures; e. g. salt and meat.

a. Positive and direct self-conservation belongs immediately to no creature, even in partial sense, because creature would be ens a se.

b. God immediately conserves all, because dominion demands it.

c. Sometimes He conserves by Himself alone, e. g. primal matter, angel, soul.

d. At other times with the help of creatures, e. g. light and sun, image and object. Their esse is situated in their fieri.

J. Things cannot conserve themselves, though they can conserve others. They cannot produce themselves, though they can produce others.

K. Annihilation is denial of conservation, no positive act. God alone can annihilate, because God alone can conserve. God never annihilates. Absolute power can, ordered power cannot do it. Against nature of spirit, against nature of primal matter, which always endures, most fit to exist, made and destroyed by God alone. God's power and goodness are more manifest in conservation than in annihilation. Ergo, by miracle.

L. God can annihilate. Finis respondet principio. Like beginning, like end. God alone in the beginning. Ergo, God alone in the end.

Answer. Creation declares power, annihilation would deny it. Creatures have infinite passive potency, enough for unending duration, not infinite active potency required for eternal duration. Forms and accidents are destroyed, but not annihilated, because subjects from which educed and substances in which they inhere remain.

II. Creatures, to act, need physical and immediate coöperation on the part of God.

TERMS

Coöperation with second causes is what we mean by God's concurrence with creatures, Dei concursus. It can be supernatural, natural; immediate, mediate; physical, moral. *Supernatural* has to do with the order of grace, and belongs to dogmatic theology. *Natural* has to do with deeds in the natural order, and belongs to our thesis. *Immediate* touches or influences the creature's activity in such a way that the whole result, act and effect alike, depends of itself and directly on God's conjoined efficacy. *Mediate* reaches the cause alone, not the cause's effect. Mediate coöperation begins and ends with the bestowal of energies on creatures. Mediate puts the sword in a man's hand, immediate helps wield the sword; one prepares the cause, the other works in conjunction with cause. Physical is here opposed to moral. *Moral* influence affects the agent's will, and through it the effect he produces. It can be extrinsic by advice, or intrinsic by predisposing, and God alone enjoys second power. It is always mediate, regarding the outward act. *Physical* influence affects the agent's outward act. It is immediate, and contributes to the agent's outward act the same kind of force the agent himself contributes.

N.B. God's moral coöperation extends to only good acts, His physical to good and bad acts. Other meanings of moral and physical. Moral activity is free activity; physical is determined or necessary activity. A man acts morally; a brute, physically. In matter of certainty, moral, physical and metaphysical have their own meanings. Physical is likewise opposed to logical. The physical exists as a matter of fact and is independent of all thought. The logical is dependent on thought for existence, and as a matter of fact exists nowhere outside of thought, e. g. the world and being in general, particulars and universals, this man and man. In compounds, parts are physical, metaphysical and logical; or really distinct, virtually distinct with foundation, and without foundation in fact. In our thesis physical is opposed to moral, without reference to other meanings.

PROOFS

II. 1°. A thing's activity follows the nature of its existence or being. But creatures, because contingent existences, depend for their continued existence on God's physical and immediate conservation or preservation. Ergo, creatures, because contingent activities, depend for their activity on God's physical and immediate coöperation.

With regard to the Major. Agere sequitur esse — Sicut res est, sic agit; are axioms in philosophy. They mean activity follows existence; in what measure a thing is, in that measure it acts.

With regard to the Minor, preceding thesis.

2°. Whatever is a being by participation depends on God for its existence. But the acts of creatures are accidents, imperfect beings by participation. Ergo, they depend on God for their existence or production, and God is part cause of them, cooperator.

3°. It would otherwise be hard for God to hinder or restrain the activity of His creatures, and that would destroy supreme dominion. To prevent a certain thought or wish, God would have to do away with an intellect or a will, and immortality forbids.

N.B. God as first cause is complete in His own order, i. e. no other first cause is needed. Creature as second cause is complete in its own order, i. e. no other second cause is needed. Nor one nor other is superfluous, e. g. writer and pen; phantasm and working intellect; image and receiving intellect. Difference between God and examples: No dependence in God, all the dependence is in creatures. Ergo, the relation is nonmutual. In examples the dependence is mutual, equally affecting the two terms of the relation. God alone of His very essence acts without dependence. Creatures essentially act with dependence, because they exist with dependence.

PRINCIPLES

A: If God were single cause of creature's acts, no act would be immanent, because principle would be outside of agent. This is not the case when God acts as first cause only, leaving to creatures all the activity attaching to second causes.

B: Free will remains unharmed, because God's coöperation is simultaneous with wish, not prior to same.

C: One and the same act can immediately and wholly proceed from two agents of different orders, not from two agents of the same order. God and creature are subordinates, not coördinates.

D: God permits sin, refrains from preventing it; and this is the whole extent of His coöperation with sin. Sin is not necessarily mixed up with God's part of the work, it lies in abuse of will; and God is not bound to physically hinder free exercise of the will, whether it be use or abuse of the faculty. God's coöperation is indifferent to use and abuse, man makes it one or the other.

E: God gives to every nature all it needs. Ergo, no coöperation. *Answer:* Always in accordance with quality of nature. To contingent natures He gives contingent or dependent activity.

F: Creatures are by themselves sufficient. Cause is often equal or superior to effect. Ergo, no need of outside help. *Answer:* Coöperation is not needed because effect surpasses created cause, it is due entirely to intrinsic want of creature as a contingent being. Angel cannot create another angel or a fly; father alone cannot produce a son.

G. Creatures are superfluous, because God can produce whole effect. Ergo.

Answer: God uses creatures not because He needs them, but to show forth His goodness.

H: Creatures are God's images. Ergo, they act like God, with independence.

Answer: Creatures are like God, they are not equal to Him.

I: God uses creatures as instruments. Ergo, coöperation is not immediate.

Answer: Creatures are not instruments in strict sense; and God's immensity makes God everywhere present. Like and unlike instruments. Free will moves itself. Instrument makes effect like principal. Not so creatures.

J: God ought to be able to vest a created cause with independent activity. Ergo.

Answer: Square circle, necessary contingent, could not hinder.

K: Infinite power would be needed for every effect. Ergo.

Answer: On part of first cause, not on part of second. Things are hard and easy with regard to second causes, not with regard to first.

L: God coöperates with matter and form as efficient cause, not as matter and form.

THESIS VII

God's coöperation with man's free will is no physical predetermination.

Boedder, pp. 370–381.

QUESTION

We have to choose between physical predetermination of the Thomists and simultaneous coöperation of the Jesuits.

TERMS

Simultaneous coöperation means that God's act on the outside is simultaneous with creature's act; neither before, nor after, but along with it. There is nothing in the effect but what proceeds from the creature, nothing but what proceeds from God. The whole effect begins with both and depends on both, e. g. pen, penman and writing. God's intermediate knowledge saves free will from harm.

Physical predetermination is actio Dei qua voluntatem humanam, priusquam ipsa se determinet, ita ad actum movet insuperabili virtute, ut voluntas nequeat omissionem sui actus cum illa praemotione conjungere. (Gonet.) *Gonet, therefore, and he is a representative Thomist, thus describes physical predetermination: Before the will determines itself, God moves it to act with such irresistible force that it cannot combine omission of the act with God's intervention.* Thomists reject intermediate knowledge in God, and make no provision for free will beyond a mere assertion. All Thomists maintain that God predetermines the will to every act in such a way, that the will, too, freely determines itself, and vote the whole question of free will an insoluble mystery. Praedeterminatio is not praemotio in strict sense, though Thomists confound the two. One means predetermination and it destroys free will, makes it a necessary agent; the other means antecedent influence, and it influences free will without destroying it, secures a set act put with entire freedom by the will. Whatever act God wants He can get from a man, and get it without danger of failure. Otherwise men would be outside His supreme dominion. He can refuse coöperation to every wish but the wish He wants. With the help of indeliberate acts, provoked in the man, God can morally entice and physically drive the will to good acts prior to its self-determination. In this sense God can physically predispose the will, exert prior influence on it, but He cannot determine or predetermine it.

PROOF

According to Thomists themselves, these are characteristic features of physical predetermination. It is concerned with a specific and individual act; it depends on God's will alone; it is an essential prerequisite for the act, and is essentially conjoined with the act.

But where an essential prerequisite for the act is not in the agent's power, where a condition of such sort, that the act cannot be omitted in the event of its fulfillment, is not in the agent's power, freedom is out of the question, and beyond understanding.

Ergo, God's coöperation with man's free acts is no physical predetermination.

With regard to the Minor. Evident from the very concept or idea of freedom. Explanation of St. Thomas: Man would have no free will, unless it rested with himself to determine his act in such a way that he chooses this or that according to his own judgment. Two things in every act, substance of act and determination of agent. Act is in agent's power only when agent determines himself, and freedom means dominion over act. Unless man determines himself, he is not free. Instinct rules brutes. A condition which makes something necessary never destroys freedom, when it is in our power. A condition which makes something necessary always destroys freedom, when it is not in our power, e. g. if you run, you must move. If God foresees that you are going to sin, you must sin. With the Thomists the condition, namely, physical predetermination, is not in our power, it is altogether dependent on the will of God. In the event of such or such predetermination, such or such an act must follow; and, whether we have such or such a predetermination, depends on God, not on ourselves.

Here is another sad consequence. In physical predetermination God would not merely permit sin, He would determine or compel man to the commission of sin. According to the Thomists the matter of sin, the physical act, is willed and predetermined by God; its form alone, its malice, is merely permitted. But in willing the matter of sin, God necessarily wills its form, since matter and form are metaphysically conjoined, and therefore inseparable in the order of reality. Man himself never wills the formal malice of sin, that would be to wish evil. He wishes the good involved in the sinful act, and he incurs blame because malice is inseparably connected with the good he wishes. God would therefore be as much in the wrong as man, and therefore unholy. We make the whole sinful act, matter as well as form, substance as well as malice, proceed from God by the single way of permission without approval.

Scholion — How God moves or influences the will in its free acts. St. Thomas: God implants in every will a tendency toward, a natural craving for, complete happiness, universal good, the summum bonum, Himself; and without this tendency man can desire nothing. In this single respect is man's will predetermined by God. With regard to particular goods, man determines himself, with the help of his intellect, to wish this good or that good, real good or apparent good. 1–2; q.9; a.6; ad.3.

N.B. A real good is good in itself, good as a matter of fact; an apparent good is evil in itself, good in the mind, e. g. revenge. Real good helps to last end; apparent good turns agent aside from last end. Every agent under man seeks real good, because nature or an unerring God fixes and rules its appetite. Man can seek real or apparent good, because his will or appetite is fixed and ruled by a reason capable of error and mistake. God's coöperation with man's free acts has a parallel in the case of a ship, the wind and its pilot. If the boat goes wrong and breaks on the rocks, the fault is not with the wind, but with the pilot who made poor use of the wind. The wind is man's tendency towards universal good, implanted in him by his creator, the pilot is free will in its selection of particular good. With the Thomists the wind would be God and free will acting in concert, or the wind would be the pilot.

PRINCIPLES

A: God's activity is simultaneous with man's in every free act. First cause is prior to second by nature, not in time. Priority of nature means simply that man's wish is more dependent on God than on man himself, because man gets all his activity from God.

B: God and man are partial causes of man's every wish, from the viewpoint of cause only. From the viewpoint of effect they are total causes, one subordinate to the other, like phantasm and working intellect with regard to the image; like pen, penman and writing. God produces the whole effect, man produces the whole effect, the whole wish, but under different aspects; God under universal aspect, man under particular aspect.

C: Man cannot wish without God, but God need not predetermine man.

D: The indifference we ascribe to free will is active, not merely passive. Active indifference can be removed by the agent; passive must be removed by another.

E: Man's will is in potency to second act, not to first act. Its actuality in first act can change to actuality its potency to second act.

THESIS VIII

God and Evil

Boedder, pp. 393–412.

QUESTION

Coöperation of God in metaphysical, physical and moral evil.

TERMS

Evil is opposed to good. Good is perfection, whatever contributes to a thing's finish or completeness. *Evil* is privatio boni debiti; it is absence or want of a good that ought to be present, e. g. blind man. Defect is absence of good that ought not to be present, it is limitation, or metaphysical evil, e. g. blind stone. Every creature is a metaphysical evil because of limitations or finite nature. *Peccatum* means slip of the mind, mistake, beside agent's end or purpose, e. g. poor scribe, ignorant doctor. *Culpa* is slip of the will, fault, sin, blameworthy, in power of agent. A slip of the tongue is no fault of the heart. Metaphysical evil is defectus, want, limitation. Physical evil is malum or peccatum, or absence of a good in the physical order, that ought to be present. Moral evil or sin is culpa, act of will opposed to rectitude or virtue. Moral evil has to do with the man's will; physical, with any other faculty of the man, e. g. blind, deaf, sick. God has to wish metaphysical evil every time He creates. Limitation is of the essence of a creature. God can wish physical evil not in itself, but as a means to some moral good or to some greater physical good. God cannot wish moral evil as an end or as a means. He can however permit or allow it. God's permission of moral evil is always physical, never moral. We distinguish two kinds of such physical permission, negative and positive. Negative is the policy of doing nothing, leaving things alone, letting a thing happen without at all desiring it. Positive is the policy of doing something negative, actively leaving things alone, letting a thing happen with bias in its favor. Negative permission is extrinsic to the permitting agent, positive permission is intrinsic to him. To be negative and nowise positive, permission must have two requisites. 1. No approval of the thing permitted, but displeasure. 2. The thing permitted must not necessarily follow from what the agent does. If it necessarily follows, the agent must not be bound to refrain from doing what he does. If he is bound to refrain, the origin of the obligation must be something other than the evil that follows. God's permission of evil is purely negative. 1. God, far from approving of moral evil or sin, threatens it with the heaviest sanction conceivable, the pains of hell. 2. Sin never necessarily follows from what God does, but from abuse of free will, for which man himself is alone responsible. God's coöperation is indifferent, the same for virtue and the same for sin, man's free will makes the difference. God is not bound to physically hinder man's abuse of his free will from a motive of justice to man, because man of himself can avoid the calamity. His own holiness is no constraining motive, because, far from approving the sins of men, God detests them; and the sins of men never prejudice the holiness of God. God's goodness simply holds Him to the duty of sharing His gifts with free agents to whatever extent these free agents desire. His goodness holds Him to good, not to better or best. His wisdom could be no motive for the physical prevention of sin, because He can derive good from even moral evil.

Two questions:

I. *Can God wish to do evil Himself?*
II. *Can God wish others to do evil?*

PROOFS

I. God can wish neither physical nor moral evil per se, because they are opposed to good, the will's object.

God can wish physical evil per accidens, because it is not evil simpliciter, but evil conjoined with good, greater than the good the evil opposes.

Physical evil sometimes contributes to restoration of moral

order, to establishment of justice and preservation of order in the world. Pain leads to medicine and cure.

God can wish moral evil neither per se nor per accidens. He can permit it. He cannot wish to sin Himself, He cannot wish others to sin; beause against His holiness.

Not per se, because otherwise men could without blame wish sin. Not per accidens, because no conjoined good can be superior to the good opposed by sin. Divine good and right order are opposed by sin, and no good can be greater. And yet sins happen. God cannot wish them. Ergo, He permits them; and to permit sin is good, not evil.

Four good things in permission of sin:

1. Good, to let free will choose between good and evil, while forbidding evil and supplying needed means for its avoidance.
2. Good, to refrain from means and helps that would force free agent to avoid sin.
3. Good, to bestow means and helps that God foresees will prove inefficacious because of man's malice.
4. Good to afford general coöperation, dependent on man's free will for good or evil.

PRINCIPLES

A: "The Lord hath bid Semei curse David." II Kings xvi, 10.

Answer: Bid means permit. Other meaning absurd. Bid and permit interchanged. St. Mark x, 3. Reason enough for permitting is the fact that they can be directed to higher purposes of providence. Not reason enough for wishing them. Same true of martyrs and Passion of Christ. Sin is not on this account good, because capacity for direction is not in sin, but outside.

B: Men are hardened by God, blinded, led into sin, e. g. Pharao. Exodus iv, 21; People, Isa. vi, 10; Egypt, Isai. xix, 14; hardeneth, Rom. ix, 18.

Answer: Permits, allows, denies more abundant helps, sends occasions He knows men will abuse. All men get sufficient grace, not all get efficacious grace.

C: One sin is often penalty of another. God can wish penalty. Ergo, He can wish sin.

Answer: Commission of sin no penalty, but the denial of more abundant graces or helps that could impede sin.

D: Sins would be outside the order of providence, beyond God's power.

Answer: The physical act needs His coöperation, deformity is in human will. Besides, God permits them for good purposes. He never wishes them. To wish by consequent will is to permit.

E: God causes sin by coöperation. What He causes, He wishes. Ergo.

Answer: He causes sin in the sense of permitting, not in the sense of loving or wishing.

PROOFS

II. God cannot wish others to do evil. God cannot wish sin to be committed.

1°. No difference between wishing sin and wishing sin to be committed. Qui facit per alium, facit per se. Men would do no harm, if God could wish them to commit sin. No harm to do what God wants done.

2°. God forbids sin. Ergo, He cannot wish sin to be committed.

PRINCIPLES

A: Either God wishes sin to be committed, or He wishes sin not to be committed. But He does not wish sin not to be committed. Ergo, He wishes sin to be committed.

Answer: Enumeration is not complete. Datur tertium. There is a third alternative, He permits sin. God's will regarding the non-existence of sin is not absolute and efficacious. It is not will of good pleasure; but antecedent and inefficacious, will of symbol. His will to permit sin is absolute and efficacious.

B: Commission of sin and non-commission of sin are contradictories. Ergo.

Answer: To wish commission of sin, and to wish non-commission of sin are not contradictories. Two affirmations cannot be contradictories. God neither wishes sin to be committed, nor does He wish sin not to be committed. He wishes to permit sin to be committed. He does not wish sin to be committed, and that is different from He wishes sin not to be committed.

C: Sins are committed. Ergo, it is impossible for God to wish no sin to be committed. Ergo, He wishes sin to be committed.

Answer: With consequent and efficacious will, I grant; with antecedent and inefficacious will, I deny.

The commission of sin, and the non-commission of sin are contradictories. To wish the commission of sin, and to wish the non-commission of sin are not contradictories.

D: St. Aug. Evil is not good, but the existence of evil is good. Enchir. c. 96. Ergo, God can wish sin to be committed.

Answer: To permit evil to exist is good. Enchir. c. 27. "Nullo modo sineret aliquid mali esse in operatione, nisi, etc." St. Aug. would not say sineret but vellet; because God can wish good and not merely allow it.

E: St. Aug. Sin helps to order and beauty in the world. Enchir. c. 10. Ergo.

Answer: Per se, no; per accidens, yes. Per se, sin destroys order; per accidens, it is an occasion for higher good. O felix culpa.

THESIS IX

God's coöperation, viewed as something outside of God, is the creature's act, proceeding at one and the same time from the creature as from second or particular cause, and from God as from first and universal cause.

Boedder, pp. 344–370.

QUESTION

God's coöperation, viewed as something in God, is His eternal decree, and we are not at present concerned with that. We now study God's coöperation in term or in effect; and we maintain that it is the creature's act. The creature's coöperation in term is likewise the creature's act. In other words the creature's act is the whole effect of God, and the whole effect of the creature. The whole act must be ascribed to God, and the whole act must be ascribed to the creature, not a part of the act to each, e. g. pen and penman in writing. Therefore God's coöperation, viewed in term, connotes nothing distinct from the creature's act, and the physical predetermination of Thomists is ruled out.

PROOF

Really and truly to coöperate, God and creature must combine to produce the effect, and by way of term nothing but the creature's act need result, to the utter exclusion of any predetermination or extra principle. Ergo, God's coöperation is the creature's act. *With regard to antecedent:* This view of God's coöperation keeps intact the creature's essential dependence on God for its causative virtue, the creature's dependence on God in process of its exercise of activity, and God's ownership of the whole act or effect. The creature not only exists in virtue of God's conservation, it acts in virtue of God's coöperation. By virtue of His immensity God is immediately present to the creature at three different periods, before the act begins, while the act is in progress, and when the act is completed. Before the act begins, He gives the creature causative virtue; while the act is in progress, He gives the creature help; and when the act is done, the whole thing is God's. The creature moves and applies itself to the act's accomplishment only by virtue of help borrowed from God. God performs the act, as first cause; the creature, as second cause. God is not only the principle of man's causative virtue, He is also the principle of man's act.

On the other hand, all the creature's essential dependence on God in process of its exercise of activity is kept intact. St. Thomas in different places describes this dependence as fivefold. *God coöperates with creatures, (1) by giving them their nature and its forces; (2) by preserving them in being; (3) by applying them to actual work; (4) by vesting them with the capacity of instruments; (5) by moving them in quality of their last end.* This fivefold dependence calls for no physical predetermination.

Besides, these three axioms need explanation: (a) Second causes never act without motion from the first cause. (b) Second causes must be applied to actual work by the first cause. (c) Second causes act only in virtue of the first cause. Explanation: (a) No motion is required beyond the reception of being and connatural activity. Creation and conservation are themselves motion. Motion is a metaphor derived from artist's use of his tools, and employed to express creature's dependence on God. The real and proper sense is, second causes never act without help from the first cause. (b) The word application is as much a metaphor as motion. It is a figure used to portray the superiority of the first cause, which directs second causes and prescribes their appointed ends. (c) The power attaching to every creature is God's power, because He preserves all and coöperates with all.

THESIS X

Physical predetermination is a, useless in necessary agents; b, useless in free agents, and destructive of free will. Simultaneous coöperation is right.

Boedder, pp. 439–448.

QUESTION

Two parts: I. Physical predetermination. II. Simultaneous coöperation.

TERMS

I. Physical Predetermination

Thomists teach two kinds of predetermination; one eternal, in God, a decree; the other temporal, in creature, motion impressed on creature; and this is physical predetermination. Second is instrument of first, and is likewise called antecedent influence. Predetermination and antecedent influence are synonymous with Thomists, not in themselves. Predetermination is infallible, influence not. Grace is influence, not predetermination. Predetermination is different from influence of object, e. g. intellect moves will objectively; different from moral influence, e. g. invitation; different from simultaneous coöperation, or help. *Physical predetermination can be best described as (1) a true push, real motion, (2) proceeding from God alone, (3) received in second cause, (4) gotten and kept without power of choice, (5) prior to act and cause of act, (6) absolutely necessary to every act of every creature, (7) brooking no denial and infallibly connected with the creature's act, (8) supplied by God, not to make the creature proximately able to act, but to make it actually active; to put it not in first or second act, but between the two.* It supposes fire equipped with natural power to burn (remote first act), and with all conditions dependent on other second causes (proximate first act), like dry wood applied. Over and above all this, physical predetermination is required, to save God's dominion over His creatures. With all these requisites fulfilled, creatures cannot act unless they are applied, excited, moved, actuated, determined by God. Physical predetermination is intrinsic to second cause. Another kind is extrinsic, due to act of God's will and to a mysterious sympathy or harmony in second cause; and we are not concerned with this extrinsic kind. Yet another kind of antecedent influence is indifferent to will's consent and dissent; and we are not dealing with this kind either. We all contend for physical and immediate coöperation on the part of God, not content with mere moral coöperation. Two classes of creatures, necessary and free. Hence our thesis.

PROOFS

(a) 1°. God's supreme dominion and the dependence of creatures are secured by simultaneous coöperation. Three things in second cause, power, exercise of power, and resulting effect. All three depend on God in simultaneous coöperation, because of creation, conservation and coöperation. No act is possible without physical and immediate coöperation.

2°. Physical predetermination is not needed to apply, to move, to excite, determine creature.

Apply means to unite; union between creature and God secured by immensity; union between creature and effect secured by inclination stamped on nature.

Move means no local motion needed, like cook setting meat to fire.

Excite means inclination stamped on nature.

Determine in specie means inclination stamped on nature. Creatures rather determine God's coöperation e. g. Sun to shine; sun to produce wheat, pears, roses.

Determine in individuo means simultaneous coöperation and decree.

(b) *Useless in free agents.* 1°. Free will can do nothing without simultaneous coöperation. God can refuse it, and will becomes helpless.

2°. Will would have only passive and negative indifference,

like intellect: freedom demands active indifference. Free will means dominion over act, and there is no such dominion where will must wait for determination by another.

Destroys free will. 1°. Physical predetermination is not in our power. With it, the act must follow; without it, the act cannot be placed. This is clear from qualities of physical predetermination enumerated above. We cannot fly without wings, read without light, walk when chained. Vain distinctions used by Thomists, originative et terminative; sensu diviso et sensu composito. N.B. Simultaneous coöperation goes always with foreknowledge, and never affects man's freedom.

2°. No violation of a commandment could be imputed to man. Ad impossibile nemo tenetur — infinite series.

3°. God determines the will; and, to be free, the will must determine itself. Necessary agents would determine themselves to the same extent as man.

4°. God would be the author of sin. Formal wickedness of act is inseparably connected with material entity of act. It is worse to physically drive a man to sin than to morally incite him. God advises against sin, and cannot drive to sin. N.B. Simultaneous coöperation is material, not formal. It is giving necessary help according to agent's nature. Physical predetermination is formal coöperation. It is giving unnecessary help, against agent's nature.

PRINCIPLES

A. Second causes act with motion, application, virtue of first. Ergo.

Answer: Motion of first is creation and conservation of second cause and its energies. Application of first is union with help of another second cause, and God is its author. God's eternal decree bearing on simultaneous coöperation moves and applies second cause from eternity. Aristotle proves God from need of a first mover. Virtue of first is creation and conservation of second cause and its energies, along with simultaneous coöperation.

B. To act, a thing must actually exist. Ergo.

Answer: Second cause actually exists and has natural energies. Nothing more is required. First act is not a mixture of potency and act, even in case of the soul's faculties. Actuality is present before exercise of faculty.

C. Second causes are instruments of first, and must be applied. Ergo.

Answer: True of artist's instruments, not of others. Creatures are not instruments of God in strict sense. Instrument contributes to likeness with principal in effect. Creatures contribute to likeness with themselves, not with God. Instruments have no dominion over act, men have.

D. God must cause the creature's act. It is something.

Answer: He causes it by creation, conservation, and coöperation. He gives the creature being and natural energies, and exerts His omnipotence.

E. Will is indifferent and needs to be determined. Ergo.

Answer: With active indifference. It determines itself.

F. God has charge of the universe, and must direct things. Ergo.

Answer: He directs men as general directs army. He gives soldiers being and natural energies, encourages them, advises, promises reward. He does not haul them around physically.

G. God must arrange things without danger of mistake. Ergo.

Answer: God must leave men free. Simultaneous coöperation with the help of intermediate knowledge secures all this. Consequent and extrinsic necessity needed, not antecedent and intrinsic.

H. In simultaneous coöperation God is first cause, first mover, first free, first to determine, first cause of whole thing, Lord of man and all creation besides. Decree exists before second cause. Actual coöperation is first in dignity, necessity and independence; not in fact, nature or causality. Man's freedom is from God, and determines coöperation in decree. God gives everything to creature. God is Lord of all; negatively, by refusing coöperation; positively, necessary agents act according to nature, free agents can be led with the help of intermediate knowledge. And so simultaneous coöperation, the system advocated by Molinists, neither unduly exalts nor unduly depresses the dominion of God or human endeavor; and furnishes forth a rational explanation of human conduct without detriment to the majesty of God or the liberty of man.

II. Simultaneous Coöperation

TERMS

Right doctrine teaches that God's act on the outside is simultaneous with creature's act, neither before nor after, but along with it; that there is nothing in the effect but what proceeds from the creature, nothing but what proceeds from God; that the whole effect begins with both and depends on both. This is coöperation in second act. Coöperation in first act is God's act on the inside, it is God's power determined by an eternal decree, and applied to coöperation with creature. It is eternal and not simultaneous; precedes the creature's act in time and in nature; cause of act destined to follow in course of time. Simultaneous in second act is creature's act inasmuch as it proceeds from God. No act of creature but it proceeds, without possibility of division, from simultaneous coöperation of God and creature. In second act it is prior in dignity, universality, necessity, and consequence to creature's act; not in nature or in time. Coöperation in first act is a decree formulated with help of intermediate knowledge, by which God knows what the free agent will do in the event of divine coöperation. This becomes coöperation in second act without more ado, as soon as the creature exerts its activity. In the case of necessary agents this decree is absolute and necessarily conjoined with a fixed effect. In the case of free agents it is efficacious but indifferent, neither wholly antecedent nor wholly absolute, but virtually and equivalently conditional. Efficacious, because it will secure a fixed effect without being necessarily conjoined with it. Indifferent, because the will in second act remains intrinsically indifferent or free.

PROOF

The decree is meant to constitute the will in nearest first act to operation, and in this phase the will must be free. Not antecedent, because of intermediate knowledge; virtually conditional for same reason. Of course, such a decree leaves free will unharmed. The will determines itself with God's coöperation. God and will are cause of determination in such a way that determination is left to the will's dominion and choice. Simultaneous coöperation in first act, though prior to creature's act, is not physical predetermination, because intermediate knowledge shifts the creature's act from time to eternity, and in this way the eternal decree is simultaneous with the creature's act. God is after a manner determined by creatures, but this implies no imperfection. It is objective determination and extrinsic. It effects nothing in God physically or morally. It arises from God's wish to suit Himself to the natures of things, and depends altogether on His own free-will and energy.

About God's Coöperation with Sin

Matter of sin is the physical act; form of sin is its malice, deformity. God coöperates with sinner, and wishes the act; because no effect of creature exists without God's physical and immediate coöperation. God wishes the physical act permissively, not approvingly; because to wish it otherwise would be to contract the malice of sin. In a lie the physical act is identical with the malice, and God would wish a man to commit sin, He would wish something dishonorable. God is not the cause per se of sin, but only its cause per accidens. Per se means with full intent and approval. God merely permits, disapproves, detests, threatens. Examples of causes per accidens: musician and builder with regard to house; builder and legal quarrel over house; two incendiaries; against wishes and beyond expectations. God is not the author of sin, because on no score can it be imputed to Him. Not because He gave man free will. He gave it for good purpose, strengthens it with grace, rewards its right use with Heaven. Not because He refrains from preventing sin. He prevents sin in a way suited to free nature; not held to prevent it every possible way. Not because He produces the physical act. He has a right to produce it as universal providence, and He is far from approving or encouraging it. He is the author of virtue, because He coöperates approvingly with virtue.

Scholion — Thomism and Molinism Compared

According to the Thomists, who reject Molina's middle or intermediate knowledge in God, every thing, apart from His own divine essence and purely possible beings, is open to the eyes of God in His decrees. All the future then is destined to come to pass because God has so decreed, and in that decree God foresees every minute detail of the future. In this state of things God must evidently have at His disposal means calculated without fail to bring about these future events, and on the other hand these means must not rob man of liberty. On this difficulty the whole question hinges, and the explanation offered by the Thomists is necessarily weak. God has decreed, they say, that somewhere in the course of time a certain free agent is to acquit himself of a certain act and no other. This divine decree is sure of fulfillment, because it proceeds from omnipotence and includes the application of means, that simply render any other course of action utterly impossible. These means are gathered up in the one word physical predetermination. In the supernatural order this physical predetermination or necessitating bias is nothing other than efficacious grace. They opine that in any other hypothesis God would not be the first, primary and immediate cause of human activity, and that the created human will would of its own unaided forces pass from a state of rest to activity, and would be the first, primary and immediate cause of its own salvation. The Thomists conjure up this process in the affairs of grace. Man has these four gifts from God, 1°, existence; 2°, sufficient grace; 3°, efficacious grace or physical predetermination; 4°, simultaneous coöperation, as between will and grace. The sureness of the future event, the impossibility of its failure, assumes a threefold guise as considered resident in the act itself, in the will of God, and in God's knowledge.

These three guises are distinguished by the titles, objective, affective and intellective. The first, in the Thomistic system, is derived from their physical predetermination, or bias exerted by God on the will; the second, from the divine decree antedating foreknowledge of the man's consent, and ordaining the bestowal of that same physical predetermination; the third, from the knowledge God has of the said decree. In God's regard, therefore, the connection between grace and the act elicited under its influence, is not one of foreknowledge, but of causality. The sureness of the act leans not on God's foreknowledge of the man's proffered consent; but God's foreknowledge of the proffered consent is wholly founded on God's omnipotence. Human liberty, the Thomists say, emerges unhurt from this forcing process, because God deals throughout with the will in a way suited to its inherent freedom. The way itself is strange, mysterious, inexplicable. To make the will appear capable still of choice under pressure from physical predetermination, they employ the time-honored distinction turning on divided or separate and united or conjoined senses. Under its protecting fold, they say that the will, though unable to choose in a united or conjoined sense, is still able to choose in a divided or separate sense; and human liberty remains intact. It may be well to set down here what some eminent Dominicans have said of this distinction. Cajetan says, "It fails to satisfy the mind"; Aravius, "I set small store by it"; Albertini, "When it comes to answering difficulties, we abandon the system with as much piety as wisdom"; Billuart, "My answer is, that it is a mystery"; Bannez, "Ignorance and rashness. We believe the Trinity, though we do not understand." N.B. The Trinity contains no element which renders the mystery absurd or contradictory. The Trinity is revealed doctrine. The Thomists can appeal to no revelation for their physical predetermination. Grace borrows none of its strength from free will. Its efficacy is its own intrinsic property. Neither is its bearing on the will's free consent based on what the Thomists style God's physical predetermination.

Here we are face to face with two systems of theology, that had their origin in attempts to reconcile the action of God's grace with human liberty. Like the Trinity, the question is, and must forever remain, a mystery. But nothing prevents us from endeavoring here, as we endeavor in the case of the Trinity, to show that the mystery involves no contradiction and violates no principle of reason. Mysteries are superior, not hostile to reason. Faith is higher homage of the mind, not its stultification.

What we call actual grace is an indispensably necessary help to salvation. This actual grace, one and always the same in itself, sometimes meets with resistance in the soul, sometimes with welcome. Men at times under stress of temptation reject the help offered by Almighty God, and walk the ways of the devil. Men at other times in spite of temptation yield to the saving influence of grace, and keep the straight and narrow path. Theology calls resisted grace merely sufficient, it calls grace welcomed, cherished, put to good account, efficacious. Man's unaided will, however, is far from raising merely sufficient to the dignity of efficacious grace. Man's will must be conceived as under the influence of grace even before the act of consent is placed, and grace under this aspect is named preventing. No matter, therefore, what part human activity plays in its accomplishment, salvation always remains the free and gratuitous gift of God, rooted in the bestowal of this preventing grace. The will thus elevated makes choice of virtue, spurns aside sin, and straightway what was preventing grace becomes assisting grace. Therefore, the will in putting a salutary act, an act tending towards salvation, passes not from complete quiet or rest to action, but from an indeliberate to a deliberate act. On this account divine grace and the will operate together in the production of a salutary act, when that act is considered in its formal or distinctively last stage; when it is considered in its totality or from beginning to end, grace must be said to antedate the will. In other words, grace is first merely preventing grace, to become later on assisting grace.

These truths well in mind, to answer future difficulties, we can now draw nearer the central problem. As a matter of fact, God has determined from all eternity to confer on certain sinners and on all His elect efficacious graces, helps to the performance of virtue they shall not, yea cannot, even though free agents, reject or fail to use. It is the province of theology to save God from the reproach of doing violence to human liberty in this saving process. God's omnipotence must not be exalted at the expense of His creatures' inalienable prerogatives, that would be to insult God's wisdom; nor must the creature's activity be unduly exaggerated at the risk of belittling God's supreme dominion. Salvation must be so explained that it remain at one and the same time the free and gratuitous gift of God, and the reward due in justice to a man's hard efforts. The Thomists, it seems to us, ascribe too much to God's omnipotence, and leave too small play for human endeavor, reducing free will to something dangerously like a necessary agent, without choice, and consequently without merit. We seem to them to emphasize beyond measure the energies of free will, and relegate God's omnipotence to too obscure a corner in the scheme of salvation and sanctification. Whether Thomists or Molinists, we are all of us Catholics, and we are agreed about such defined points of doctrine as the gratuity of grace, the nature of merit and the continued existence of liberty alongside of efficacious grace. Our Church is a unit on these matters, and leaves no room for doubt or discussion. But condescending, as it were, to reason, she leaves a wide field for argumentation, when methods of explanation are to be adopted. She has condemned neither Thomists nor Molinists, and even encourages them to pursue their investigations without limit, provided always that due deference be paid to the demands of faith. Hence the Thomists, though they seem in as many words to deny free will when grace exacts consent, are nevertheless careful to always close their remarks with the saving statement that, though God forces or determines the will, He always does so in some mysterious way, escaping our powers of perception, but adapted to a free agent, and leaving the agent's liberty inviolate and intact. The statement saves their faith, and puts their orthodoxy beyond suspicion; but it is far from satisfying, and leaves the mystery just as much a mystery as ever. The Molinists have no such subterfuge to offer; and, while vindicating to free will all its vast prerogative, they in no whit diminish the Creator's supreme and universal dominion.

In our exposition we begin with the system of the Thomists, remarking that, though they profess to derive their doctrine from passages in the writings of St. Thomas, the Molinists are just as loud in declaring that the Angelic Doctor is authority for their position. Since, however, the illustrious St. Thomas was himself a Dominican, the Thomists, belonging to the same Order, wear his proud name with a peculiar grace, and nobody disputes the title with them. We are ourselves Molinists, casting our lot with that leader among Jesuit theologians on questions of grace, Father Molina of Spain. God's knowledge of things plays an important part in the two systems; and, as explained by Thomists and Molinists, presents the first marked difference. To keep God's independence of created things safe, we must hold that God knows everything in His own essence, without in any way leaning on things themselves for that knowledge. In the universe of things we distinguish these several categories, 1°, Necessary things, things such of their very nature that they cannot not be. God Himself and pure possibles are instances. 2°. Contingent things, things that can with equal indifference be or not be. Past, present and future occurrences are instances. Some future events are subject to conditions, they are dependent for their existence in time on certain circumstances. If these circumstances have place, then the future events follow as a matter of course; if the circumstances are wanting, the future events likewise fail of actual being. Besides, some of these future events are the effects of necessary causes; others are the effects of free causes. Events of the first kind present no difficulty, and fall under our second category or contingents. Events of the second kind present a difficulty, and constitute a third class. 3°. Futuribles, or future events derivable from free agents, that would indeed have place under certain fixed conditions, but never as a matter of fact happen because these conditions are never fulfilled. The conversion of the Tyrians as described by Our Lord in St. Matthew xi, 21, is an instance in point, "Wo to thee, Corozain; wo to thee, Bethsaida; for if in Tyre and Sidon had been wrought the miracles that have been wrought in you, they had long ago done penance in sackcloth and ashes." The conversion of Tyre and Sidon belongs to what we call futurible events. In other words, it never happened, but would certainly have happened, were the miracles forthcoming. We distinguish, likewise, between a futurible only and a futurible future. The former never happens, the latter happens, and is considered futurible, only under the aspect of complete independence from its occurrence.

To embrace these different objects of knowledge, theologians agree to recognize in God different ways of apprehending the truth. Of course, this agreement is a matter of mere convenience. All theologians are satisfied that everything in God is absolute unity, and they speak of multiplicity only to bring God into closer range with our feeble intellects. The Thomists limit God's knowledge to two kinds, vision or seeing, and intelligence or understanding. Every object in the field of knowledge, they contend, is attainable by these two processes. Intelligence grasps things possible, and future events dependent on a condition. Vision grasps existences, whether necessary, like that of God Himself, or contingent, like that of aught else in the universe of facts. What we described as futuribles, if admitted at all as objects of God's knowledge, are referred partly to intelligence, partly to vision.

The Molinists, admitting intelligence and vision, introduce a third kind of knowledge, labeling it middle or intermediate. They hold it necessary for the understanding of events styled futuribles, and derive its name from the circumstance that it partakes at the same time of intelligence and vision. The Thomists are up in arms against this third kind of divine knowledge, branding it an unnecessary and dangerous innovation. That it is a necessary feature of God's knowledge, may be easily seen from these three examples, supposing an individual, Peter, under the influence of efficacious grace,

1°. *Intelligence.* Peter, looking merely at the essences of things, can with this grace be converted.
2°. *Vision.* Peter, acting as a necessary agent, shall with this grace necessarily be converted; i. e. Peter with this grace cannot possibly escape conversion.
3°. *Middle or Intermediate.* Peter, acting as a free agent, shall with this grace be converted; i. e. Peter even with this grace could still escape conversion and embrace damnation.

We, therefore, define middle or intermediate knowledge as the certain and infallible knowledge by which God is acquainted with futuribles, with events destined to happen only on the fulfilment of a condition, that has a bearing indeed on their occurrence, but no necessary connection with same. This knowledge in God has accordingly for object future acts springing from free agents, in the event of a certain condition's fulfilment. It is easy, therefore, to see that it has for object acts in a double sense contingent. They are contingent on the condition, which may or may not be verified; and, even after the verification of the condition, they are contingent on the choice made by the free will of the free agent. To illustrate, we take again that Scriptural example of the Tyrians, "The Tyrians would be converted, if given the grace bestowed on the people of Corozain." This conversion of the Tyrians falls into the class of objects known by God with that knowledge described as middle or intermediate. It is a futurible, and in only a half-sense of the word a mere conditional future. Were it a mere conditional future, the Tyrians on the acceptance of such grace would be converted in spite of themselves, and would be practically deprived of freedom. But the Tyrians are men, vested with free will; and, therefore, even in the presence of efficacious grace, they are at liberty to choose either conversion or damnation. Their conversion becomes a necessary fact only after they have rendered full and free consent to the inspiration of grace. Grace, therefore, as far as their ultimate conversion is concerned, is a condition with a bearing, indeed, and a very vital bearing, on their conversion, and yet not necessarily connected or bound up with it. In other words, grace can still be present, and the conversion of the Tyrians can fail of effect. The one thing in the whole affair that caps and finishes the business, is the free and unconstrained consent of the Tyrians to act as grace prompts. And this is our whole reason for saying that one element of grace's efficacy is derived from a source outside of grace. That element we call its efficacy of connection. The other element, called its efficacy of force or strength, is intrinsic and wholly native to grace itself.

That God has knowledge of futuribles, and therefore middle or intermediate knowledge, is evident from the express declaration of Christ concerning the Tyrians. St. Matthew, xi, 21. Besides, futuribles are capable of being known, and God knows everything such. God knows these futuribles neither in their proximate cause, nor in His own decrees; but in themselves, as they exist previous to any divine decree, formulated in their regard. Knowledge of a thing always presupposes the thing's existence. We are, however, far from maintaining that the futurible is the cause of God's knowledge. It is a mere condition, but a condition indispensably and unqualifiedly necessary. God, therefore, knows a futurible beforehand, because it is in reality going to happen. The futurible is going to happen, not precisely because God knows it is going to happen. Or, as St. Justin says, "The future reality of a futurible does not follow after God's foreknowledge, but God's foreknowledge follows after the futurible's future reality."

We have these several counts against the system of the Thomists:

1°. The divine decrees, in which according to this system God sees futuribles, are described as subjectively and on the part of God absolute, objectively and on the part of the futuribles themselves conditional. Such mixed decrees are offenses against common sense. God cannot absolutely decree a thing diametrically opposed to another divine wish. This would be a fair instance of such a decree. I absolutely and without condition decree the conversion of the Tyrians, and I at the same time absolutely withhold from the Tyrians the grace of conversion or efficacious grace.

Besides, since the fulfillment of the required condition is, according to the Thomists, entirely independent of free will, and altogether dependent on God, these decrees could be with more justice called even subjectively conditional, or conditional on the part of God. This grace, they say, has all its double efficacy of force and connection from within, and comes in its entirety from God. It may be here remarked that some Thomists venture the opinion that God seriously wishes some men to be sinners, to secure variety in the universe. We heartily disagree with the sentiment.

Again, were God capable of having the decrees postulated by the Thomists, there would exist in God a decree without any corresponding result in nature. The Thomists are fond of quoting these as parallel examples, "I intend to give Lorenzo a thousand dollars, if he marries my daughter." "I intend to make a present of a horse to Egbert, if he meets me to-morrow." These are not parallel examples, because in these two cases the condition is in the power of the parties on whom the favor is to be conferred, in the power of Lorenzo and Egbert; not altogether in the power of the man who pledges himself to confer the favors. The reverse happens in the case of efficacious grace. God decrees the favor, and the condition, too, proceeds wholly from God, being put outside the reach of the human will, when constituted by God's physical predetermination. To make the above cases parallel, they would have to read in this absurd way, "I intend to give Lorenzo a thousand dollars, if he marries my daughter; but at the same time I am going to take efficacious means to prevent the marriage." "I intend to make a present of a horse to Egbert, if he meets me to-morrow; but I am at the same time going to take efficacious means to prevent his meeting me." Surely, this is not the way God offered the grace of conversion to the Tyrians, this is not the way He offers grace to any sinner.

2°. Human liberty is done to death by the Thomists. It is robbed of active indifference. In other words, when hard pressed by physical predetermination, it no longer remains mistress of its own acts. It is wholly without freedom of choice, because it is forced by an antecedent, intrinsic and insurmountable necessity, i. e. physical predetermination.

3°. There would be no such thing as sufficient grace properly so-called, because without this physical predetermination, which at once constitutes grace efficacious, the grace present would not proximately equip the agent for action.

Passing now to the Molinists, it is easy to show that their system is free from every reasonable objection. We have already said that the sureness of the future event, the impossibility of its failure, assumes a threefold guise, as considered resident in the act itself, in the will of God, and in God's knowledge. The corresponding titles are, objective, affective and intellective. With the Molinists, the first is derived from the free act of the will, already elevated and ennobled by preventing grace, and choosing of its own inherent virtue; the second, from an absolute decree of God, elicited under the guidance of middle or intermediate knowledge antedating the decree itself; the third, from middle or intermediate knowledge as above described. The objective sureness, therefore, arises from the relation of fitness in force between the grace bestowed and the free consent of the will, based on the fact that the will is in reality of its own free choice going to embrace the grace offered. "In this way," says Suarez, "grace will infallibly meet with consent, not because the will cannot act otherwise, even when confronted with this grace, but because the will as a matter of fact is not going to act otherwise." The divine decree constituting affective sureness is called predefinition or predestination, though predestination is more properly said of glory in Heaven than of any single grace. The Molinists thus describe predefinition, "A divine decree or wish, by which God prior to the act itself decrees from all eternity, positively, absolutely and efficaciously that the will shall in time acquit itself of a certain good act." This, then, according to Molinists, is the order and process followed in the conversion of an individual, say Peter:

1°. God by means of simple intelligence knows all possible helps and knows the possibility of Peter's conversion.
2°. God by means of middle or intermediate knowledge foresees what helps Peter will freely embrace or reject.
3°. Of these helps, God chooses, e. g. A, one He foresees Peter will freely embrace if put in his way.
4°. God now by means of vision knows that Peter's conversion is absolutely going to happen in time.
5°. At the proper moment God sends Peter the help A, Peter embraces it, and is converted.

GOD'S PROVIDENCE, HIS GOVERNMENT AND OWNERSHIP

THESIS XI

Providence belongs to God.

Jouin, pp. 253, 254; *Boedder,* pp. 381–393.

TERMS

Providence is from providentia, compounded of porro and videre, and means to see from afar. It is therefore a part of prudence, which orders things to their ends, and has to do with future contingents, not with pasts or presents. It can turn on one's own acts or on another's. In the matter of one's own acts providence is the prudence of the monk or solitary. In the matter of another's acts, it can be domestic or family prudence; political, state or civil prudence; prudence of the king. God's prudence or providence deals with the acts of others, not with His own. He is His own last end, and there can be no question of ordering His own acts. His end and His acts are God Himself. Providence includes knowledge and will, and is essentially resident in knowledge, practical not merely speculative. Government presupposes providence. Providence plans order, government executes the plans of providence, and ownership is a corollary of both. Providence is from eternity, government is a matter of time, and presupposes creation. *Physical providence* extends to all creatures without exception, the quick and dead. *Moral* embraces only men and angels, beings with free wills. *Supernatural* touches the order of grace; natural, the order of nature. *Natural* or physical providence turns on creation, conservation and coöperation, along with times and places best suited to the accomplishment of God's designs in the universe, e. g. men of providence in Church history, like St. Ignatius. Moral or supernatural turns on God's laws and precepts, promises, threats, rewards, punishments, graces, miracles, gifts. Briefly, moral has to do with man's elevation, redemption, justification, decrees regarding men's virtuous acts, permission of sin, grace's helps, Heaven, hell.

Providence means a plan and its infallible accomplishment, with a distinction. God's providence, like His will, is twofold, antecedent, conditional and inefficacious as well as consequent, absolute and efficacious. Predestination of the elect is a manifestation of God's consequent providence, while the loss of the damned and God's wish to save all mankind are manifestations of His antecedent providence. Hence the distinction, God's plans are infallibly fulfilled, I distinguish. Regarding supreme end of everything, God's glory, I grant; regarding other ends, not supreme or simply last, I again distinguish. In question of consequent and absolute providence, I grant; in question of antecedent and conditional providence, I deny. Whether men are lost or saved, God gets from creation the very measure of glory He meant to have from the beginning; goodness and mercy in Heaven, justice in hell. Man's salvation depends on his own free will, and God's providence regarding it is antecedent and conditional, not consequent or absolute. God is held to supply of means and nothing more.

Three opinions about divine act in which providence formally resides, in intellect and will both, in will alone, in intellect alone. In second opinion will wishes end and chooses means; in third, intellect foreknows creatures, ends and means, with the decree to create and choose set means for measure of glory God freely purposes. The Thomists, with a view to physical predetermination, introduce a third act of intellect ordering the accomplishment of preconceived plans; and this third act formally constitutes providence. Providence connotes two things, foreknowledge and care; first belongs to intellect; second, to will; and from the very term, providence, it would seem to formally reside in intellect. There must be no suspicion of physical predetermination. St. Thomas puts it in intellect. Intermediate knowledge certainly enters providence. The Vatican defined providence an article of faith, Denziger, 1933. Deists and Fatalists deny, with Democritus, Epicurus, and their chance-grouping of atoms. Aristotle and Cicero are under suspicion. Ancients separated incorruptible from corruptible things in this matter.

PROOFS

1°. Order in world calls for government, and this in turn calls for providence. Ergo.

2°. Providence is a great perfection in God. Ergo.

3°. Nothing in providence surpasses God's power or knowledge, nothing conflicts with His dignity. Ergo.

4°. Providence in last analysis means conservation and cooperation. Ergo.

PRINCIPLES

A. God takes counsel without doubt or hesitation. His knowledge is intuitive. No formal study of means, but virtual. Our study without its imperfections.

B. Providence is eternal with regard to substance of act, temporal with regard to execution or outward terms.

C. No composition in God, because intellect and will are one thing in God, His substance.

THESIS XII

God's providence a, extends to everything created, and b, touches man in a very special way.

Boedder, pp. 381–393.

PROOFS

a, 1°. God's providence is coextensive with His causality. Ergo.

2°. Every agent works unto an end, and God is of all agents the most perfect. Ergo.

3°. God's providence ought to be the most perfect conceivable. Ergo.

4°. Birds of the air, lilies of the field, grass in the meadow. St. Matt. vi, 26. Hair of the head. St. Matt. x, 29.

N.B. Regarding good, God's providence is approving; regarding evil, permissive.

PRINCIPLES

A. No chance in the world.

Answer: Respecting God, I grant; respecting man, I deny. Chance with man is what happens ex inopinato, beyond expectation.

B. A good provider excludes evil. Ergo, no providence.

Answer: A particular provider, I grant; a universal provider, I deny. Destruction of individuals contributes to perpetuity of species. A king looks to the community, not to individuals. Evil is from God, as darkness is from the sun.

C. Doth God take care for oxen? I Cor. ix, 9.

Answer: No care at all, I deny; no special care as for men, I grant. St. Jerome says, it is beneath God's majesty to care for gnats, bugs, fleas, flies. Same distinction as above.

D. God left man in the hands of his own counsel.

Answer: No determination, I grant; no providence, I deny.

E. God does no evil. Ergo.

Answer: Approvingly, I grant; permissively, I deny.

F. A prudent man permits no subject to commit evil. Ergo.

Answer: To obtain greater good, I deny; otherwise, I grant. It is of the nature of free agents to be able to do evil; and providence never destroys, it respects natures.

G. It is easier to get good from good, than good from evil. Ergo.

Answer: Every good can be gotten from good, I deny; some goods can be gotten from evil alone, I grant; e.g. patience, repentance, martyrdom.

H. Nobody gets evil from good. Ergo, nobody ought to get good from evil.

Answer: Wrong to make good subserve evil, right to make evil subserve good.

I. Man must not do evil to procure good. Ergo, nor God.

Answer: Man cannot permit evil, when it is in his power to prevent, and prevention is a duty, without approving of it and therefore doing it. God can permit evil without approving of it. To do evil and to permit evil are two different things.

J. Man is able to take care of himself.

Answer: Sufficiently, I deny; insufficiently, I grant.

K. Men's acts are oftener crooked than brutes'. Ergo.

Answer: Providence is to blame, I deny; free will is to blame, I grant.

L. Sin is most hateful. Ergo, God cannot permit.

Answer. Sins are greater and lesser. He can without approval permit a lesser sin to avoid a greater. In this case He chooses not between good and evil, but between two goods. He chooses the greater good, rejects the lesser, because absence of the greater evil is a good. In permitting the lesser evil He is rejecting the lesser's absence. Besides, no harm attaches to the permission of evil, when approval is withheld and prevention is no duty. God threatens sin, and He made men free.

M. Providence is eternal. Ergo, predetermination.

Answer. It antedates man's act in time, I grant; in nature and causality, I again distinguish, foreknowledge of act with help of intermediate knowledge presupposed, I grant; otherwise, I deny.

N. Miracles are departures from regular order. Ergo, no providence.

Answer. Departures with a just cause, I grant; without a just cause, I deny.

PROOFS

b, 1°. *Special providence for man,* because highest of visible creatures, and closest to God, and a good provider attends to dignity of objects he manages.

2°. God loves man in a special way, that of friendship, and the world was made for man.

3°. Man needs providence more than other creatures. The others are ruled and determined, they cannot go astray. Man is free and can disturb order. Hence manifestation of providence in natural law, religion and worship, instinct for good, stings of conscience, society, rewards, punishments.

4°. History is witness. Church overcame enemies in spite of their greater strength. Roman emperors, heretical countries never prevailed. Endurance of Church is a lasting miracle.

PRINCIPLES

A. God hath equally care of all.

Answer. Equally, I grant; equal, I deny.

B. Man's solicitude would be idle. Ergo.

Answer. Undue, I grant; due, I deny. God gave man reason, to use it and look out for himself. His industry coöperates with God's providence. Work hard, as if everything depended on yourself; trust in God, as if nothing depended on you.

C. "We would have cured Babylon, but she is not healed; let us forsake her," Jer. 51.9. Ergo, God has no care for sinners.

Answer. No care in comparison with saints, I grant; in comparison with lower creation, I deny.

D. Greek Fathers deny providence in evil acts. Ergo.

Answer. Deny approving, I grant; deny permissive, I deny.

E. Good suffer, wicked prosper. Ergo.

Answer. Not always the case. Good must atone for lesser faults. In many things we all offend, St. James 3.2. Just man shall fall seven times, Prov. 24.16. If we say that we have no sin, the truth is not in us, 1. St. John 1.8. Wicked do some good and deserve a reward. None in next life. Ergo, here. Providence bears on last end or next life, not on proximate end or this life. Adversity tests virtue; perfects justice, fortitude, contempt of world, meditation, love of God. Seneca, and the uses of adversity. Jove, and the spectacle of a just man in conflict with trouble. Horace, and his man of principle face to face with a cracked world. Prosperity ought to drag wicked back to God's feet, He is an indulgent Father. Horace's pedagogue and cakes.

THESIS XIII

X. God's providence over all is immediate and particular. Y. God's (a) government of the world is (b) in part immediate, in part mediate.

Boedder, pp. 381–393.

QUESTION

X. Plato teaches three kinds of providence. God cares for spiritual things, genera, species, universal causes. Inferior deities in planets care for matter, things that are born and things that die. Demons, midway between the gods and ourselves, care for human affairs. Plato is wrong when he removes planets and men from immediate providence of God.

PROOF

God provides for things as He knows them. He knows them immediately and particularly. Ergo. Kings fail to provide immediately for details because of their limited ability. God's ability is absolutely unlimited.

PRINCIPLES

A. St. Augustine says, "Better not to know things than to know them." Ergo.

Answer. True of men, I grant; true of God, I deny. Better for men not to know vice and sin, because we are of limited intellectual capacity, and knowledge of evil and sin crowds out knowledge of better things. Besides, knowledge of evil drags down the will. God is of infinite capacity, and God is above tempting.

N.B. God's providence imposes necessity on necessary agents, none on free agents, because providence respects natures, it does not destroy them. All the order in the world, with respect to necessary agents, is such by virtue of providence that it cannot be other; with respect to free agents, its necessity is not antecedent, but consequent; and this consequent necessity presupposes God's intermediate knowledge of what act a free agent would put, and put freely, in such and such circumstances, if suited help and coöperation were granted. No physical predetermination. The order of providence is not uncertain or inefficacious, because God gets what He wants from all creatures with either antecedent or consequent necessity. Consequent is as infallible as antecedent. Creation supposed, providence in God is a necessity; because creation and conservation without providence would be against God's goodness and wisdom. St. Ambrose says, "Though to refrain from making a thing contains no wrong, to take no care of what you make is the height of unkindness or cruelty."

Y. (*a*) *God governs the world.*

QUESTION

Government is execution of plans which constitute providence. Boethius says, "You bind the elements to keep cold and hot, dry and wet together, lest subtle fire escape, or its heavy weight bury the earth in the sea."

PROOFS

(1) Actual order in the world proves God's government. Order in house bespeaks owner's management.

(2) Government touches whatever agents tend to an end. All agents work unto an end. Men work with knowledge of end and self-motion; other creatures, without knowledge of end and with motion communicated by God, or instinct, or nature. God governs lower creation as the bowman governs the arrow. The arrow is ignorant, but the bowman knows.

N.B. One God governs the world, not many, in spite of opposites; because universal and last end harmonizes particulars and proximates. Nothing in the world happens out of accord with God's government, because nothing can escape God's knowledge or purpose; nothing can oppose His will or omnipotence, which are all infinite.

PRINCIPLES

A. A just king punishes only transgressors of his law. Nobody transgresses God's law, because everything happens in accord with His government.

Answer. To do what God permits without approval is to transgress God's law.

(b) *God governs some things immediately, others mediately.*

PROOFS

1°. God governs the world by others as He causes by second causes.

2°. Better to be good in self and good to others than to be merely good in self.

3°. A good teacher makes not only wise pupils, but able teachers.

4°. God uses intellectual beings to govern lower orders. Hierarchy among angels, guardian angels for men, rulers among men; minerals, plants, brutes, men; hierarchy of universe.

N.B. God's dominion extends to ownership and jurisdiction; and it is essential. Man's ownership in the concrete is accidental and from diverse titles, occupancy, purchase, gift and the like. God's ownership is essential because rooted in creation, conservation and coöperation. Lessius says, "Subjection or dependence is measure. Man's ownership of internal acts is fuller than his ownership of external acts. First are free from organs, second dependent on organs. Man's ownership of senses and limbs is fuller as compared with fortune and wealth. First are intrinsic, others are from extrinsic title, like inheritance, purchase, occupancy." Men are always relative owners with regard to God. In disposing of their property as they like, they can offend God without harming their neighbor. God's ownership is basis and foundation of man's ownership. Jurisdiction likewise belongs to God. The right to rule and govern men belongs to their maker. "King of kings, Lord of lords." 1 Tim. 6.15. "By me kings reign." Prov. 8.15. "No power but from God." Rom. 13.1. "All power in Heaven and in earth." St. Matt. 28.18.

INDEX

C

E

F

PRINTED IN THE UNITED STATES OF AMERICA